THE LONGEST ROMANCE

THE LONGEST ROMANCE
The Mainstream Media and Fidel Castro

Humberto Fontova

ENCOUNTER BOOKS • *New York* • *London*

First American edition published in 2013 by Encounter Books, an activity of Encounter for Culture and Education, Inc., a nonprofit, tax exempt corporation. Encounter Books website address: www.encounterbooks.com

Manufactured in the United States and printed on acid-free paper. The paper used in this publication meets the minimum requirements of ANSI/NISO Z39.48 1992 (R 1997) (Permanence of Paper).

FIRST AMERICAN EDITION

LIBRARY OF CONGRESS CATALOGING-IN-PUBLICATION DATA
Fontova, Humberto.
The longest romance : the mainstream media and Fidel Castro / Humberto Fontova.
pages cm
Includes bibliographical references and index.
ISBN 978-1-59403-667-5 (hardcover : alkaline paper)—ISBN 978-1-59403-668-2 (ebook) (print) 1. Castro, Fidel, 1926—Relations with journalists. 2. Castro, Fidel, 1926—Public opinion. 3. Press and politics —United States. 4. Mass media—Political aspects—United States. 5. Cuba—Foreign public opinion, American. 6. Public opinion— United States. 7. United States—Relations—Cuba. 8. Cuba— Relations—
United States. I. Title.
F1788.22.C3F664 2013
972.9106′4—dc23
2012038952

CONTENTS

PREFACE The Connections You Don't See................vii

CHAPTER 1 The Golden Anniversary: A Half-Century of Loyal Service....................................1

CHAPTER 2 Communist Omelet: The Unreported Cost in Life and Treasure.................................7

CHAPTER 3 The "World's Luckiest People," or So Says *Newsweek*.......................................21

CHAPTER 4 Here Come the Sharks. Where's the Discovery Channel?...............................35

CHAPTER 5 The Discovery Channel Spins the Missile Crisis.......................................47

CHAPTER 6 Castro's Running-Dogs: Herbert Matthews and *The New York Times*.........................53

CHAPTER 7 To Kill a Labor Leader: Manhunt in Buenos Aires......................................69

CHAPTER 8 Papa Hemingway Admires Death in the Cuban Afternoon.................................77

CHAPTER 9 Castro's "Revolution of Youth"—Imprisoning the Young...83

CHAPTER 10 Jon Stewart to Don Fidel: Thank You, Godfather...95

CHAPTER 11 Not Your Father's Hit-Men: Gangsters in Cuba Today......................................109

CHAPTER 12   How Barack Obama Tried to Lose Honduras to the Dictators...................................127

CHAPTER 13   Keep Your Pants On, Stephen Colbert. Che Wasn't That Hot...........................135

CHAPTER 14   Sickos! The Cuban Health-Care Hoax, Directed by Michael Moore.............................159

CHAPTER 15   The Cuban "Embargo"—Are You Kidding?.................................177

CHAPTER 16   "Agents of Influence"—Castro's Ladies and Men in the U.S. Media.........................195

CHAPTER 17   Barbara Walters, Charmed by the Hemisphere's Top Torturer of Women.......................205

CHAPTER 18   Dan Rather on Castro: "This Is Cuba's Elvis!".....................................215

ENDNOTES 223

INDEX 235

The Connections You Don't See

He jailed political prisoners at a rate higher than Stalin during the Great Terror. He murdered more Cubans in his first three years in power than Hitler murdered Germans during his first six. He came closer than anyone in history to starting a worldwide nuclear war. In the above process Fidel Castro converted a nation with a higher per-capita income than half of Europe and a huge influx of immigrants into one that repels the poorest people in the region and boasts the highest suicide rate in the Western Hemisphere.

Who would guess any of this from reading the mainstream media? Instead we read almost exclusively about how Castro freed Cuba from the greedy clutches of U.S. robber barons and mobsters and rewarded his downtrodden countrymen with free health-care and education. A scornful Uncle Sam then retaliated with a vindictive embargo, still in place. Topping off a half-century of tortured history, *Newsweek* hailed Cuba as among "the best countries in the world to live."

In July 1958 an excited American magazine reporter climbing his way up to Castro's guerrilla hideout in Cuba's mountains for a supposedly exclusive interview with the elusive guerrilla chief stopped and gaped at another reporter passing him on the way down. The reporter coming downhill, clutching a secret interview of his own, worked for *Boys' Life* magazine, the official publication of the Boy Scouts of America.[1]

Farther along the curiously well-trod trail, the reporter stopped and gaped again. Straight ahead was a huge sign reading "Press Hut—This Way." Castro had recently installed it to accommodate the throng of journalists seeking interviews at his "secret camp." By then reporters from *The New York Times* to CBS, from *Look* and *Life* to *Reader's Digest* and *Boys' Life*, had all managed the terrifying trek to the remote hideout while evading Batista's brutal army and police and obtaining exclusive interviews with the furtive guerrilla commander.

Two years later, in his *Reminiscences of the Cuban Revolutionary War*, Che Guevara snickered: "Foreign reporters—preferably American—were much more valuable to us than any military victory. Much more valuable than recruits for our guerrilla force were American media recruits to export our propaganda."

Five years earlier, in a letter to revolutionary colleague Melba Hernandez, Fidel Castro had laid down his movement's mission statement: "We cannot for a second abandon propaganda. Propaganda is vital—propaganda is the heart of our struggle. For now we use a lot of sleight of hand and smiles with everybody. There will be plenty of time later to crush all the cockroaches together."[2]

After so many fake smiles and crushed cockroaches, you'd hope journalists would be on their guard when accepting Castro-regime press releases. But history records few media recruitment drives as phenomenally successful or as enduring as Castro and Che's.

"Cuban mothers, let me assure you that I will solve all Cuba's problems without spilling a drop of blood." Upon entering Havana on January 8, 1959, Cuba's new leader Fidel Castro broadcast that promise into a phalanx of microphones. "Cuban mothers," he continued as the jubilant crowd erupted with joy, "let me assure you that because of me you will never have to cry."[3]

The following day, just below San Juan Hill in eastern Cuba, a bulldozer rumbled to a start, clanked into position and pushed dirt into a huge pit with blood pooling at the bottom from the still-twitching bodies of more than a hundred men and boys who'd been machine-gunned without trial on orders of the Castro brothers, as many wives and mothers wept hysterically from a nearby road.

On that very day the prestigious *Observer* ran the following: "Mr. Castro's bearded, youthful figure has become a symbol of Latin America's rejection of brutality and lying. Every sign is that he will reject personal rule and violence."

These two events epitomize the Castro phenomenon, even half a century later. The Cuban regime oppresses and murders while issuing a smokescreen of lies not merely devious but positively psychopathic. The international media abandon all pretense to be investigators or watchdogs (or even reporters); they become not merely sycophants but publicists.

On April 21, 1959, Fidel Castro said to Americans: "I am not a communist for three reasons: communism is a dictatorship and for my entire life I have been against dictatorships. Furthermore, communism means hatred and class struggle, and I am completely against such a philosophy. And finally because communism opposes God and the Church. I say this to set your minds and spirits at rest."[4]

For three months prior to that date, Fidel Castro and his Stalinist partners, Raul Castro and Che Guevara, had already been hosting Soviet GRU agents in their respective stolen mansions and buttoning down the Stalinization of Cuba. Fidel's brother Raul and sister-in-law Vilma Espin had had assigned KGB handlers since 1953.[5]

A half-century of relentless Castroite Communism later, one could have hoped that mainstream journalists would adopt a more prudent approach in reacting to this regime's statements.

This book will show how utterly vain is that hope.

The media's heraldry of Fidel Castro in 1957 or 1959—though often based on reflexive anti-Americanism, laziness, stupidity and condescension towards Latins (maybe a taste of the lash is what those volatile and frivolous people need)—was in some ways excusable. "A man of many ideals, including those of liberty, democracy, and social justice," gushed *The New York Times* about Castro in February 1957. Many prominent Cubans, after all, were equally deluded. But the same theme over half a century later can only be described as the journalistic version of battered-wife syndrome. Among historical figures, Fidel Castro wins hands down as the most persistently effective liar of modern times.

"Castro's use of propaganda-assets—interviews with journalists, radio broadcasts—during his guerrilla war against Batista contributed in a major way to his victory and was a preview of the methods he would use so successfully after coming to power," states a declassified CIA document from 1984 titled "Castro's Propaganda Apparatus." "Immediately after assuming power," it continues, "Fidel Castro set out creating a propaganda empire that today is perhaps the most effective in the Western Hemisphere."

Sadly, the CIA itself is a victim of Castro's effectiveness. In 1987, Cuban intelligence officer Florentino Aspillaga defected in Prague and revealed that every Cuban agent (four dozen of them) the CIA had recruited to spy on the Castro regime since 1962 was a double agent controlled personally by Fidel Castro.[6]

But according to Norman Bailey, formerly of the U.S. office of the Director of National Intelligence: "For Castro, being able to influence U.S. policy and elite opinion-makers is even more important than recruiting spies with access to intelligence information."[7] Foremost among his successes is Castro's penetration of U.S. media.

For close to a decade, most of what Americans have read about Cuba has been doctored by Castro-regime "agents of influence" working in concert with the regime's intelligence service. Let's hope the CIA has finally caught on. "Useful idiocy" is one thing, deliberate collaboration quite another. We'll introduce you to the folks in both camps.

In 1984, KGB defector Yuri Bezmenov wrote: "Cynical, egocentric people who can look into your eyes with angelic expression and tell you a lie—these are the most recruitable people for us;

people who lack moral principles—who are either too greedy or who suffer from exaggerated self-importance. These are the people the KGB wants and finds easiest to recruit."[8]

As if nothing in the intervening half-century had called into question the veracity of Castro regime press releases, on August 8, 2009 a CNN "Special Report" on Cuba's health-care gushed about the island nation's "impressive health statistics." The show featured clips from Michael Moore's so-called documentary *Sicko*, while CNN's Morgan Neill, on location at a for-show Havana hospital, reported live. "Cuba's infant-mortality rates are the lowest in the hemisphere," he recited, "in line with those of Canada! Cuba can boast about health-care, a system that leads the way in Latin America."

Besides plugging Moore's *Sicko*, CNN's "Special Report" also featured medical expert Gail Reed, introduced on screen as "someone who's lived and worked in Cuba for decades." "They [the Cubans] concentrate on prevention," she explained to CNN viewers. "They concentrate on bringing services closer to people's homes. When I first came to Cuba in the 70's, I was very impressed with their efforts in building a new kind of society," Reed explained.

Most of her companions at the time were also impressed; like Bill Ayers's wife Bernardine Dohrn. As it happens, Gail Reed visited Cuba as a member of the *Venceremos* Brigades, the starry-eyed college kids who visited ostensibly to cut sugar-cane and help build Cuban socialism, a volunteer Peace Corps of sorts. Or so we were led to believe.

In fact the *Venceremos* Brigades were a joint venture between Castro's KGB-mentored DGI (Central Intelligence) and the U.S. terrorist group known as The Weathermen, which included Bill Ayers, Bernardine Dohrn and Larry Grathwohl.[9]

You've probably never heard of Grathwohl. But he looked just the part at the time. He was a ringer for Country Joe McDonald of Woodstock fame ("well it's one two three, what are we fighting for"). But Grathwohl was actually a proud Vietnam combat veteran recently recruited by the FBI and tasked with penetrating the Weathermen.

CNN's Morgan Neill could have fluffed up *Venceremos* brigadista Gail Reed's credentials by adding that from 1993 to 1997 she was a regular correspondent for *Business Week* magazine; that from 1994 to 1996 she served as a Havana-based producer for NBC News; and that today she contributes to *The Huffington Post*. When Andrea Mitchell, NBC's chief foreign-affairs correspondent, interviewed Gail Reed in Havana in April 2012 for an MSNBC report, Mitchell introduced her as "international director of the nonprofit group Medical Education Cooperation."

All true. But for the past 34 years Havana resident Gail Reed has also been married to an officer of Cuba's DGI named Julian Torres Rizo. Reed is also a regular contributor to *Granma*, which is the *Pravda* of Cuba. In 1991 Reed was tasked by the Castro regime with writing its official "Island in the Storm: the Cuban Communist Party's Fourth Congress," a not inconsiderable honor.[10]

She served in all these capacities while working for *Business Week* and NBC, by the way. Not that any American reader or viewer imbibing her reports on the marvels of Cuba's health-care and the wicked U.S. blockade of her adopted country might have guessed her background.

In early 1983, when Grenada's Marxist leader Maurice Bishop was planning a propaganda tour of the U.S., Castro appointed Gail Reed as Cuba's special emissary to his new ally. Her job was to advise Bishop on how to handle (i.e., charm and bamboozle) the U.S. media. And let's face it; who better than Reed's boss to proffer such advice?

The partnership between this future CNN, NBC and *Business Week* correspondent with Castro's secret police began in 1969 with those visits to Cuba as a member of the (DGI-created) *Venceremos* Brigades. This was also the beginning of Reed's romance with DGI officer Julian Torres Rizo. The terrorist offshoot from the SDS (Students for a Democratic Society) known as the Weathermen, and staffed most famously by Barack Obama's future neighbors Bill Ayers and Bernardine Dohrn, served as the DGI's U.S. recruitment officers, and their job proved easy. In that heady Age of Aquarius, hundreds of starry-eyed college kids were volunteering to "help build Cuban socialism" and "fight U.S. imperialism," mostly by joyfully cutting Cuban sugar-cane.

Castro's DGI had other goals in mind. "The ultimate objective of the DGI's participation in the setting up of the Venceremos Brigades," says an FBI report declassified in 1976, "was the recruitment of individuals who are politically oriented and who someday may obtain a position, elective or appointive, somewhere in the U.S. Government, which would provide the Cuban Government with access to political, economic and military intelligence. . . . A very limited number of VB members have been trained in guerrilla warfare techniques, including use of arms and explosives," the report said. "This type of training is given only to individuals who specifically request it."

"I don't regret setting bombs," Bill Ayers wrote 30 years later. "I feel we didn't do enough."[11] Three months after Dohrn's return from a *Venceremos* junket to Cuba, the Weathermen were busy in their Greenwich Village townhouse dutifully constructing a huge bomb destined for the Officers Club in Fort Dix, New Jersey.

But the bomb went off in their hands, blowing three of them to smithereens. So maybe Castro's bomb-trainers didn't do enough either? That, or their Weatherman pupils were tragically inattentive during an important session.

A week earlier, however, a Weatherman bomb had gone off as planned in San Francisco's Park Police Station, wounding nine and killing police officer Brian V. McDonnell. Larry Grathwohl, the Country Joe look-alike and the FBI's top mole within the Weathermen at the time, testified under oath that Bill Ayers boasted to him that Bernardine Dohrn had planted the bomb. When police raided the Weathermen's San Francisco bomb-factory they found Dohrn's fingerprints everywhere, along with those of Bill Ayers himself.[12]

Claims years later (especially during the first Obama presidential campaign) by Ayers and Dohrn, that their bombs were merely overgrown firecrackers meant to make noise and attract attention to their humanitarian cause, don't pan out, Grathwohl says:

"Bill Ayers specifically stated that the bombs should be placed when and where the greatest number of police officers would be killed. He specified that they should contain shrapnel, nails and wood staples, and should fire off propane tanks. Their intention was unmistakably to kill people. In fact, one of the devices found in the Pine Street bomb-factory location was a voice-activated detonator, meaning that it was designed to explode only at the nearby sound of a human voice."[13]

In September 1970 Larry Grathwohl foiled two more attempts with similar bombs. These were against the Detroit Police Officers Association, whose building was adjacent to a Red Barn Restaurant usually packed with diners, mostly blacks.

"When I objected to Billy Ayers that more innocent people would be killed in the restaurant," recalls Grathwohl, "he replied, 'Innocent people have to die in a revolution.'"

After the bombings and an FBI crackdown, the Weathermen went underground. According to Grathwohl, this is when Bill Ayers's services as a conduit between his fellow terrorists and Castro's DGI really kicked in. The heat was on, so Ayers instructed all comrades, including Grathwohl, to contact the Cuban embassy in Canada and use the code name "Delgado" to communicate with each other and for safe passage to and from Cuba through Czechoslovakia.

"They weren't out to change the system," testified Grathwohl. "They were out to destroy it, to completely destroy it. That's what they said the first time I met them, and that's what they said the last time I was with them."

"You come from a society that must be destroyed," stressed Julian Torres Rizo to the *Venceremos* brigadistas he was training in Cuba to make bombs, as he'd been trained by the KGB. This boyfriend and future husband of CNN, *Business Week,* NBC and *Huffington Post* correspondent Gail Reed then admonished: "It's your job to destroy your society."[14]

CHAPTER 1

The Golden Anniversary: A Half-Century of Loyal Service

The proverbial Man from Mars visits New York in February 1957, picks up the world's most prestigious newspaper and on the front page reads: "Fidel Castro is humanist, a man of many ideals including those of liberty, democracy and social justice . . . the need to restore Cuba's constitution and to hold elections."

Herbert Matthews, Latin America expert for *The New York Times,* had briefly "embedded" himself in Cuba's hills during a guerrilla war, interviewed the Cuban guerrilla leader himself and come away with the scoop. "Cuban Rebel Is visited in Hideout," reads the headline.

"You can be sure we hold no animosity towards the United States," he quotes Fidel Castro. "Above all we are fighting for a democratic Cuba and an end to dictatorship."

"What we do know today, in spite of the censorship, is that Cuba is undergoing a reign of terror," reports Herbert Matthews in the same piece. "This is an overworked phrase, but it is a literal truth so far as the regime of General Batista is concerned. . . . " "It amounts to a new deal for Cuba," Matthews said of Castro's program, "radical, democratic and therefore anti-Communist."

Visiting two years later the Martian discovers from another *New York Times* Latin America expert that Fidel Castro assumed power and events are playing out exactly as predicted by his colleague: "Castro's promise of social justice brings a foretaste of human dignity for millions of Cubans who had little knowledge of it in Cuba's former *near-feudal* economy," wrote New York Times' reporter Tad Szulc from Havana in February 1959. (emphasis mine)

"Cuba is now a happy island," chimed in Herbert Matthews. Happily that "reign of terror" was finally over and done. Dickey Chapelle over at *Reader's Digest* concurred. "The Cuba of Fidel Castro today is free from terror," she wrote in April 1959. "Civil liberties have been restored in Cuba and corruption seems to be drying up. These are large steps forward, and they were made against fearful odds."

Putting down *Reader's Digest* the Martian picks up *The Washington Post* to read from renowned pundit and Pulitzer Prize-winner Walter Lippmann: "It would be a great mistake even to intimate that Castro's Cuba has any real prospect of becoming a Soviet satellite."

Moving over to *Newsweek,* our Martian reads that "Castro is honest, and an honest government is something unique in Cuba. Castro is not himself even remotely a Communist."

The Martian visits again a generation later, in 1996, to find that this same Fidel Castro is visiting New York for the UN's 50th-anniversary celebration. "The Toast of Manhattan!" reads the *Time* magazine headline covering the visit. "The Hottest Ticket in Manhattan!" reads the one by *Newsweek.* He reads on to learn that parties, luncheons and assorted celebrations rage in Fidel Castro's honor Manhattan-wide, with millionaire pundits, businessmen and politicians spanning the American political spectrum clamoring for his autograph, everywhere from the head offices of *The New York Times* and *The Wall Street Journal* to the Council on Foreign Relations.

First, there was a luncheon at the Council on Foreign Relations. After holding court there for a rapt David Rockefeller, along with Robert McNamara, Dwayne Andreas and Random House's Harold Evans, Castro flashed over to Mort Zuckerman's Fifth Avenue pad, where a throng of Beltway *glitterati,* including Mike Wallace, Peter Jennings, Tina Brown, Dan Rather, Bernard Shaw and Barbara Walters, all jostled for photo-ops and Castro's autograph. Diane Sawyer was so overcome in his presence that she rushed up, broke into that toothy smile of hers, wrapped her arms around Castro and smooched him warmly on the cheek.[1]

Fast-forward to 2009, and the Martian again visits the U.S., which recently elected the candidate of its majority political party as president. "How can we help President Obama?" he reads that Fidel Castro is asking from Cuba. "Fidel Castro really wants President Obama to succeed," continues the article, quoting officials from one of the U.S. legislature's most powerful assemblies, the Congressional Black Caucus, who were visiting Cuba.[2]

"He [Fidel Castro] looked directly into my eyes!" the Martian reads from a member of this Congressional Black Caucus named Laura Richardson.

"It was quite a moment to behold! Fidel Castro was very engaging and very energetic," he reads from yet another powerful U.S. lawmaker and Congressional Black Caucus member named Barbara Lee.

"He [Fidel Castro] is one of the most amazing human beings I've ever met!" the Martian reads from Emanuel Cleaver, the chairman of this powerful legislative group belonging to America's majority political party.

The Martian hurries back to the U.S. in 2011. He (or perhaps, by now, she) turns on the TV to find former U.S. president Jimmy Carter, acclaimed as the elder statesman of America's majority political party, hugging Fidel Castro on a visit to Havana and gushing: "We greeted each other as old friends."[3]

On this same visit the Martian picks up a copy of *Newsweek* magazine, which happens to be choosing the "Best Countries in the World." "If you were born today," asks America's second-highest circulation weekly, "which country would provide you the very best opportunity to live a healthy, safe, reasonably prosperous, and upwardly mobile life?"

Intrigued, the Martian turns the page. "Ah!" he nods. "Why, of course!" *Newsweek* has crowned the citizens of Castro's Cuba among the world's luckiest people. Quality of life was the magazine's paramount issue in choosing Cuba among its "Best Countries in the World." "In quality of life," explains *Newsweek,* "Cuba outdoes its fellow middle-income countries."[4]

Among the panel of experts tasked with this daunting evaluation by America's second-biggest weekly journal were Nobel laureate and World Bank chief economist Joseph E. Stiglitz, working along with Byron Auguste and James Manyika of McKinsey & Co., ranked the most prestigious consulting firm in the world.

"How 'bout that!" the Martian marvels. "That *New York Times* nailed it when I was here half a century ago. Looks like Castro indeed liberated and enriched Cubans. And he's still enamored of the U.S. Wow! *The New York Times* was right on the money—and right from the beginning!"

Besides living up to those ideas of liberty and democracy, besides ending dictatorships and fulfilling that promise of social justice, while abolishing Cuba's shameful near-feudalism, after providing that foretaste of human dignity, after eschewing the slightest animosity towards the U.S.—during, between or after these amazing accomplishments, did anyone notice Fidel Castro and his henchmen engaging in anything else during this past half-century?

And has anyone noticed those acclaimed as "the world's luckiest people" acting in any matter that might call into question their being so honored by *Newsweek*?

Here's a hint. In 27 years, between 200 and 300 people died while trying to breach the Berlin Wall. In twice that period, about 30 times that number—between 65,000 and 80,000 people, men, women, and children, entire families at a time—have died trying to escape from Castro's Cuba.[5]

CHAPTER 2

Communist Omelet: The Unreported Cost in Life and Treasure

Bill O'Reilly: *He [Fidel Castro] has murdered people. He's imprisoned people.... He's a killer. He's a killer. And you admire the guy?"*

Ted Turner: *"To my knowledge, that's never been proven.... I admire certain things about him. He's trained a lot of doctors...."*
(Fox News, December 2008)

"There are no credible reports of disappearances, extrajudicial killings and torture in Cuba since the early 1960s, according to human rights groups."
(Anthony Boadle, Reuters Havana Bureau, December 2006)

"During the 1980s, one could still conceivably argue that Cuba's dictatorship was preferable to its US-backed counterparts in Chile, Argentina, Nicaragua or El Salvador, which went one step farther by murdering thousands of their citizens." (*The Sunday Times*, August 2006)

Forget for a second that none of the regimes denounced above by *The Sunday Times* abolished private property, free travel or free speech. None abolished free enterprise and mandated slave-era food rations for its subjects. None set up Stasi-mentored snitch groups on every city block. Forget that far from being "U.S.-backed counterparts," Pinochet's Chile and Somoza's Nicaragua had economic sanctions slapped on them by Jimmy Carter. Forget the peripheral ignorance; let's look at the central stupidity.

You long to believe otherwise, you grope for an extenuation, you hope you misread—but it's inescapable: The editorial staff of one of the world's most prestigious newspapers (*The Sunday Times*) seems unaware that Castro's regime killed people.[1] And yet:

Fidel Castro's regime jailed political prisoners at a higher rate than Stalin's during the Great Terror and murdered more people (out of a population of 6.5 million) in its first three years in power than Hitler's regime murdered (out of a population of 65 million) in its first six.

If this sounds like typical hype from an embittered and over-emotional exile with an axe to grind, let's consider some figures.

In his book *Against All Hope*, Armando Valladares—who suffered 22 years in Castro's prisons, forced-labor camps, and torture-chambers, then served under President Reagan as U.S. ambassador to the UN Human Rights Commission—reveals how at one point in 1961 Castro's *gulag* held 350,000 political prisoners. Freedom House estimates that half a million Cubans have passed through Castro's *gulag.* That's out of a Cuban population at the time of 6.5 million.

In her book *Gulag*, Anne Applebaum estimates that at any one time, two million people were incarcerated in Stalin's *gulag.* That was out of a Soviet population of 220 million.

Now punch your calculator . . . see? It turns out that calling Castro a Stalinist (as will occur often in this book) slightly low-balls his repression. Fidel Castro jailed and tortured Cubans at a higher rate than Stalin jailed and tortured subjects of his Soviet empire.

The Black Book of Communism, written by French scholars and published in English by Harvard University Press (neither an outpost of the vast right-wing conspiracy, much less of embittered

Cuban exiles) estimates that Castro's regime murdered 16,000 Cubans by firing squad, mostly during the 60's. Again, Cuba was a nation of 6.5 million in those years. Given the U.S. population, a proportionate bloodbath would approach one million firing-squad murders.

I write murders because the term execution implies some form of judicial process. Che Guevara laid down this process one week after entering Havana. "Judicial evidence is an archaic bourgeois detail," he sneered. "We execute from revolutionary conviction."

His boss Fidel Castro (a lawyer who abolished *habeas corpus* immediately upon assuming power) followed up: "Legal proof is impossible to obtain against war criminals. So we sentence them based on moral conviction."

According to the Cuba Archive Project, headed by scholars Maria Werlau and the late Armando Lago, the Castro regime—with firing squads, prison tortures, forced-labor camps and drownings at sea—has caused an estimated 100,000 Cuban deaths.

According to the *Harper Collins Atlas of the Second World War,* Nazi repression caused 172,260 French civilian deaths during the occupation.

France was nation of 42 million in 1940. Punching my calculator now reveals that Fidel Castro caused an enormously higher percentage of deaths among the people he made among the luckiest in the world with free and exquisite health-care than the Nazis caused among the French they enslaved and tortured with the SS and Gestapo.

Many opponents of the Cuban regime qualify as the longest-suffering political prisoners in modern history, having suffered prison camps, forced labor and torture-chambers for a period three times as long in Castro's *gulag* as Alexander Solzhenitsyn suffered in Stalin's (eight years). Several black Cubans suffered longer in Castro's prisons than Nelson Mandela spent in South Africa's (27 years). Surely you're familiar with Solzhenitsyn and Mandela. Now let's see if you recognize some of the Cuban ex-prisoners:

Mario Chanes (30 years), Ignacio Cuesta Valle (29 years), Antonio Lopez Munoz (28 years), Indasio Hernandez Pena (28 years), Alberto Fibla (28 years), Pastor Macuran (28 years), Roberto Martin Perez (28 years), Roberto Perdomo (28 years), Teodoro Gonzalez (28 years), Jose L. Pujals (27 years), Miguel Alvarez Cardentey (27 years), Eusebio Penalver (28 years).

No? None of these names rings a bell? And yet their suffering took place in a country only 90 miles from U.S. shores, in cells and torture-chambers off-limits to inspection by the Red Cross and Amnesty International, unlike apartheid South Africa's. An association of these Cuban heroes, representing 3,551 years in Castro's prisons and torture-chambers, resides in the U.S. today.

Shortly before his death in 2006, one of those ex-prisoners, Eusebio Penalver, granted this writer an interview. "For months I was naked in a six-by-four-foot cell," recalled Eusebio. "That's four feet high, so you couldn't stand. But they never succeeded in branding me as common criminal, so I felt a great freedom inside myself. I refused to commit spiritual suicide."[2]

In light of this totalitarian secrecy by their torturers, these revelations would seem of immense interest and value. In fact most of the ex-prisoners reside in New York City and Miami, a short cab ride from most mainstream media studios. They'd be easy to contact for dramatic interviews, inspirational human-interest segments, etc.

Also note that all of the above suffered prison as long as or longer than Nelson Mandela. Ninety or more miles from U.S. shores, they suffered at the hands of a Stalinist regime that craved to nuke the U.S. But none has ever been featured in a U.S. mainstream media report. Apparently the media perceive no human-interest quotient for U.S. viewers in any of this.

Yet when Nelson Mandela, who suffered his prison term at the hands of a segregationist regime eight thousand miles away, first visited the U.S. in 1990, the media-watchdog group Accuracy in Media termed his tumultuous media coverage "Mandela Mania."

"The hero of oppressed people everywhere!" hailed ABC. "A larger-than-life figure!" gushed CNN. "A virtual symbol of freedom!" crowed CBS. "His name has a mystical quality!" gushed Dan Rather. "A worldwide hero!" continued "Gunga Dan" Rather, who went on to compare Mandela to Mother Teresa.

Other reports compared Mandela to the Pope, Jesus Christ and Moses. *The New York Times* devoted 23 pages to laudatory articles on Saint Mandela in one single week. Ted Koppel hosted an ABC "Town Meeting" with Mandela where every question was sugar and spice and everything nice.[3]

All the networks that were responsible for the tumultuous coverage of a South African political prisoner have been granted news bureaus in Havana by the regime that created the longest-suffering political prisoners in modern history. But none of the latter has ever been featured in those networks' reporting.

Interestingly, at the very time of his adulatory U.S. media coverage, the U.S. State Department listed Mandela's African National Congress (ANC) as a terrorist organization. Today the U.S. State Department still lists Cuba as a State Sponsor of Terrorism.

Moral: if you want U.S. mainstream-media encomiums, be a foreign terrorist rather than a Cuban-American victim of the terrorists who craved to nuke the U.S.

OK, let's try the names of some women political prisoners who were jailed and tortured for years and even decades by Fidel Castro's regime. This totalitarian horror, by the way, was utterly unknown in the Western Hemisphere until introduced by the man swooned over by Barbara Walters and Andrea Mitchell and Diane Sawyer. Here's a handful of the thousands of ladies who suffered in Castro's prisons and torture chambers: Ana Rodriguez, Miriam Ortega, Isabel Tejera, Nelly Rojas, Olga Morgan, Maritza Lugo, Georgina Cid, Caridad Roque, Sara Del Toro, Mercedes Pena, Aida Diaz Morejon, Agata Villarquide, Alicia Del Busto, Albertina O'Farrill.

Again the names are all unfamiliar, right? Yet these ladies all live in the U.S. today, mostly minutes from mainstream media studios. But no producer for Oprah or Joy Behar or Katie Couric, none from the Lifetime or Oxygen TV, much less the History Channel, has ever called them. No writer for *Cosmo* or *Glamour* or *Redbook* or *Vogue* has bothered either. And for obvious reasons; "The Real Grandmaws of Miami" just doesn't interest Bravo TV.

Women's prison conditions were described by former prisoner Maritza Lugo. "The punishment cells measure three feet wide by six feet long. The toilet consisted of an eight-inch hole in the ground through which cockroaches and rats enter; especially in cool temperatures the rats come inside to seek the warmth of our bodies, and we were often bitten. For week's we'd be locked up in total darkness with a little cup of filthy water daily to drink. Nothing to wash or to flush the excrement and vermin-crammed hole that passed for a toilet. Nothing to wash away the menstrual fluid that caked to our legs. The suicide rate among women prisoners was very high."

Indeed a study found that, by 1986, Cuba's suicide rate reached 24 per thousand—making it double Latin America's average, making it triple Cuba's pre-Castro rate, and with Cuban women the most suicidal in the world.[4]

How these women survived years and even decades of such horrors, then "taken charge of their lives" and "gotten their groove back," might seem newsworthy and inspirational. Indeed, their stories fairly epitomize the most popular themes of women's chatshows. You can almost hear Gloria Gaynor's "I Will Survive" as Joy Behar, Barbara Walters and Whoopi Goldberg greet these long-suffering but somehow-surviving Cuban ladies on stage with a standing ovation, sniffles and teary hugs.

Instead, "the national media have never shown the slightest interest in any of our stories," shrugs Caridad Roque from Miami today. Ms. Roque was arrested by Castro's KGB-trained police at the age of 19 and suffered 16 years of prison and torture in Cuba.

Her torturer, on the other hand, has been fawningly interviewed by feminists from Barbara Walters to Andrea Mitchell, from Maria Shriver to Oriana Fallaci. On a visit to Cuba in 2002 feminist pioneer Carole King sang Fidel Castro a personal and heartfelt "You've Got a Friend."[5]

THE UNREPORTED COST

The Stalinist regime Fidel Castro imposed on Cuba stole the savings and property of 6.4 million citizens, made refugees of 20 per cent of the population from a nation formerly deluged with immigrants and whose citizens had achieved a higher standard of living than those residing in half of Europe. The Castro regime also tripled Cubans' pre-revolution suicide rate. The editors of *Newsweek*—the defenders of Cuba as the land of opportunity in which "to live a healthy, safe, reasonably prosperous, and upwardly mobile life"—might take note.

Fidel Castro converted a nation with double Spain's per-capita income, with the 13th-lowest infant-mortality rate in the world, whose industrial workers earned the eighth-highest wages in the world, whose peso was valued higher than the U.S. dollar, into a pesthole that repels Haitians.[6]

"I can see that Cuba is much more impoverished than Haiti," observed Gelsy Leveque, a recent Haitian visitor to Cuba. "People here in Cuba are all sad. I watch on Cuban TV how they say Haitians are all poor. But in reality we're less poor than Cubans. Yes, my family is poor but we have a car. We're never hungry and we're free and generally happy. Cubans, come to Haiti, we have a country much better and happier than yours."[7]

And this after the Soviets lavished Castro's Cuba with subsidies that totaled almost ten Marshall Plans (into a nation of seven to ten million). This Castroite economic feat defies not only the laws of economics but seemingly the laws of physics.

This revolutionary process also graced Cuba with a lower credit rating than Somalia, fewer phones per capita than Papua New

Guinea, fewer internet connections than Uganda, and 20 per cent of her population gone—all at the total cost of their property and many at the cost of a horrible death by exposure, drowning and/or sharks. This from a nation that formerly enjoyed a higher influx of immigrants per-capita (primarily from Europe) than did the U.S.[8]

WHO KNEW?

Who knew? Certainly no one who relied on the mainstream media for news about Cuba.

"But come on, Humberto!" you might retort. "If everything was so hunky-dory and peachy-keen in Cuba, then how on earth did Castro manage take over? Why did so many Cubans initially back him? Huh?"

Thought you'd never ask.

Upon its release in 2006 Andy Garcia's Movie *The Lost City* ran into a media buzz-saw for failing (in media-critic eyes) to answer that very question. "In a movie about the Cuban revolution, we almost never see any of the working poor for whom the revolution was supposedly fought," sniffed Peter Reiner in *The Christian Science Monitor*. "*The Lost City* misses historical complexity."

Actually, what's missing is Mr. Reiner's historical knowledge. Andy Garcia and screenwriter Guillermo Cabrera-Infante knew full well that the working poor had no role in that part of the Cuban revolution. The anti-Batista rebellion was led and staffed overwhelmingly by Cuba's middle class and, especially, upper class. To wit: In August 1957 Castro's rebel movement called for a national strike against the Batista dictatorship—and threatened to shoot workers who reported to work. The national strike was completely ignored.

Another was called for April 9, 1958. And again Cuban workers blew a loud and collective raspberry at their liberators, reporting to work *en masse*.

"Garcia's tale bemoans the loss of easy wealth for a precious few," harrumphed Michael Atkinson in *The Village Voice*. "Poor people are absolutely absent; Garcia and [screenwriter Guillermo Cabrera] Infante seem to have thought that peasant revolutions happen for no particular reason—or at least no reason the moneyed one per cent should have to worry about."

What's absolutely absent is Mr. Atkinson's knowledge about the Cuba Garcia depicts in his movie. His crack about that "moneyed one per cent" and especially his "peasant revolution" epitomize the clichéd idiocies still parroted by the media about Cuba.

"The impoverished masses of Cubans who embraced Castro as a liberator appear only in grainy, black-and-white news clips," snorted Stephen Holden in *The New York Times*. "Political dialogue in the film is strictly of the junior high-school variety."

It's Holden's education on the Cuban revolution that's of the junior high-school variety, probably thanks to colleagues such as Herbert Matthews, Tad Szulc and Anthony DePalma.

"It fails to focus on the poverty-stricken workers whose plight lit the fires of revolution," complained Rex Reed in *The New York Observer*.

Here we see the effectiveness of a 50-year-long propaganda campaign. You're generally better off attempting rational discourse with the Flat Earth Society, but nonetheless I'll try to dispel the fantasies of pre-Castro Cuba still cherished by the mainstream media and Hollywood. Here's a report from the International Labor Organization on Cuba circa 1957: "One feature of the Cuban social structure is a large middle class," it starts. "Cuban workers are more unionized (proportional to the population) than U.S. workers. The average wage for an 8-hour day in Cuba in 1957 is higher than for workers in Belgium, Denmark, France and Germany. Cuban labor receives 66.6 per cent of gross national income. In the U.S. the figure is 70 per cent, in Switzerland 64 per cent. Forty-four per cent of Cubans are covered by social legislation, a higher percentage than in the U.S."[9]

In 1958 Cuba had a higher per-capita income than Spain, Austria and Japan.[10] Cuban industrial workers had the eighth-highest wages in the world. In the 1950's Cuban stevedores earned more per hour than their counterparts in New Orleans and San Francisco. Cuba had established an eight-hour workday in 1933—five years before FDR's New Dealers got around to it. Add to this a one-month paid vacation. The much-lauded (by liberals) social democracies of Western Europe didn't manage this till 30 years later.

These labor-friendly policies naturally had their cost; chiefly in moderately high unemployment. "It would not be an exaggeration to say that Batista, during his second period of power, ran Cuba by means of an alliance with organized labor," writes Hugh Thomas in *Cuba or The Pursuit of Freedom*. "In return for the support of labor, Batista underwrote the vast number of restrictive practices, the limitation on mechanization and the bans on dismissals that were such a characteristic of the Cuban labor scene."

"It's easier to get rid of a wife than an employee!" was a lament said to be heard in the Havana Yacht Club during those years. So Cuba's pre-Castro economy certainly needed tweaking. But hardly because a handful of "billionaire oligarchs" controlled the island, as *The Atlantic's* Jeffrey Goldberg claimed in an article after interviewing Fidel Castro in September 2010, wherein this newly-minted Cuba expert denounced "the thugocracy of Batista, who was a friend only to a handful of oligarchs and American mafia leaders."[11]

FRIEND OF OLIGARCHS?

Granted, *The Godfather II* is a superb film. But better educational sources on pre-Castro Cuba *do* exist, though the fact seems to be lost on Jeffrey Goldberg of *The Atlantic,* among most other self-appointed Cuba experts. Batista, the alleged friend of oligarchs, was the mulatto grandson of slaves, born on the dirt floor of a palm-roofed shack in the Cuban countryside. Cuba's oligarchy in fact denied Fulgencio Batista admittance into their Havana Yacht Club and largely bankrolled his violent overthrow. From Cuba's richest man, sugar magnate Julio Lobo, to Pepin Bosch of the Bacardi dynasty, and hundreds of oligarchs in between, the very people whom the learned Mr. Goldberg claims were Batista's friends were funding Castro's July 26 Movement.

In fact—contrary to the propaganda-fueled superstitions of most academics and pundits—the economic adjustments needed in Cuba at the time were more along the lines of what Governor Scott Walker recently achieved in Wisconsin than what the "Occupy" movement prescribed.

"A new hour has arrived for the world," wrote Communist poet Pablo Neruda in 1944 as Batista stepped down from his first term as Cuba's president. "The hour of the people, and of the men of the people, the hour of figures like Tito, *La Pasionaria* [Spanish Stalinist Dolores Ibarruri] and the important American figure Fulgencio Batista, who included two Cuban Communist party members in his Cabinet."[12]

In fact, despite the media's universal and Pavlovian response of "U.S.-backed" to any mention of Fulgencio Batista, this backing amounts to another Castroite fable spread by his media auxiliaries. If Batista was a U.S.-backed dictator, then Yugoslavia's Tito was a U.S.-backed dictator squared, receiving over $3.5 billion in U.S. economic aid during the 50's. Communist Tito was receiving essentially free U.S. arms shipments at the same time that anti-

Communist Batista was denied delivery of U.S. arms his government had actually bought and paid for.[13]

Given that Cuba always maintained a favorable balance of trade with the world, and that the Cuban peso was equal (and briefly more valuable) than the U.S. dollar during Batista's term, this (black) Cuban dictator never saw a need to step and fetch or roll over and beg in front of U.S. officials. Obama's bowing to Hu Jintao just wasn't Batista's style, or remotely called for in view of Cuba's economic condition during his term. Since 1933, when he took over Cuba's military at the age of 32, Batista had been known as *El Hombre*—the man, after all.

Batista's trouble with the State Department actually started with some of his nationalist (in the liberal sense of the term) policies of import-substitution and trade diversification, which is to say the precise opposite of lackeyism. The contract to build the Havana Tunnel in 1956, for instance, was granted by the Cuban government to a French engineering firm, though several U.S. firms were bidding. In the late 1950's Batista's government was also shopping around for locomotives and General Motors assumed they had a done deal.[14]

Instead Cuba bought the locomotives from a West German manufacturer. The U.S. farm lobby got up in arms when a wheat mill was planned for construction in eastern Cuba, accompanied by higher tariffs on U.S. wheat. U.S. paper mills grumbled when Cuba instituted a process for converting bagasse (the residue from sugar-refining) into newsprint. Cuba had 58 daily newspapers and 126 weekly magazines at the time. So the eventual loss to U.S. paper suppliers would not be paltry.[15]

The anti-Batista rebellion (not revolution) of the late 50's was staffed and led overwhelmingly by college students and professionals—and financed by Cuba's wealthiest men, sugar magnate Julio Lobo and rum magnate (Bacardi) "Pepin" Bosch among them.

Here's the makeup of the supposed peasant revolution's first Cabinet, drawn from the leaders in the anti-Batista fight: seven lawyers, two university professors, three university students, one doctor, one engineer, one architect, one former city mayor and a colonel who defected from the Batista army. A notoriously bourgeois bunch, as Che Guevara himself put it.

By 1961, however, workers and *campesinos* (country folk) made up the overwhelming bulk of the anti-Castroite rebels, especially the guerrillas in the Escambray mountains. So Andy Garcia showed it precisely right. In 1958 Cuba was undergoing a *rebellion*, not a revolution. Cubans expected *political* change and economic tweaking, not a socioeconomic cataclysm and catastrophe. But most film critics and reporters still rely on boneheaded clichés.

Oh, and as previously asked—during the past half-century, has anyone noticed those people, whom *Newsweek* termed the world's luckiest, acting in any matter which might call that label into question? Let's look further into it.

CHAPTER 3

The "World's Luckiest People," or So Says *Newsweek*

On July 14, 2011, only six months after Tina Brown's *Newsweek* had pronounced Cuba among the "Best Countries in the World," an Iberia Airlines jet left Havana and landed in Madrid with a member of the "world's luckiest people" stowed away. The 23-year-old Cuban man, named Adonis G.B., was curled in the landing gear, crushed to death.[1]

Adonis joined an estimated 70,000 Cubans dying (literally) to leave Fidel Castro's handcrafted kingdom. Almost two million Cubans have made it out alive, from a nation formerly swamped with immigrants.

On Christmas Eve 2000, a British Airlines jet flying from Havana opened its landing-gear near Heathrow airport, and out dropped two corpses, frozen solid. They were shortly identified as 16-year-old Miguel Fonseca and 17-year-old Alberto Vazquez.

"Crazy blokes!" some of the passengers probably huffed, oblivious or uncaring that all those pounds they'd just spent on their Cuban vacations had gone straight into the coffers of the Stalinist military and police who drove the Cuban boys to such deadly desperation.

On July 21, 1991, the frozen corpses of Alexis Hernandez, 19, and Jose Acevedo, 20, plopped onto Madrid airport's tarmac from the landing-gear of another Iberia Airlines flight.

On August 22, 1999, the frozen cadaver of Felix Julian Garcia dropped from a British Airlines plane onto the tarmac of Gatwick airport as it landed from Havana.

In July 2002, the frozen and battered corpse of a of 20-year-old Cuban identified only as "Wilfredo D." was found in the landing-gear of a Lufthansa Airlines plane at Dusseldorf airport.

In December 2002, a 20-year-old Cuban who worked at Havana airport snuck into a pressurized compartment of Canadian Airlines, just under the cabin. Four hours later he scurried out alive in Montreal's international airport.

On June 4, 1969, an Iberia Airlines plane, just landed in Madrid from Havana, was taxiing to the terminal when the frozen corpse of 16-year-old Jorge Perez dropped out. His partner in escape, Armando Socorras, 17, somehow survived in what Spanish medical authorities described as a form of "human hibernation."[2]

In September 1999, an unpleasant stench led airport officials near Milan, Italy to the decomposed corpse of Roberto Garcia Quinta in the landing-gear of an Alitalia Airlines flight that had landed from Santiago, Cuba ten days earlier. In 1958 the Cuban Embassy in Rome had a backlog of 12,000 applications from Italians clamoring to immigrate to Cuba. "A simple way to take measure of a country is to look at how many want in, and how many want out," famously quipped Tony Blair. Millions of people "voted with their feet" in favor of *The New York Times'* near-feudal Cuba. Then came Castroism.

Pre-Castro Cuba took in more immigrants per-capita (primarily from Europe) than the U.S., including the Ellis Island years. In the 1950's, when Cubans were perfectly free to emigrate with all their property and U.S. visas were issued to them for the asking, about the same number of Cubans lived in the U.S. as Americans lived in Cuba. This phenomenon was so alarming that in 1933, as a stopgap against foreign rascals horning in on the "Cuban dream," the Cuban government passed laws more draconian than Arizona's and Georgia's today: a majority of employees at all Cuban businesses had to be Cuban natives.

Would our construction, service and hospitality industries survive the enforcement of such a law nowadays?

In 1992 former East German dictator Erich Honecker was tried (to no avail) for the deaths of 192 Germans killed while attempting to cross the Berlin Wall. Some human-rights groups estimate that actually 300 people (out of an average East German population over the decades of 18 million) had died trying to breach the Berlin Wall or otherwise escape East Germany—no runner-up in the "quality-of-life" awards, even by *Newsweek* standards. (The Wall's official name was the "Anti-Fascist Protection Rampart.")

As mentioned, an estimated 70,000 people (out of an average population of seven to ten million over the decades) have died trying to escape Castro's Cuba, *Newsweek's* quality-of-life winner. After so many machine-gun blasts of their frontier "guards" disturbed their coastal subjects, the Castro brothers hit upon the expedient of having helicopters hover over the escaping freedom-seekers, who often comprised whole families—but to hold off on shooting.

Instead of machine-gunning the families to death as years of tradition called for, they switched to dropping sandbags onto the rickety rafts and tiny boats to demolish and sink them. Then the tiger sharks and hammerheads could do the Castroites' deputy-work. Screams, groans and gurgles, after all, don't carry nearly as far as machine-gun blasts.

"The best revolutionary German man I've ever known was Erich Honecker," tweeted Fidel Castro on June 1, 2012 commemorating the 18th anniversary of the East German Stalinist's death. "I maintain feelings of profound solidarity with Honecker."

"What a chump," Castro was probably thinking. "A measly 192?"

"In one week during 1962 we counted more than 400 firing-squad blasts from the execution yard below our cells," recalled former Cuban political prisoner and freedom-fighter Roberto Martin-Perez to this writer.

"This is the most savage kind of behavior I've ever heard of," said Robert Gelbard, deputy assistant Secretary of State for Latin America during the Clinton administration. "This is even worse than what happened at the Berlin Wall!"[3] Gelbard had watched desperate Cubans trying to swim to our Guantanamo Naval Base when machine-guns opened up and the water around them frothed in white, then red.

The corpses were retrieved by Cuban guards on boats, with the same kinds of gaff hooks the lucky contestants in the regime-sponsored "Hemingway Fishing Festival" were using in nearby waters to yank thrashing tunas and marlins aboard their Cuba-registered yachts.

In September 2011 Spanish medical examiners found that stowaway Adonis G.B.'s throat had been crushed. He probably died on takeoff, meaning he died more quickly and painlessly than the tens of thousands of others who perished while running from Cuba's free and fabulous health-care.

It was a different story for the tens of thousands of dead Cuban rafters. Most of these desperate rafters probably died like captives of the Apaches, staked in the sun and dying slowly of sunburn and thirst. Others perished gasping and choking after their arms and legs had finally given out and they had gulped that last lungful of seawater, much like the crew in *The Perfect Storm*. Still others were eaten alive—drawn and quartered by the serrated teeth of hammerheads and tiger sharks, much like Captain Quint in *Jaws*. Perhaps these last perished the most mercifully. As we've seen on the Discovery Channel, sharks don't dally at a meal.

"In space no one can hear you scream," says the ad for the original *Alien*. Same is true for the middle of the Florida Straits; except, of course, for your raft-mates. While clinging to the disintegrating raft, while watching the fins rush in and water froth in white, then red, they hear the screams all too clearly. Elian Gonzalez might know.

All during the decades coinciding with Castro's rule, the Coast Guard has documented hundreds of such stories. Were the cause of these horrors more "politically incorrect," we'd have no end of books, movies, documentaries, TV interviews, survival-story specials, etc. We'd never hear the end of it. Alas, the agents of this Caribbean holocaust are the Left's premier pin-up boys.

So what's the alternative if you can't flee Cuba, among "the Best Countries in the World" according to Tina Brown's *Newsweek* and a "happy island" according to *The New York Times?*

Well, in 1986, Cuba's suicide rate reached 24 per thousand—double Latin America's average, triple Cuba's pre-Castro rate, *Cuban women the most suicidal in the world*, and suicide the primary cause of death for Cubans aged 15 to 48. At that point, the Cuban government ceased publishing the statistics on the self-slaughter. The figures became state secrets. The implications horrified even the Castroites.[4]

But apparently they did not faze *Newsweek*.

During the summer of 1961, as the Berlin Wall went up, Miami's Cuban Refugee Center started keeping records of the refugee wave then setting out from Herbert Matthews's "happy island." By late 1964 they recorded 1,002 boats and rafts of various types carrying more than 10,000 bedraggled Cubans to Florida. Approximately 800 of these craft were first spotted in mid-passage by the Coast Guard's two Grumman Albatross planes patrolling the Straits. These then notified the U.S. Coast Guard, who escorted the escapee crafts to U.S. shores.

Too often, however, upon being alerted and guided by their airborne colleagues, the cutter would pull up to an empty boat or one filled with corpses. At the time, the Cuban Refugee Center and the U.S. Coast Guard estimated that, for every Cuban who made it to the U.S., three died—by drowning, exposure, sharks or bullets. The odds were well known in Cuba. And still they came.[5]

Arturo Cobo, who runs a refugee center in Key West (*Hogar de Transito para los Refugiados Cubanos*), says the number of dead freedom-seekers tops the 70,000 figure often cited. "Word eventually reached Cuba that our group was helping rafters here in Key West," says Cobo, a Bay of Pigs veteran. "So there came a point in the 80's when we started getting calls from Cuba saying so and so just left on a raft from such and such a place. Can you please notify us when they reach the U.S.?"

"Usually my heartbreaking notification to the Cuban relatives came a few weeks later," says Cobo, "meaning that that no people by those names had ever been rescued or processed. The vast majority never reached the U.S. At first it was an informal tally. But finally I began posting the names and the dates of their departure from Cuba on a wall and running them against the names of those who we rescued at sea or helped and processed when they somehow made it to land. My informal study showed that right around three-quarters of the freedom-seekers never made landfall. And many who did we had to rush to local hospitals—dehydration, sunburn, dementia, all of that for sure, but also add gunshot wounds from Castro's police, shark attacks, etc. I well remember processing Ivette Molina who arrived horribly sunburnt, delirious and dehydrated. She had several bullet wounds and was also pregnant. Why does the world ignore this? I still wake up often in the middle of the night and find it impossible to sleep.

"That cemetery-without-crosses as we started calling it is a huge one. And this holocaust is still being denied—not by a few nutcases as in the one during WWII, but by most of the world."[6]

Landfall itself doesn't always ensure survival. On May 15, 1997 a Brothers to the Rescue flight-crew noticed people waving frantically from tiny key called Dog Rock in the southernmost Bahamas. Following their standard rescue pattern, the crew banked, came in on a lower pass and dropped water, food and a radio.

In minutes the plane's radio crackled with the news from below that the family of six rafters had languished on that blazing rock for 17 days. Three of them were still alive. The Brothers notified the Bahamian Coast Guard which arrived on a windless day to find a dreadful stench hovering over the little rock island. Two of the freedom-seekers had perished days before and been crudely buried under rocks, the only burial possible. One was a four-year-old moppet named Camila Martinez Rodriguez, the other a 13-year-old girl named Adianet Tamayo Rodriguez. The captain of the tiny raft, 26-year-old Leonin Rivas, had also perished. The Cuban American National Foundation recovered the bodies and gave them a proper burial in Miami. The three survivors were granted asylum in the U.S.

"Multiply that horror hundreds of times," says Arturo Cobo, "and you'll get an idea of what many of us witnessed from Key West during the 90's. And it's still going on today, though mercifully more infrequently."

During the first five months of 2012 the U.S. Coast Guard interdicted close to one thousand Cubans at sea. These were all shuttled back to Cuba, as mandated by U.S. law.

CASTRO'S WALL

"Mr. Gorbachev, tear down this wall!" Who can forget the famous line? In fact most people forgot it shortly after President Reagan detonated the words at the Brandenberg Gate in June 1987. At the time they got little press-play, and what they got was mostly negative. President Reagan's own advisors, Colin Powell and Howard Baker, denounced as "unpresidential" and "extremist" the proclamation that would become President Reagan's most admired and famous.

It was only in November 1989, as the wall was finally torn down, that Reagan's proclamation was recalled, dusted off, and festooned with the fame now almost universal—at least among conservatives.

The people of the Free World were thrilled *en masse* when the wall finally came down. To lay eyes on the Berlin Wall provoked shame and horror. Here was stark and perfect proof of what divided the world. No amount of paint or plaster to pretty it up could disguise what it was doing. Reagan saw it and outspokenly called it by its name—diplomatic peck-sniffs be damned.

And two years later Mr. Gorbachev complied, to much acclaim worldwide, though his compliance may have been unwitting.

Down in Cuba at this very time, Raul Castro was warning: "If any Gorbachev raises his head around here, we'll promptly chop it off! We would rather see Cuba sink into the ocean, like Atlantis, before we see the corrupting forces of capitalism prevail!"[7] Raul Castro's boasts came safely from behind a Communist barrier that had murdered (by the *lowest* estimate) more than 20 *times* the number of innocents as the one Gorbachev had been petitioned to tear down.

At the time of Raul Castro's characteristically bloodthirsty boast and during the wholesale murder by his military of hundreds of Cubans for the crime of voting with their feet (and paddles) against him, thousands of tourists from Western Europe, including many from West Germany, were already pouring into Castro's island fiefdom.

Every Mark, Lira, Pound, Franc and Schilling of their expenditures landed in the pocket of the Soviet-trained outfit which owned and operated the Soviet helicopters and gunships that helped fill the cemetery-without-crosses where 20 times as many freedom-seeking Cubans were buried as freedom-seeking Germans lay in all of Berlin's cemeteries. And machine-gun bullets kill relatively quickly compared to sunburn, dehydration and tiger sharks.

Upon the Soviet Union's collapse, and in the nick of time, the overlords in this Caribbean outpost of the Evil Empire had a lifeline thrown to them—and they clutched it eagerly. This financial lifeline for Cuban Stalinism was thrown in large part by European witnesses to the Holocaust, *gulag* and Cold War. Starting in 1991 and continuing to throng the island today, free-spending tourists from Europe have swarmed to Castro's rescue. Which brings us to the military-tourism complex.

CUBA'S MILITARY-TOURISM COMPLEX

The only income-producing activity properly describable as an industry in Cuba is tourism. And the Cuban military owns Cuba's tourist industry almost lock, stock and barrel. So the only outfit in Cuba with guns is also the richest, thanks in large part to people who shuddered and grimaced at the Berlin Wall.

Castro's Cuba is a military dictatorship in the most genuine sense of the term. Raul Castro and his military cronies have been running Cuba for more than two decades and doing quite well in the process. Of the 19 members of Cuba's *Politburo,* nine are military men. That is more than was the case for the typical Soviet-bloc nation, and more than for the Soviet Union itself.

A Castro-regime bureau known as GAESA (*Grupo de Administracion Empresarial S.A.*) does much of this running. It controls 300 different companies or state agencies, which often operate in partnership with minority-owning foreign investors. Among GAESA's subsidiaries are Gaviota S.A., which runs the island's tourist industry; hotels, restaurants, car-rentals and nightclubs; and TRD-Caribe S.A., which runs all retail operations. In brief GAESA controls virtually every economic transaction in Cuba, making it by far the most powerful company in Castro's Stalinist fiefdom.

Gaviota also owns the domestic airline, Aerogaviota, which uses Cuban air-force pilots flying refurbished Soviet transport airplanes. The U.S. Army's *Military Review* describes Cuba's Revolutionary Armed Forces and its GAESA operation as "one of the most entrepreneurial, corporate conglomerates in the Americas."

In a November 18, 2010 hearing by the House Foreign Affairs Committee debating the (so-called) U.S. travel ban to Cuba, Lieutenant Colonel Christopher Simmons, a recently retired Defense Intelligence Agency Cuba specialist, explained the issue in detail. He showed how Raul Castro's military owns virtually every corporation involved in Cuba's tourism industry, which in turn is the regime's top money-maker.

The Cuban military's Gaviota tourism group is a corporate umbrella encompassing: Aerogaviota SA (airlines), Almest SA Hoteles Gaviota (hotels), Gaviota Tour (bus touring company), Marinas Gaviota (marinas), Tiendas Gaviota (tourist souvenir stores, restaurants) and Parques Naturales Gaviota (national parks, museums).

The presentation also revealed something that goes a long way towards explaining Raul Castro's confident entrenchment and recent brazen murder of dissidents. Last year Cuba enjoyed record tourism revenues: 2.7 million tourists leaving almost $3 billion in military-regime coffers, and precious little to other sectors of society, owing to the regime's tourist apartheid, where Cubans (especially darker-skinned ones) are strictly segregated by billy club and at gun-point from tourist areas, except as waiters, maids, bellhops, shoe-shine boys, masseuses, etc.

With this tourist-revenue windfall going on for almost two decades, Cuba's ruling military robber-barons are making a killing. Why would they voluntarily upset their own apple-carts by democratizing the system and opening it to competitors?

As GAESA's chief executive officer we find Raul Castro's son-in-law, Maj. Luis Alberto Rodriguez *Lopez-Callejas*. Lately—and seemingly out of the blue—one of the U.S. media's most-beloved and oft-quoted experts on U.S.-Cuban relations is a lecturer on Latin American politics at the University of Denver named Arturo *Lopez-Levy (Callejas)*, who happens to be Maj. Luis Alberto's cousin.

In 2005, Arturo Lopez-Levy *(Callejas)* received the Leonard Marks Essay Award of the American Academy of Diplomacy. He has also been a fellow of the Inter-American Dialogue and the (Jimmy) Carter Center. Let the issue of U.S.-Cuba relations blip on the media radar nowadays and, given his supposed expertise on Cuban matters, *The New York Times* almost immediately reaches out to Arturo Lopez-Levy, Raul Castro's nephew-in-law—not that anyone would guess it anywhere in his media bio.

"Mr. Lopez-Levy is a former secretary of the B'Nai B'rith Lodge in Cuba." That's how *The New York Times* introduced him in a story of March 2012. "A Cuban-born academic who left the island ten years ago and lectures at the University of Denver," is how *The New York Times* described its valued source in another article three weeks later.

"Arturo Lopez Levy is Ph.D. candidate at the Josef Korbel School of International Studies of the University of Denver, Colorado," is how CNN summarizes its frequent contributor.

Professor Arturo Lopez-Callejas's media-soundbites, lectures, articles, papers and speeches all stress a common theme: namely, that the U.S. should allow unfettered travel to Cuba. "Canadian respect for the human right to travel, as it is defined in the Universal Declaration, is a model to be emulated by the United States."

Despite the general fetish to consult and quote him, no mainstream media outlet has ever mentioned Arturo Lopez-Callejas's kinship with Cuba's dictator, much less his closer kinship with the Cuban dictator's son-in-law, much less this son-in-law's position as chief of the Castro regime's business monopoly over Cuba's tourist industry.

In brief: the head of Castro's tourist industry, through the good offices of the mainstream U.S. media, has his cousin constantly lobbying for more U.S. travel to Cuba. And the U.S. public for the most part remains utterly oblivious to his background and possible motives, much less to what tourism in Cuba might mean to the Cuban people's prospects for freedom.

"We don't need no stinkin' registration with the U.S. Justice Department as agents of a foreign government!" could well be the chuckle of Castro's U.S. agents; and for going on half a century now.

JUVENILE VICTIMS

A 17-year-old named Orlando Travieso was armed with only a homemade paddle when he was machine-gunned to death in March 1991. His crime was trying to flee Cuba on a tiny raft. Loamis Gonzalez was 15 when he was machine-gunned to death for the same crime the same year. Owen Delgado was 15 when Castro's police dragged him out of the Ecuadorian embassy, where he had sought asylum, and clubbed him to death with rifle-butts.[8]

Yes, behind those statistics lie people, often children. Carlos Anaya was three on July 13, 1994 when Castro's Coast Guard rammed and sank the escaping tugboat that held his mother and 70 other desperate Cubans. His boatmate Yisel Alvarez was four. Helen Martinez was six months old. Forty-three Cubans drowned, 11 of them children. Fidel Castro personally decorated the boat captain responsible for the ramming, sinking and drownings. The premeditated Castroite atrocity and deafening media silence outraged even Ted Koppel.

"Three and a half years ago, in the summer of 1994, something terrible happened out there, seven or eight miles out at sea, off the northern coast of Cuba," he broadcast from Miami on ABC's "Nightline," January 20, 1998. "It was an incident that went all but unnoticed in the U.S. media. The Cuban-American community protested but they protest a lot and, as I say, we in the mainstream media all but ignored it."

And they're still ignoring it. Cubans had the misfortune of being born on a picturesque island. "The most gorgeous land human eyes have ever seen," Columbus is fabled to have said when he first saw it. Location, location, location, as real-estate folks say. Flying or boating into Cuba, then sipping *mojitos* along its beaches while gazing north just doesn't provoke the same emotions as sipping *Schnapps* in a cafe near the Brandenburg Gate and gazing east.

The *mojito* goes down smoothly, the Cohiba smoke curls languidly through the air, the salsa music pulses in the background, the mulatto prostitutes beckon. Unlike the vista in Berlin, the panorama in Cuba gives no hint of anything like the barbed wire and machine-gunners of the murderous Wall, portions of which remain for the very purpose of reminding tourists of the recent horror.

Very few visitors to Cuba conjure how those gorgeous emerald, blue and cobalt waters reap the name of "cemetery without crosses." It's a Cuban thing, apparently.

"I HATE THE SEA"

"I Hate the Sea" is the title of a gut-gripping underground essay by Cuban dissident Rafael Contreras. It's about the young men Rafael met on the beach west of Havana. Some were building a raft while another stood off by himself at the edge of the waves and stared out to sea. "It incarcerates us worse than prison bars," fumes the loner as he curses and spits into a receding wave along the shoreline.

Mankind has always been drawn to the sea. For most of us the sea soothes, attracts, infatuates. The most expensive real estate always faces the sea. "Water is everywhere a protection, like a moat," writes anthropologist Lionel Tiger." As a species we love it."

Yet Cubans now hate it. Che was right. The Cuban revolution indeed created a "New Man"—but one more psychologically crippled than even Che imagined. In Cuba, Castro and Che's totalitarian dream gave rise to a psychic cripple beyond the imagination of even Orwell or Huxley: the first people in the history of the species to hate the sea.

"I hate the sea because it took away the only thing I had after living so long in Cuba—the hope of leaving it," the young man, Roberto, tells dissident journalist Contreras. "Drowning doesn't scare me much. By merely living here in Cuba you're drowning in a sense. We live in a jail-cell but with bars of salt water and sharks."

"The sea had already swallowed his girlfriend and only brother," explains Contreras; the journalist has spoken with many foiled rafters who tell of the enormous waves, of the constantly-circling sharks, of terror almost unimaginable, before their "rescue" by the U.S. Coast Guard which then returned them to Cuba as mandated by a treaty President Clinton signed with Castro in 1994.

"You're playing Russian roulette when you paddle off from here in a raft," the boy tells Rafael Contreras. "But at least there's a chance. Staying here in Cuba means slowly choking to death anyway, at least for people like me."

Roberto could come across as a contestant on "Survivor," or as a thrill-seeking fan of "X-treme" sports as featured on MTV—that is, except for the Cuban setting. "Here in Cuba I'm drowning on the surface, right here on dry land," continues Roberto, stomping his feet on the sand. "The way I feel right now, I'd rather live out there on the bottom with my girlfriend and brother than continue drowning by inches in this piece-of-shit country. Good-bye," he says, running towards his friends.

Contreras then realized that Roberto was part of the group assembling the ramshackle raft. They pushed it out over the small waves, clambered on board and started paddling north.

A few weeks later Rafael Contreras finished his piece. "Nobody around here has heard anything about Roberto and his friends," he wrote. "Perhaps he's happy out there on the bottom of the sea with the silence of the fishes while the rest of us continue drowning by inches here in Cuba."

The quip "sleeping with the fishes" never quite caught on in Cuba. It hits too close to home for too many families. But Castro rolls out the red carpet for Francis Ford Coppola on every one of his frequent visits to Cuba. "Fidel, I love you," gushed a young Francis Ford Coppola. "We both have beards. We both have power and want to use it for good purposes."[9]

CHAPTER 4

Here Come the Sharks.
Where's the Discovery Channel?

Edward O. Wilson calls the shark "the most frightening animal on earth . . . a killing machine, the last free predator of man." Yet fully aware of the high odds of being eaten alive by sharks, hundreds of thousands of Cubans have taken to the sea in flimsy rafts to escape what *Newsweek* magazine hails as among the "Best countries in the world to live," what Jack Nicholson calls "a paradise," and what Bonnie Raitt commemorates in song as a "happy little island."

"I'd just joined Freedom Flight International when my colleagues came in from a flight with a video, " recalls Matt Lawrence, who flew rescue flights over the Florida straits in the 90's in conjunction with Brothers to the Rescue. "On this video one could see a tiny raft. Then the plane came in for a lower pass and I expected to see the typically heartbreaking empty raft, as happened so often.

"But something was moving on this raft. Now I expected to see a desperate rafter waving a shirt or anything else that might have been available to him in order to get the plane's attention. This was also routine, and not as heartbreaking. But then I noticed the water all around the raft turning red . . . the cloud spreading . . .

"Then as they came in for a lower pass and an even closer look, I saw that this rafter wasn't focused on the plane at all, wasn't even looking up at them. He was in frantic motion all right, but not waving. Instead he—she, actually—was bashing the water with an oar. Then

I could see the shark—a shark about the same length as the raft.

"The rafter was in fact a Cuban woman in her early twenties. Upon her rescue we found she had two bullet wounds in her legs from Castro's frontier police. All others in the raft including two infants had died, as had the shark, which had been repeatedly stabbed by the pointed end of a broken oar by Maria. The shark had broken it with a bite, we later learned. I started flying rescue missions full-time after that."[1]

Matt's life-changing rescue mission took place as much of the world rejoiced over the fall of the hated Berlin Wall.

CROSSING THE FLORIDA STRAITS FOR FUN AND GLORY

"I just want to be crystal clear about how my team will handle sharks on our upcoming attempt to make history in swimming the 103 miles from Cuba to Florida," wrote the popinjay recreational swimmer and *Huffington Post* contributor Diana Nyad in July 2011. "No shark will be harmed at any time during our event. I am humbly asking the sharks of this particular ocean to allow me to skim across the surface of their home for about three days. I am duly respectful of them, their habits and their habitat."[2]

Maria viewed the matter differently, while stabbing the ten-foot bull shark through the gills with her broken oar. "Humbly asking" the shark to allow her family to reach freedom safely probably never occurred to the Cuban woman.

And despite her humble entreaty during her celebrated attempted swim from Cuba to Key West, Diana Nyad was protected by an electrical device or "shark shield" that surrounded her with an invisible electrical field to repel sharks. She was also shadowed by a little fleet of boats full of divers tasked with warding off any sharks that ventured too close.

A month earlier, in June 2011, another open-water swimmer,

Penny Palfrey, had made a similar trip south of Cuba, swimming some 68 miles between Little Cayman and Grand Cayman islands. As the Cayman News Service reported on June 14: "Palfrey's swim was not only an incredible feat of endurance but pretty dangerous as she said one shark cruised under her throughout the night."

Much like Diana Nyad a month later, the showboating Australian swimmer was escorted the entire way by three shark-watching inflatable boats and surrounded by a shark shield. Even so, two sharks got too close to Palfrey, so her escorts hooked them, towed them away from the swimmer and hacked them to death with machetes.

"One of the white tip sharks, it just shadowed me the entire night—I could see it sort of five feet away, maybe more," Palfrey said. "I had the (electronic) shark shield on so it was just outside the range of the shark shield and it was just cruising underneath me all night long."

Explains Christine Ambrosino, zoologist at the University of Hawaii: "Shark shields come in different forms, including ones that strap to the ankle, attach to a surfboard, and can be affixed to small vessels like canoes and kayaks. They set up such a strong electric pulse in the water that, as the shark swims toward it, it's like punching them in the face with a cattle prod. If you're out there and you see a big shark coming, that's security that you probably want to have."

Point is, the waters surrounding Cuba are famed for their hordes of sharks. Most people entering them for extended periods insist on a defense against them. Yet from a quarter- to a half-million Cubans have crossed these waters with little more between them and the sharks than thin rubber or canvas—and knowing the odds were close to 50-50 that their craft would overturn or crumble.

"Sharks Attack Boat!" videos abound on YouTube. Recently a bull shark bit the welded aluminum swimming platform off a 22-foot luxury boat near the Florida coast. Imagine those teeth and jaws crunching into the rubber, canvas or styrofoam that keep precariously afloat the typical escapees from that happy little island.

Many of those freedom-seekers have also "seen big sharks coming," including perhaps Elian Gonzalez's mother, who unlike Nyad and Palfrey got precious little empathy from the media.

"Why did she [Elian's mother] do it?" asked NBC's Jim Avila in April 2000. "What was she escaping? By all accounts this quiet, serious young woman, who loved to dance the salsa, was living the good life, as good as it gets for a citizen in Cuba. . . . An extended family destroyed by a mother's decision to start a new life."

So according to NBC (the recipient of a Havana bureau, by the way), Elian's mom had lived the "good life" in Cuba, and irresponsibly "destroyed her extended family's life." Got that?

If only 99.99 per cent of the people who precariously cross the Florida Straits got the media attention of Diana Nyad. Actually, Ms. Nyad herself could help. "As someone who grew up with many Cuban friends in South Florida, *someone who has now visited Havana some 30 times. . . .*" (emphasis mine). So she starts a recent article in *The Huffington Post*.

First off (and this is for the brain-dead): You're not welcomed into the Castros' totalitarian fiefdom 30 times if you're not blatantly helping the regime.

"With each stroke as I head north will also be the love of Cuba," she continues. "Millions of us worldwide, but especially here in the United States, have been fascinated by the mystique of this 'forbidden' island so close to our shores.

"We have become raging fans of 'The Buena Vista Social Club,' among other famous Cuban artists: painters, poets, photographers.

"We have installed proud posters of Che on our college room walls.

"We are aware of the advanced level of medicine and general education on the island."[3]

Wouldn't Nyad's swim be a great way to honor those tens of thousands of dead Cubans? She boasts that she grew up in Miami surrounded by Cuban friends. Can she be oblivious to what drove them to Miami? Wouldn't her swim be a great way to focus some much-needed media attention on this 'cemetery without crosses' and on the oppression that drove so many to throw themselves into the sea on craft most of us wouldn't board outside a backyard swimming pool?

Maybe for some, but not for someone who proudly installed Che Guevara posters on her dorm wall and has been welcomed into Stalinist Cuba more than 30 times. Obviously Nyad feels greater affection for the uniformed Cubans who welcome her in Cuba than for the ones in rags who jump on rafts.

"His body was torn by sharks almost beyond recognition," reported *The Miami Herald* about 23-year-old Juan Carlos Rodriguez-Bueno who had fled Cuba in a tiny boat a week earlier. "U.S. Coast Guard officers were unable to retrieve the body of the man's brother after a tiger shark dragged him underwater about 20 miles off Looe Key on Thursday. The stepbrother showed the picture to his father, Carlos Rodriguez, 59, of Hialeah, who identified the badly mutilated man."

"My father is devastated," said his son. "Twenty-two years ago he lost another son and I lost another brother in the same manner. My father doesn't even want to hear the word Cuba anymore. He shuts himself off from any mention of its tragedy."

This was reported twelve years after the fall of the Berlin Wall and within sight of the U.S. coast. Only *The Miami Herald* saw fit to report it.

The thrill of the Discovery Channel's "Shark Week" is totally lost on Eliecer Castillo, former heavyweight boxing champ, so not exactly a wimp. "I get goose-bumps whenever I see anything with sharks and turn it right off," he says.[4] The Cuban boxer and four partners, including his two brothers, lashed together an inner-tube and canvas raft in 1994, hopped aboard and paddled north into the

Gulf Stream as part of a small fleet of similar floating contraptions filled with similar desperate Cubans.

As usual, within hours sharks were trailing and circling the rafts. The current carried the ramshackle flotilla away from the U.S. and Castillo spent five days at sea. He recalls watching many of the rafts around him capsizing and falling apart in the waves. The sharks would rush in immediately, their patience and diligence paying off. Castillo would see the water frothing white, then red as his fellow rafters yelled for help. But what could anyone do? Hence the goose-bumps and squeamishness of a professional heavyweight boxing champ who specialized in brutal knockouts in the first round.

"I'll never forget the case of the two teenagers who came ashore sunburnt, malnourished as usual, but also in a state of near hysteria," recalls Arturo Cobo. "After a while they could finally explain how their father, in a delirious state from thirst and exposure, finally jumped in the water. They threw him a rope tied to the raft and he clutched it. So they turned away for a second, slightly relieved—but only to spot a huge shark approaching, then another. Soon an entire school was around their raft.

"And almost before they could react, the sharks ripped into their father from all sides. From what they told me days later at the local hospital, what erupted around their tiny raft was a feeding frenzy, like the ones you see on those shark shows where they bait the water for hours to attract the sharks. The water turned red as their father was eaten alive. . . . I can tell you from decades of heartbreaking work from our center here in Key West that in the Florida Straits every week is shark week. . . . "

"People who are attacked by sharks are exceptionally, almost absurdly unlucky," writes Michael Capuzzo, author of *Close to Shore: The Terrifying Shark Attacks of 1916*. From 1979 to 1986 Capuzzo worked at none other than *The Miami Herald*. So probably thousands of (extremely unlucky) people had been attacked by sharks not far from his office. Arturo Cobo and Matt Lawrence were a brief phone call and short drive away. Instead Capuzzo wrote about an attack 1,300 miles away and 60 years earlier.

"I kept waiting and waiting and waiting for this decades-long and seemingly never-ending horror to burst upon the national media," says Matt Lawrence. "I mean, here are thousands upon thousands of people—men, women, children—right off our coast braving dangers as bad as, if not worse than, those of hundreds of East Germans five thousand miles away. And the Berlin Wall was just coming down when I started my rescue flights.

"Where's the outrage? I kept asking. . . . And on every flight, upon every sighting of another empty boat, another tombstone at sea as I started calling them, and imagining what might have become of the occupants—of another body bobbing in the water surrounded by sharks—upon every encounter with the emaciated, sunburnt, delirious survivors, upon hearing their stories, upon watching them—in their stumbling, stuporous, emaciated condition—still dropping to the ground to kiss U.S. soil, mostly sand actually, when they reached Key West . . . well . . . my outrage grew worse and worse—against the Castro regime for sure, but also again Castro's accomplices, witting and otherwise, in the international media.

"Well, it never did burst upon the media," continues Matt. "This astounding insensitivity still troubles me deeply, breaks my heart. I'd come in from those flights every evening and simply break down. Many of us would, and I'm talking tough guys, Bay of Pigs veterans, former Cuban political prisoners who stood up stoically to KGB-tutored torture. Just about anyone who would see what we saw on those rescue flights, and hear what we heard from the survivors, would break down.

"That said, helping save a few thousand lives still made it the most rewarding experience of my life. In fact maybe the knowledge that no one else would be coming in to help us, or to publicize this horror, hardened my determination to keep flying even in the most horrible weather, with Castro's MiG's constantly menacing us, and continue saving the lives of people who, after I got to know so many of them, seemed no different from my own family and friends. Their only crime was having been born in Castro's Cuba."

SO WHERE'S THE DISCOVERY CHANNEL?

For 25 years The Discovery Channel has charted its highest rating during its "Shark Week," which exclusively features documentaries on sharks, especially the frequent attackers. Every year, tens of millions of viewers have tuned into the Discovery Channel to watch such programs as "Teeth of Death," "Sharkbite Summer," "Anatomy of a Sharkbite" and "Blood in the Water." Indeed, the bloodier the better, as Discovery Channel producers well know.

These shows feature, in gruesome detail, shark attacks from Australia to South Africa to California to *northern* Florida. "Australia records 56 fatal shark attacks between 1958 and 2008!" gasps one show's narrator.

"The Florida Straits probably record 56 fatal shark attacks every few years," says Matt Lawrence. "Probably every month during the early 90's," adds Arturo Cobo.

Right off the southern Florida coast an estimated 70,000 people have perished since 1961 on the high seas, a large but unknown number of these at the hands (jaws, actually) of sharks. To this day, most airborne rescuers report seeing sharks in the vicinity of Cuban rafters. Many have observed attacks. Most survivors mention sharks and shark-attacks often during their terrible voyage.

So here's one of America's most populous states and one bounded by beaches crammed with tourists. You'd really think this setting could provide the Discovery Channel with material much more dramatic and relevant (titillating) for its U.S. audience. So where's the Discovery Channel on this?

In Cuba, partnering with the Castro regime, that's where.

The Cuban press reports very little about rafters. In his tell-all about reporting from Cuba, long-time Havana correspondent for Spain's *Television Espanola* Vicente Botin reports that he never saw a mention of rafters in the state-run media. It's obviously embarrassing.

And for the benefit of those who came of political age after the fall of the Iron Curtain, Communist regimes do not issue media, academic or scientific visas (as in the Discovery Channel's) randomly. "The vetting procedure starts when the regime receives your visa application," reports Chris Simmons, once the Defense Intelligence Agency's top Cuban spycatcher, now retired. "When your smiling Cuban guide greets you at the airport he knows plenty about you, and from several angles."

Often they learn much more about you during your stay. "First thing I advised visiting Americans," an official at the U.S. Interests Section told this writer, "was to check their rooms for bugs—the electronic surveillance type. One of these visitors later told me he'd just fallen asleep when he heard a loud thump from the closet. He opened the door and somebody ran out of the closet almost between his legs and scooted out of the room."

"My job was to bug visiting Americans' hotel rooms," confirms high-ranking Cuban intelligence defector Delfin Fernandez, "with both cameras and listening devices. And famous Americans are the priority objectives of Castro's intelligence."[5]

In brief, if you're not there to help the regime's image abroad, you're not getting a visa, at least more than once. And if in the Stalinist regime's estimation you helped their image insufficiently, a little "prodding" might be applied, via blackmail. Upon publishing his book, for instance, Spanish reporter Vicente Botin promptly lost his Cuban visa. The Discovery Channel, on the other hand, seems to have a perpetual red carpet into Castro's fiefdom.

"Discovery Channel Returns From Underwater Scientific Expedition Off the Coast of Cuba," read the *Science Daily* headline in January 1998. "Crew of scientists received a surprise visit from Cuban President Fidel Castro. . . . Castro has long been interested in underwater expedition and he spent two hours on the boat talking with the scientists about their findings and about the issues of underwater conservation." The Castro regime touts scuba diving as among Cuba's top tourist attractions, in case the Discovery Channel hadn't guessed.

The Discovery Channel has also featured sport-fishing videos filmed in full partnership with the Stalinist regime's ministry of tourism. The obvious purpose is to attract a large number of well-heeled sport fishermen from around the world to Cuba's unspoiled and fish-filled coastal waters.

By the simple expedient of banning boat-ownership under penalty of prison or firing squad for everyone except high-ranking government officials, many other nations could boast fishing grounds every bit as unspoiled as those surrounding the Castro brothers' fiefdom. On June 20, 2012, for instance, the Stalinist regime held a huge and public bonfire; not of illegal books like *Animal Farm*—as in the bonfire of 2005 that prompted Ray Bradbury to denounce the Castro regime's book-burning—but of illegal floating devices. These floating devices (mostly one-man contraptions fashioned from styrofoam and wood) belonged to what the regime deplores as "illegal fishermen," Cubans who paddle out at night in desperate hope of supplementing their slave-era government rations with some of the delicious fish that swarm off Cuba's coast.

These Cubans' paddling and fishing is often hampered by huge wakes thrown by magnificent yachts captained by fat foreign millionaires who roar past them in quest of marlin and wahoo for the walls of their trophy-rooms. But the foreign magnates usually roar by with a friendly wave, perhaps even lifting their *mojitos* in salutation. Given their docking fees and other expenses at the regime-run Hemingway Marina, the "nationalist" regime which hosts and pampers them would never think to admonish any discourtesy they might show to the gnarled, dusky, hungry natives in their path.

Castro's nationalist regime burned the pathetic little Cuban craft almost within sight of the hundreds of foreign millionaire-owned yachts tethered at Hemingway Marina just east of Havana.

Such a surefire tourism-booster (outlawing fishing by their own countrymen) never seems to have occurred to any of those dreaded right-wing dictators, so vilified in the media. Under Batista, for instance, boat ownership for coastal Cubans was regarded as almost a birthright. During the 50's foreign fishermen clamored for a chance to fish with Cubans aboard their often spacious and luxurious boats. If you're ever in Miami, ask around.

As a five-, six- and seven-year-old I well remember the weekend ritual of fishing with my grandfather. He'd rent a boat much like the one in *The Old Man and the Sea* and not far from where Hemingway's old man set off every morning. He'd row us out a few hundred yards to hand-line for *ronquito* (yellow grunt), *rabi-rubia* (yellowtail snapper) and *cabrilla* (grouper).

I also remember the morning the grimacing fisherman told us the trip was off. He motioned us over to his boat which was over-turned in the sand and riddled with bullet-holes. Too many people were going fishing and winding up in Key West, Castro's guards had explained to him as they reloaded their Czech machine-guns with fresh clips.

In brief, Discovery Channel personnel have no trouble obtaining Cuban visas, which in turn drop much tourist currency in regime coffers. Would this continue if their ultra-popular programs "Teeth of Death" or "Blood in the Water" featured the death and blood of men, women and children driven to near-suicidal desperation by the Stalinist regime with which they partner for videos and infomercials of mutual benefit? Would the gracious host and president, who paid the Discovery Channel producers a surprise visit, be cool with those types of shows? The question answers itself.

CHAPTER 5

The Discovery Channel Spins the Missile Crisis

To its partnership with Castro's ministry of tourism, in October 2008 the Discovery Channel added Castro's ministry of history. The program was entitled "Defcon-2" and covered the Cuban Missile Crisis. "DEFCON-2, the official term for the highest level of U.S. military readiness short of nuclear war, goes back to the tension-filled days of the Cuban Missile Crisis," reads the trailer. "Author Tom Clancy hosts an analysis of key participants on both sides of the confrontation."

The tension-filled program, complete with a *Jaws*-type soundtrack, features interviews with some of Cuba's highest-ranking apparatchiks, though not Fidel or Raul. Conspicuously absent (for those who know the matter) was the most tension-filled incident of all. Think of what the Discovery Channel's crackerjack writers and producers could have produced using the following incident starring Soviet Premier Khrushchev, as witnessed and later described by Sergei Khrushchev, the premier's son:

"'Nikita Sergeyevich, a very disturbing message has also come in from Castro.' Oleg Aleksandrovich [Troyanovsky, the premier's assistant] again spoke in quiet and measured tones. 'The text itself is still at the Foreign Ministry, but I have written down its main points.'

"'Yes?' asked Father impatiently.

"'Castro thinks that war will begin in the next few hours and that his source is reliable. In the opinion of the Cuban leadership, the people are ready to repel imperialist aggression and would rather die than surrender. We should be the first to deliver a nuclear strike.

"'WHAT?!'

"'That is what I was told,' Troyanovsky responded, without visible disquiet.

"'What?' said Father somewhat more calmly. "'Is he proposing that we start a nuclear war? That we launch missiles from Cuba?'

"'Apparently.'

"'That is insane!' Whatever doubts Father might have had about his decision to remove the missiles had vanished completely. 'Remove them, and as soon as possible. Before it's too late. Before something terrible happens.'

"The meeting's participants stared at one another incredulously. To start a world war so cavalierly! Obviously events were slipping out of control. Yesterday the Cubans had shot down a plane without permission. Today they were preparing a nuclear attack.

"To general approval, Father ordered that an immediate order be sent to Pliyev through military channels: 'Allow no one [Castro or his people] near the missiles. Obey no orders [from Castro or his people] to launch and under no circumstances install the warheads.'"[1]

So much for JFK cowing Khrushchev with his bluster and naval blockade. Khrushchev was cowed all right, but by the genocidal lust of his errant Caribbean satrap (and Discovery Channel business partner), not by the commander-in-chief of a nation with a nuclear warhead superiority over his own by a margin of 5,000 to 300.

Khrushchev snickered the truth in his memoirs: "It would have been ridiculous for us to go to war over Cuba—for a country 6,000 miles away. For us, war was unthinkable." So much for the threat that rattled the Knights of Camelot and inspired such epics of drama and derring-do by their court scribes and court cinematographers (i.e., the mainstream media and Hollywood).

Considering the U.S. nuclear superiority over the Soviets at the time of the so-called Missile Crisis—5,000 nuclear warheads for us, 300 for them—it's hard to imagine President Nixon, much less President Reagan, quaking in front of Khrushchev's transparent ruse as Kennedy did. The genuine threat came not from Moscow but from the Discovery Channel's production partner, Fidel Castro.

So naturally there is no mention in the Discovery Channel's "Defcon-2" of how Che Guevara—thinking he was off-the-record a month later—fully confirmed Khrushchev's fears (and prudence). "If the missiles had remained, we would have used them all and fired them against the heart of the United States, including New York."[2]

"What we contend is that we must walk the path of liberation," wrote Che in Castro's house organ *Verde Olivo* a week later, "even if it may cost millions of atomic victims . . . . What we must consider is the ultimate the victory of socialism."

Khrushchev's response to Castro was low-key and diplomatic: "In your cable of October 27 you proposed that we be the first to launch a nuclear strike against the territory of the enemy. You, of course, realize where that would have led. It would have been the start of a thermonuclear war. Dear comrade Fidel Castro I consider this proposal of yours incorrect."[3]

Did Stanley Kubrick realize he had directed a documentary entitled *Dr. Strangelove* rather than a fiction? He simply got a few scenes wrong. The real-life General Ripper and Major T. J. Kong were both in Havana, not at Burleson Air Force Base or Washington, D.C.

The Discovery Channel somehow "omitted" the most dramatic scene from the entire crisis, just as they omit the daily sanguinary drama of the half-century-long "Shark Week" in the Florida Straits. There was no hint in the Discovery Channel special of Fidel Castro's raging lust to fire the missiles preemptively against the nation in which the Discovery Channel dwells.

Castro's image as the plucky David surviving decades of bullying and brutalization by the Yankee Goliath also emerged intact from the Discovery Channel program. There was no mention whatever of Khrushchev's snickering with satisfaction about the Missile Crisis resolution. "We ended up getting exactly what we'd wanted all along," he wrote in his memoir. "Security for Fidel Castro's regime and American missiles removed from Turkey. Until today the U.S. has complied with her promise not to interfere with Castro and not to allow anyone else to interfere with Castro."

So far from defying a superpower, Fidel Castro has poked along lo these many years by hiding behind the skirts of the U.S., the U.S.S.R. and the British Empire. After the Missile Crisis resolution, Castro's defiance of the U.S. took the form of protection by the U.S. Coast Guard and also by the British Navy, shielding Castro from attacks by his Cuban-exile enemies in the U.S. and the Bahamas.

So sacrosanct was the U.S. pledge to protect Castro that it even stayed Ronald Reagan's hand. When Professor Antonio De La Cova asked Elliott Abrams, assistant Secretary of State for Inter-American Affairs under Regan, about the possibility of arming some Cuban *contras* in the manner of Nicaragua's, Abrams replied: "You can't do that because of the Kennedy-Khrushchev agreement. We never got there, at least not in the period that I was involved with it. We never got to contemplating any serious action in Cuba which could be considered a violation of the agreement."[4]

Castro, on the other hand, was again itching to get his fingers on the button. A Pentagon study declassified in 2009, entitled "Soviet Intentions 1965-1985," based on extensive interviews with former Soviet officials, shows that Castro's urge to toast Manhattan flared again during the Reagan administration.

During the early 1980's—according to a former chief of the Soviet general staff, General Adrian Danilevich—"Mr. Castro pressed hard for a tougher Soviet line against the U.S. up to and including nuclear strikes. We had to actively disabuse him of this view by spelling out the ecological consequences for Cuba of a Soviet strike against the U.S."

NATIONAL GEOGRAPHIC PARTNERS WITH CASTRO

National Geographic's partnership with Castro's propaganda ministry started with a January 1977 article—really an infomercial for Castroism—called "Inside Cuba Today." The article featured an interview with Fidel Castro and proclaimed that "over half of Cubans' lives had been improved by the Revolution." The magazine's pro-Castro coverage continued in 1991 with "Cuba at a Crossroads" by Peter White, and then in 2000 with "Cuba's Reefs, A Last Caribbean Refuge" by none other than Peter Benchley, the author of *Jaws*.

"Cuba Naturally," a *National Geographic* feature presenting Cuba as a paradise of ecosystems, followed in 2003. Then in 2006 came "Castro the Conservationst? By Default or Design, Cuba Largely Pristine." Here we learn that "Cuba's land-tenure system [identical to Stalin's for the Ukraine] and relatively strong enforcement of laws [!] are all associated with its conservation achievements."

In March 2012 *National Geographic* finally dropped any pretense of objectivity and ran an unabashed tourist infomercial entitled "Falling for Cuba." The commercial was timed to kick off the joint *National Geographic*-Castro-regime tours called "Cuba; Discovering Its People and Cuba." In this joint venture, the magazine and the regime helpfully provide full-time tour-guides. Among these is *The Washington Post*'s Tom Miller, whose services to the regime began with his book *Trading With the Enemy; A Yankee Travels Through Castro's Cuba*, published in 1996, just as the regime's tourism campaign was kicking into high gear. The

Cuban red carpet—a visa for the asking—has been extended to Miller ever since.

A Canadian company runs similar junkets called "Cuba Discovery Tours." Some highlights from their brochure:

"Your tour is fully escorted by Cuban experts from the minute you touch down in Havana until you return home! You'll experience island history, social and ecological achievements first-hand from Cubans."

Among the testimonials from enchanted customers:

"So many museums and not enough time to see them all! My favorite visit was to the Fortress of San Carlos de la Cabana. We saw where Che Guevara set up his headquarters!" (Headquarters for what? No further details provided.)

"Above all, this tour was truly an education. If you go, your eyes and hearts will be opened, and you'll come home with different outlooks on many issues."

"In addition to expressing great pride in the country's low crime rate, the Cubans that we met took great pride in their successful literacy campaign, and their high investment and emphasis on education and health-care. Cuba was declared the first Illiteracy-Free Country in the Americas after its revolutionary victory!"

"The elevated status of women and health-care for women and children were also areas that Cubans spoke of with pride."

"Our guide, Reynaldo, an enthusiastic and ebullient man in his forties, was with us throughout the stay in Cuba!"

We know.

CHAPTER 6

Castro's Running-Dogs: Herbert Matthews and *The New York Times*

T*he New York Times*'s Herbert Matthews, who repeatedly denounced Batista as "tyrant, torturer, murderer, thief," etc., visited Cuba repeatedly during Batista's reign. (Try that during Castro's.) The interview and three-part fron page feature that resulted from his first trip in February 1957 "invented" Fidel Castro, according to fellow *Times* reporter Anthony DePalma. In 2006 DePalma authored a book about Herbert Matthews entitled, appropriately enough, *The Man Who Invented Fidel*.

In his book, DePalma endeavors to offer a *mea culpa* of sorts on the Matthews-Castro saga but in a highly sympathetic manner, as befits their *New York Times* fellowship. DePalma starts with a nail-biting account of the perils Herbert Matthews faced while clandestinely setting up the interviews, then clandestinely making his perilous way to those ground-breaking interviews.

"He [Matthews] did not see anyone from the Batista Government because he feared that doing so might raise suspicion about his presence in Cuba," DePalma states in his book. "Matthews had decided that that the best way of getting past the cordon of troops surrounding the Sierra [Maestra, mountains of eastern Cuba] was to bring along [his wife] Nancie and pretend to be a couple of middle-aged American tourists out with some young Cuban friends."

"Matthews confided to her that many young Cubans were risking their lives to smuggle him into the mountains, so it was important to be discreet during the long trip." Crowded into the car, they passed the hours on the rough road singing Cuban songs or talking about the revolutionary movement for which they were risking their lives. Matthews was enthralled by his secret passage through Cuba.

"A soldier stepped into the road in front of them! It was the first real test of their plan. He peered inside the car, checking out the young Cubans in the front and the American couple in the back. They all held their breath for a second, their hearts racing. . . . He took a quick look around the car and smiled, then waved them through."

Finally they reached the Sierra Maestra, got out of the car and started hiking. "The only sounds were the night-voices of the forest—the screeches of animals and the heavy drip, drip, drip of raindrops . . . finally out of the darkness came an unmistakable sound—the two flat notes of the secret code . . . the scout whispered that [Castro's] camp was nearby . . . It was just after dawn and Matthews was muddy, hungry, cold . . . but this was why he had come all the way from New York. . . . Castro strode into the clearing with the sun just breaking through the clouds and dawn seeping into the day."[1]

The New York Times' prize-winning investigative reporter Anthony DePalma wrote his book in 2006, almost exactly a half-century after *The New York Times'* prize-winning investigative reporter Herbert Matthews wrote his famous Castro articles. Which means—not to take anything away from DePalma's heart-pounding prose—that, for 48 years, sworn testimony on the public record which makes a hilarious hash of his account was available to anyone willing to devote about 60 seconds to investigating the issue.

In fact, Matthews's trip to the Sierra for the Castro interview was not only approved by Batista—who thought Castro was dead at the time so it would do no harm—but provided a police escort by Batista to insure Matthews's safety every step of the way. To wit, from hearings of the Judiciary Committee in the U.S. Senate, August 1960:

Senator Dodd: "Did Herbert Matthews ever contact you while you were the Ambassador in Cuba?"

Ambassador Gardner: "I made it possible actually for Herbert Matthews to go down and have this interview [with Castro], because he asked me."

That's Arthur Gardner, the U.S. ambassador to Cuba at the time of Matthews's early-1957 visit.

Senator Dodd: "Yes. I wanted to ask you, about that. He [Herbert Matthews] did ask for assistance in arranging an interview with Castro? "

Mr. Gardner: "He did."

Senator Dodd: "And this was arranged?"

Mr. Gardner: "Yes."

Senator Dodd: "How did you arrange it?"

Mr. Gardner: "Only under the condition that when he came back he would tell me his reactions."

Senator Dodd: "Yes. But how could you arrange a meeting with Castro?"

Mr. Gardner: "Well, I mean in those days Batista, said, 'All right, if you think it won't do any harm, it is all right,' and he let him go down."

Mr. Gardner: "Senator, to be perfectly clear about this, the only thing I could do was help him [Matthews], so that he would have a pass to go down the island, so that he could make this trip [to interview Castro]."

Senator Dodd: "I understand—whatever it was that he thought you could do, he wanted you to do it to help him get there?"

Mr. Gardner: "That is right."

Senator Dodd: "And in return for this he promised he would come back and tell you about this conversation with Castro?"

Mr. Gardner: "That is right. And to this day I never have seen him."

Senator Dodd: "He never did return and never did tell you?"

Mr. Gardner: "No. It was a big shock to me, as a matter of fact."

Senator Dodd: "Mr. Gardner, do you feel that Matthews's account of his visit to Castro, as he wrote it up, had considerable influence on the American people with respect to favoring Castro?"[2]

"Almost two years before Ambassador Gardner's testimony, my father heard the same thing from some of his government contacts," adds Manuel Marquez-Sterling, whose father Carlos was a Cuban senator at the time. "The last thing Batista wanted was Matthews, a famous *New York Times* reporter, killed and the killing pinned on his police or army—which is exactly the type of thing he suspected Castro's people would pull off," continues Marquez-Sterling. "And then naturally, the anti-Batista U.S. media would headline it everywhere. So Batista wanted to make sure Matthews got to into the Sierra safely, conducted his interview and returned safely."[3]

"Turns out he was wrong about Castro's motives," adds Marquez-Sterling. "At the time, Matthews was much more valuable to Castro as a courier and propagandist than as martyr. But the facts debunking the 'perils' of Matthews's visit with Castro stand as a matter of historical record—though no one would ever know it from anywhere in the mainstream media, especially *The New York Times*."

In sum: Herbert Matthews was protected by a Batista police escort the entire route to his interviews with Fidel Castro. And this is all a matter of sworn testimony on the public record for over 50 years, and corroborated by one of Cuba's most respected political figures of the time—an anti-Batistiano to boot. For the record, Anthony DePalma himself refers to Carlos Marquez-Sterling as "a respected politician."

By way of gratitude, shortly after the interviews, Herbert Matthews—instead of visiting with Ambassador Gardner to report on Fidel Castro as he'd promised—visited his State Deptartment cronies to urge that they fire (Republican) Arthur Gardner from his ambassadorial position, which they did.

"In Cuba itself . . . I received no help at all from the Castro regime," DePalma writes in his book's acknowledgements, "despite my repeated requests and their repeated assurances that assistance would be forthcoming."

"No journalist gets a visa to do research in Cuba without very careful vetting by the regime's intelligence services," says Lieut. Col. Chris Simmons, for years the Defense Intelligence Agency's top Cuba spy-catcher. So DePalma actually has many Castro-regime apparatchiks to thank. But let's go ahead and indulge him; maybe he doesn't have all their names.

DRINKING A LIE

A Cuban girl's coming-of-age or "sweet-sixteen" party comes at fifteen. And during the 1950's a Cuban tecnybopper's *quinceanera* (from "quince," the Spanish word for fifteen) was easily the major event of her life, usually until her big fat Cuban wedding.

Miriam Mata lived in a Havana suburb in 1957 (but wasn't fat!); she had her coming-of-age party made all the more memorable when Castro's July 26 movement, for whom *The New York Times'* Herbert Matthews was faithfully serving as propagandist and courier, sent an RSVP in the form of a bomb threat.

"Dozens of young girls would be crowded into our house on that day," recalls Miriam. "My family was obviously frightened and I was obviously devastated. But most who knew how Castro's people worked were not surprised in the least. In those days there weren't many such people—and Herbert Matthews sure didn't help matters."

Fifteen-year-old Miriam Mata's birthday greetings in the form of a bomb threat were standard operating procedure for the organization that *The New York Times'* Herbert Matthews served as flack. Bombs were exploding all over Cuba at the time, especially in crowded public places. According to Herbert Matthews, the reign of terror in Cuba at the time came from the police—the people trying to stop the bombings!

In February 1957, just as Matthews's articles on Castro were headlining in *The New York Times*, Pablo Atilano, Placido Analisio and Urbino Jerez, all teenagers, were blown to pieces by a bomb placed by July 26 agents near a farm in the Sierra Maestra.[4] These innocent boys were murdered a few miles from where Matthews had just conducted his famous first interview with the chief of this July 26 movement, whom he hailed a humanitarian hero.

A few months later, Mercedes Diaz-Sanchez was blown to pieces by one of the dozens of bombs exploding throughout Havana at the time. The one that killed Mercedes was placed in a five & dime store.

"Traitor to the July 26 Movement"—so read the sign attached to the bullet-riddled body of Daniel Sanchez Wood on a street-corner of Santiago, Cuba around the time of Matthews's famous interview with Castro. The body of 23-year-old Alcides Wood had an identical sign when found just outside a cemetery in the Sierra Maestra region, with his skull shattered by gunshots.[5]

And well before suicide bombers were cool—especially young female suicide bombers—the organization for which *The New York Times* served as unofficial press agency was putting them to use. "She always stressed that for one who dies many would rise," reads the article in Cuba's captive (literally) press from February 21, 2011. "On March 3, 1957 [a few weeks after Herbert Matthews's famous interview with Fidel Castro] after her final exam July 26 agent Urselia Diaz Baez strapped a clock-bomb to her thigh and walked into a movie theater in Havana. The device seemed to be taking too long to detonate so she walked into the ladies' restroom where it exploded. . . . Her name is registered among those heroic Cubans who fought for a better world."

For the sake of argument, let's say that Herbert Matthews remained somehow oblivious to the terrorism of his clients of the time. Now here comes *The New York Times'* Anthony DePalma, writing half a century later, in a book purportedly designed somehow to exculpate *The New York Times* from Matthews's sponsorship of Castroite terror:

"The [Castro group's] bombs were usually placed where no tourist or Cuban civilian would be hurt. . . . and they were meant not to maim or kill," he writes in his whitewashing of Herbert Matthews, published in 2006, called *The Man Who Invented Fidel.*

But too many eyewitnesses to July 26 terror, living in the U.S. today, know better. Also, not all newspapers of the time took their cue from the famous *New York Times.* Many, as seen above, were actually reporting on a reign of terror then spreading in Cuba. Not that Mr. DePalma deigned to consult with any of these.

"Batista's goons," on the other hand "killed an estimated 20,000" Cubans, according to this same book by *The New York Times'* DePalma. This meme of 20,000 Cubans killed by Batista had originated in 1957 in an article written by Enrique De La Osa and published by *Bohemia,* Havana's famous magazine. The statement quickly spread around the world. A half-century of refutations later, the lie is still parroted by *The New York Times* among many others in media and academic circles.

Fox News's Bob Beckel even picked up on it for his show, *The Five,* on September 5, 2011. "I still have my Che poster," bragged Beckel. "Che helped Fidel Castro get rid of one of the biggest thugs and murdering bastards there ever was, and that was Batista in Cuba."

A special issue of *Bohemia,* published January 11, 1959, right after Castro's seizure of power, carried an article by Enrique De La Osa, listing 898 dead, by name, on both sides of the seven-year-long anti-Batista rebellion. So the magazine's own figure of 20,000 dead had exaggerated the truth more than twenty-fold, and had placed the blame for all those deaths on one side.

The following year, *Bohemia's* owner Miguel Angel Quevedo saw his magazine stolen by the Stalinist terrorists that he and his magazine had served as dutifully as had Herbert Matthews and *The New York Times.* Quevedo, a fervent Fidelista—many called him the Cuban Herbert Matthews—quickly scurried to Venezuela just ahead of a firing squad. The Cuban revolution was just starting to devour its own children, an appetite it would indulge more voraciously than had Lenin's.

In 1969, from Venezuela, Miguel Angel Quevedo confessed that it was he himself who had invented the statement about the 20,000 dead. He also confessed tremendous regret for hatching the lie and for how it had helped the propaganda campaign to put Fidel Castro in power. The regret for the calamity he helped bring upon Cuba was such that, right after signing the letter admitting to his lie, Miguel Angel Quevedo put a gun to his head and blew his brains out.[6]

In the 55 years since the lie's inception, a reporter for the world's most prestigious newspaper, exhaustively researching Herbert Mathews's reporting on Cuba, had ample sources from which to check its veracity. The lie was of such magnitude that it forced the liar to blow his brains out. Apparently *The New York Times* had no such scruple.

In fairness, Miguel Angel Quevedo's remorse stemmed from being forced to live with the consequences of his sponsorship. Herbert Matthews, Ed Murrow, Dan Rather, Barbara Walters, Ted Turner, Andrea Mitchell, etc., on the other hand, visit Castro's fiefdom, bask in the Stalinist regime's red-carpet treatment in appreciation for their ongoing sponsorship, then scoot back to Georgetown or the Upper West side of Manhattan while sipping *mojitos* on the flight. It's a no-brainer.

Not that Herbert Matthews was alone in overlooking these matters. If the American public remained oblivious to the July 26 terrorism in the late 50's, the Associated Press merits honorable mention. But the AP has an excellent excuse: its dispatches from Castro and Che's war during 1957-58 in the Sierra, complete with rockets' red glare and bombs bursting in air, were actually written from a desk in Manhattan by *July 26* agent Mario Llerena, who snickers this admission in his book, *The Unsuspected Revolution*. Llerena was also a frequent New York contact for none other than Herbert Matthews.

MISSIONARY STYLE

During his three visits to Cuba in 1957-58, Herbert Matthews did much more than report. To wit:

In early 1958 Cuban quasi-dictator Batista, who had taken power in a virtually bloodless coup in 1952, agreed to allow elections the coming summer. A long-time and well-known political opponent of Batista's looked likely to win. Cuban senator and University of Havana professor Dr. Carlos Marquez-Sterling had an impeccable record for honesty. He had helped draft the constitution of 1940 that Batista violated with his 1952 coup and that Castro would abolish with his in 1959. In fact mere days after Batista's March 10, 1952 coup Marquez-Sterling petitioned Cuba's Supreme Court to declare Batista's rule unconstitutional. He was anti-Batista when anti-*Batistianismo* wasn't cool, five years before *The New York Times* made it so.

Great, you might think. Here's the perfect solution to Cuba's problems of the time, or so it seemed if you took Herbert Matthews's articles at face value. The ever-spiraling rebel terror and police counter-terror will finally cease. Batista will finally scoot. Peace, honesty and constitutionality will climb back into the Cuban saddle (more or less). So what's to complain?

Plenty, for Castro. In fact the prospect of Carlos Marquez-Sterling honestly replacing Batista sent Castro ballistic. Typically shrewd in these matters, Fidel Castro realized that with the fading of Cuba's political crisis another item that would quickly fade would be his own political star. Enter his star-maker.

"Herbert Matthews shows up at our door," recalls Carlos Marquez-Sterling's son, Manuel (today professor emeritus at Plymouth State University and author). "My father helped write Cuba's constitution of 1940 and our ancestors had fought in every Cuban liberation movement for 200 years. My father, a long-time opponent of Batista, was widely regarded as the candidate most likely to win the elections scheduled shortly in Cuba. So *of course* he agrees to an interview with *The New York Times's* Herbert Matthews.

"A few days later, and without calling ahead, Matthews knocks on our door," recalls Manuel. "He swaggers in with barely a greeting and quickly starts shoving Castro's July 26 pamphlets in our face! Now this is a reporter for the famous *New York Times,* remember? My father was expecting an actual interview from a re-porter for the most prestigious newspaper in the world at the time. But nothing like it ever materialized.

"'Why aren't you backing Fidel Castro?' Matthews arro-gantly asked my father. 'Why aren't you backing Castro's call for an election boycott and for a nationwide general strike?' After his initial shock wore off, my father started losing his composure. We kept waiting for the interview, for his questions on Cuba's elections and political prospects, etc. You'd really think a U.S. reporter, especially one constantly carping about democracy, would *welcome* the prospect of elections to replace the usurper Batista and hopefully solve Cuba's problems. And here he was face to face with the candidate predicted to win, and with a life-time of impeccable democratic credentials.

"But no interview ever materialized," recalls Manuel. "My father soon saw what Matthews was up to, which was certainly not what Matthews had claimed when requesting a visit. Herbert Matthews was simply on an errand as propagandist and courier for Fidel Castro. There's no other way to put it—especially by those of us who were eyewitnesses to the process.

"'Mr. Matthews, you're always denouncing U.S. meddling in Cuban politics,' my father told Matthews. 'And that's exactly what you're attempting here. Good day, sir.' And we showed Mr. Herbert Matthews the door."

If this sounds harsh, Fidel Castro himself agrees with Marquez-Sterling, the Cuban he rightly recognized as the biggest obstacle to his dictatorial ambitions at the time. Castro at first tried to co-opt and neutralize Marquez-Sterling by using Herbert Matthews as his personal envoy. When this failed, "Castro sent his men to try and murder my father," recalls Manuel. "A couple of times they came close. Needless to add, none of this was featured in *The New York Times's* reporting of the time, or ever afterward."

"Without your help," a beaming Fidel Castro said while nodding at Herbert Matthews during a visit to *The New York Times's* offices in April 1959, almost exactly a year after he'd visited Marquez-Sterling, "and without the help of *The New York Times*, the revolution in Cuba would never have been."

A week earlier, in the Cuban embassy in Washington, a beaming Fidel Castro had ceremoniously pinned Herbert Matthews with a medal cast specially in his honor. "Sierra Maestra Press Mission," read the glowing emblem. "To Our American Friend Herbert Matthews with Gratitude. Fidel Castro."[7]

When shown the door by sputtering Cuban senator, constitutionalist, Batista enemy and presidential candidate Dr. Carlos Marquez-Sterling, Herbert Matthews was fresh from another meeting, this one with Cuba's most powerful labor leader Eusebio Mujal, who headed Cuba's AFL-CIO-affiliated CTC (Confederation of Cuban Workers). Here was another vital player on the Cuban political scene of the time, an ideal source for a *New York Times* reporter to interview, you might think. He was also another prime target for Castro to co-opt and neutralize, in order to derail the planned elections.

Like many of Cuba's labor leaders, Eusebio Mujal was an ex-Communist. He had joined Cuba's Communist party almost upon its founding in 1925 by the Comintern's Fabio Grobart, who immigrated to Cuba from Poland in 1921. Mujal then cut his teeth on Cuban communism while Stalin consolidated his rule in Russia. Mujal broke with the Party in the early 1930's.

So Mujal had seen and heard plenty. Obviously he'd graduated well past Communist Tactics 101. By 1958 he had few illusions about the Gods that failed him. So he knew who was behind Fidel Castro, and he knew most of them by name—first among them Fabio Grobart.

Indeed, minutes into Matthews's visit with him, Eusebio Mujal saw what Marquez-Sterling saw a bit later. This famous *New York Times* reporter was simply a courier and missionary for the closet (but not to Mujal) communist, Fidel Castro. Needless to add, Matthews was not on an interview mission with Mujal, any more than with Marquez-Sterling.

Some background that explains these missions for Castro by Matthews: in August 1957 Castro's July 26 movement had called for a national strike—and threatened to shoot workers who reported to work. The strike was completely ignored. Castro was declaring another strike for April 9, 1958. Hence the March 1958 call by his faithful *New York Times* courier Herbert Matthews on Cuba's most powerful labor leader, shortly before his call on Marquez-Sterling.

Eusebio Mujal, lifelong labor leader and ex-Communist, instantly recognized Matthews's agitprop, quickly showed him the door, and refused to take his calls or accept his messages from that time on. None of this appears in any of Matthews's reporting, or in DePalma's book.

Came April 9 and—much to Matthews's grief—Cuba's workers *again* blew a loud and collective raspberry at Fidel Castro, reporting to work en masse. "Cuba's laborer's always maintained a stony indifference to Fidel Castro's movement," admitted Cuba's richest man and (duped) Fidel Castro bankroller Julio Lobo, who knew because he employed thousands of them.[8] Lobo himself scooted out of Cuba barely ahead of a firing squad in 1960.

With his call for a general strike, Fidel Castro was again trying to derail the forthcoming elections. The rationale for these personal calls by Herbert Matthews in March 1958 is not hard to plumb. Here was the man most likely to win a free and fair presidential election (Marquez-Sterling) and here was the head of Cuba's largest and most powerful labor organization (Mujal). At that time, by the way, according to the International labor Organization, Cuban workers per capita were more unionized than U.S. workers. Both of these men must be coopted or neutralized, as Fidel Castro well knew.

So Castro called his faithful retriever from *The New York Times*. "Heel, boy! Heel!" Then he pointed him in their direction and said, "Fetch, boy! Fetch!" All under the guise of interviews for the famous *New York Times*.

That some Hispanic politicians in some banana republic not only rebuffed his entreaties but booted him from their domiciles must have shaken the worldly, tweedy, pipe-smoking Herbert Matthews, reporter for the world's most prestigious newspaper, Polk Award Winner and friend to Ernest Hemingway. But so it came to pass.

"He really looked shocked when my dad kicked his ass out of our house!" recalls Carlos's son Manuel Marquez Sterling.

About the election itself, the story is short and not-so-sweet. General elections were held on November 1, 1958. As Castro had threatened to jail and execute any candidate who took part, the only person willing to stand for the office was a Batista partisan, Andres Rivero Aguero. Batista's flight and Castro's coup prevented him from taking office.

The very week Fidel and Che Guevara entered Havana, Carlos Marquez-Sterling received another visit from their men.

But the ones who came this time were bearded and heavily armed. Marquez-Sterling was arrested and bundled to La Cabana prison, already filled to suffocation. This was Che Guevara's command post and Havana's firing-squad central. Soon it would be known as Cuba's Lubyanka.

Shortly Che himself—sneering as usual, reeking horribly as usual—walked into Marquez-Sterling's cell and asked if he'd been the Cuban ambassador to his native Argentina in the 30's and 40's.

No, that ambassador had been his father, Carlos explained. "I'm not exactly sure of what the charges are against you yet," said Che. "Then Che was alerted that he had some phone calls back in his office and he walked out," recounts Carlos's son Manuel. "After taking these he walked back in and sneered at my father: to think that you and your politicking, you and your elections, almost derailed our revolution!"

So here was proof—and from a pretty primary source—of Castro's fears, and the motive for Matthews's visits. "Though we always suspected the rationale," says Manuel, it "was now confirmed. He was using the good and prestigious offices of a *New York Times* reporter to try and derail my father's own attempted derailment of the Castro brothers' and Che Guevara's plans to Stalinize Cuba. To the end of his life my father considered Che's remark one of the biggest compliments he'd ever received."

Further confirmation came to Argentina's ambassador, Julio Amoedo, a few weeks later. "Marquez-Sterling was the one we feared most," Castro confided to him. "Had he won the elections, I would not be here today."

So (unwittingly) from Che Guevara, Carlos Marquez-Sterling had learned of the Castroite charges against him. At a time when every media outlet and personality from *The New York Times* to Ed Sullivan was hailing the glories of the newly-democratic Cuba, a man was jailed for having taken part in a Cuban democratic process.

"In fact my father was released a few days later," says Manuel. "Che must have taken a call from someone quite high when he walked out of the cell. Remember, at the time Guevara certainly didn't take orders from too many people in Cuba. We think the call was from Fidel himself, telling him that the immediate danger from such as Marquez-Sterling was over. So he was released and put under house arrest. A few weeks later he and my mother escaped Cuba, intent on alerting the world to what was going on behind all those media headlines and to organize a resistance in exile to what he already foresaw as the Stalinization of Cuba."

So despite what Matthews and all the rest were broadcasting to the world, here was early proof that Castro had no intention of allowing any elections in his new fiefdom. The immediate danger to his rule came—as it did to Stalin's plans for Poland—from the military. "Carlos Marquez-Sterling's turn would certainly come, but for now let's get cracking against Cuba's military, the outfit with guns—especially the few who showed mettle when fighting us in the hills," Castro must have reasoned.

So Cuba's version of the Katyn massacre ensued. Within a few months, the bulk of the Cuban military officer-corps had been murdered by firing squad or imprisoned. Research by Armando Lago of the Cuba Archive project documented 1,168 firing-squad executions by the end of that first year of revolution, with another 5,000 Cubans (mostly professional military men) jailed for political crimes. With a few exceptions the international media echoed the Castroite line, rationalizing this reign of terror as "Nuremberg-type justice for Cuban war criminals."

Among the exceptions was Havana correspondent for London's *Daily Telegraph,* Edwin Tetlow, who reported on a mass "trial" orchestrated by Che Guevara in February 1959, where the reporter noticed the death-sentences posted on a board before the trial had started.

The January 1959 issue of Cuba's *Bohemia* magazine listed a total of 898 Cubans killed on all sides of the anti-Batista violence starting in 1952. How a civil war with such casualties on both sides could produce so many war criminals on one side few reporters cared to question. Their crusading journalistic zeal of a year before, with Cuba under Batista, vanished in a poof with Cuba under Castro.

Yet gripping human-interest stories were all around them. "I'm sworn not to violate my holy duties of confession," sobbed a Cuban priest named Berba Beche to Gerardo Abascal in Santiago, Cuba during the early days of the revolution. Raul Castro was machine-gunning dozens of supposed war criminals into mass graves at the time but had graciously permitted Father Beche to hear the confessions from the condemned. "Who would lie upon his last confession?" asked the shaken priest to his friend Gerardo Abascal. "Why would these men lie to me? . . . I can assure you that the Castroites are executing mostly innocent men."[9]

CHAPTER 7

To Kill a Labor Leader: Manhunt in Buenos Aires

The very week Castro took power—with everyone from Herbert Matthews to Ed Murrow and Ed Sullivan singing his praises as a "Christian humanist"—Castro's hit-teams went after Marquez-Sterling's partner in drafting Cuba's social-democratic 1940 constitution. The labor leader Mujal ducked into the Argentinian embassy just in time to escape a bullet in the neck, Lubyanka and Katyn-style. Somebody with Mujal's background, contacts and smarts might quickly let the Castroite communist cat out of the "democratic" and "humanist" bag that had been carefully sewn shut by so many in the media, starting with Herbert Matthews.

Mujal escaped to Argentina a few days later, only to meet up with fellow Cuban Carlos Bringuier, who happened to be visiting his Argentinean in-laws at the time. Finding a countryman in a foreign port always breeds quick rapport and, though they'd never met, Bringuier and Mujal had many common acquaintances back home. "The communists have taken over in Cuba and they're trying to murder me." Mujal finally told Bringuier, who was then a 25-year-old lawyer.

"At first I figured Mujal was a bit crazy," recalls Bringuier, "psychotically paranoid for sure." But twelve years earlier, University of Havana student Fidel Castro had murdered Bringuier's cousin

Manolo Castro—no relation, but a rival to him as a student leader. So Bringuier was eager to hear out the older and wiser man.[1]

"I know most of the people really in power behind Castro's façade of a democratic government." Mujal told him. "They're hard-core Stalinists I knew in the 30's. I know full well they'll now try to kill me. I've got to get to the U.S. where I'll be safer. I've already got a U.S. visa. Can you and your in-laws help me get an exit visa from Argentina?"

The more Bringuier spoke with Mujal the more he became convinced of everything he said—media and intelligence "experts" be damned. And here's what the "experts" were claiming about Castro at the time:

"We've infiltrated Castro's guerrilla group in the Sierra mountains. The Castro brothers and Ernesto 'Che' Guevara have no affiliations with any communists whatsoever." (Havana CIA station chief Jim Noel, November 1958)[2]

"Fidel Castro is not only *not* a communist—he's a strong *anti*-communist fighter! He's ready to help us in the hemisphere's anti-communist fight and we should share our intelligence with him!" (Gerry Droller, the CIA's expert on Latin American communism, April 1959)[3]

"Fidel Castro is a good young man trying to do what's best for Cuba. We should extend him a hand." (former President Harry Truman, July 1959)[4]

"Now these things [i.e., Castro is a Communist] are charged. But they are not easy to prove. The U.S. Government has made no such charges." (U.S. President Eisenhower, July 1959)[5]

More than a year and a half later, in June 1960—as Cuba crawled with Soviet agents, with Raul Castro in Moscow arranging for the delivery Soviet missiles, with Castro a mere month away from stealing more than 1,600 U.S.-owned businesses at Soviet gunpoint—a situation report by the CIA and the State Department concluded: "We are unable to answer the simplified question, Is Castro himself a Communist?"[6]

Eusebio Mujal had much to teach U.S. intelligence in early 1959—if only he'd been allowed entry to the U.S. Instead, promptly upon his arrival at Miami International Airport from Argentina, Mujal's U.S. visa was cancelled on orders of the U.S. State Department. Mujal then flew to Spain where he found asylum.

The State Department officials in charge of Cuban matters at the time were Roy Rubottom and William Wieland. According to sworn testimony by U.S. ambassadors Arthur Gardner and Earl Smith, both of those officials worked hand in glove with *The New York Times's* Herbert Matthews, who bore a grudge against Mujal. To return to the ambassadors' testimony:

Senator Dodd: "While you were the ambassador to Cuba, Mr. Rubottom was the assistant secretary for Latin American affairs, was he not?"

Mr. Gardner: "Yes."

Mr. Smith: "I believe there was a close connection . . . between the Latin American desk and Herbert Matthews."

Mr. Sourwine: "And by the Latin American desk, whom do you mean?"

Mr. Smith: "I would say the Latin American desk would go from the assistant secretary for Latin American affairs [Rubottom] right down to the man who presides over the Cuban [Wieland]."

Mr Smith: "I would say that *Mr. Wieland and all those who had anything to do with Cuba had a close connection with Herbert Matthews.* I will go further than that. I will say that when I was ambassador, I was thoroughly aware of this, and sometimes made the remark in my own embassy that Mr. Matthews was more familiar with the State Department thinking regarding Cuba than I was." (my emphasis)

Senator Dodd: "You have been quoted, Mr. Gardner, as referring to 'Castro worship' in the State Department in 1957. You are quoted as saying you fought all the time with the State Department over whether Castro merited the support or friendship of the United States. Would you explain?

Mr. Gardner: "I feel it very strongly, that the State Department was influenced, first, by those stories by Herbert Matthews, and soon [support for Castro] became kind of a fetish with them."

Senator Dodd: "Your successor as ambassador to Cuba, Earl Smith was actually [sent by the State Department] to be briefed by *The New York Times'* Herbert Matthews?"

Mr. Gardner: "Yes, that is right."

Two years ago Obama's communications director Anita Dunn denounced a dangerous political-media axis consisting of conservative Republicans and Fox News, the second of which served as "either the research arm or the communications arm of the Republican Party." No proof was provided by Anita Dunn.

On the other hand, we have sworn Congressional testimony by Republican ambassadors Arthur Gardner and Earl Smith of intimate collusion by liberal State Department officials with a liberal *New York Times* reporter (Herbert Matthews). Partly owing to this collusion, the U.S.—in the Missile Crisis—would soon face its biggest external threat since the War of 1812. This State Department-*New York Times* cronyism had completely upended the traditional process. In 1957 U.S. government officials posted to Cuba got briefings and orientation from a *New York Times* reporter. It used to work the other way: reporters got briefings from diplomats.

Not to be outdone, during a chat with Matthews in the fall of 1962 President Kennedy learned that the reporter was again heading to Cuba. So the president asked if Matthews would be so kind as to stop by afterwards to brief him. A week later the Missile Crisis put the kibosh to Matthews Cuba trip. But the point is that Matthews's clairvoyance on Cuban matters (in which he now had more than five years' experience) impressed the U.S. president.

Cuban exiles were also getting on both Matthews's and Kennedy's nerves at around this time. They were sending hate-mail to *The New York Times* and "sensationalist rumors" about Russian missiles to the White House. For weeks dozens of young

Cuban exiles had been infiltrating Cuba and bringing out eyewitness reports of Soviet missiles. In the process, dozens were also dying by firing squad and torture at the hands of Castro and Che Guevara's KGB-tutored secret police.

Matthews's insight into Cuban matters in October 1962 would have probably been welcomed among "the best and the brightest." Chances are his insights would match and confirm their own. To wit:

"There is no evidence of any organized combat force in Cuba from any Soviet-bloc country," stressed a public statement from President Kennedy in September 1962, "or of military bases provided to Russia or of the presence of offensive ground-to-ground missiles."[7]

"Our intelligence on this is very good and very hard," stressed Undersecretary of State George Ball to a Congressional committee.[8]

"Nothing but refugee rumors," sneered JFK's national security advisor McGeorge Bundy on ABC's "Issues and Answers" on October 14, 1962. "Nothing in Cuba presents a threat to the United States," continued the Ivy League luminary, barely masking his scorn for the hot-headed and deceitful Cuban exiles and their sensational reports of missiles. "There's no likelihood that the Soviets or Cubans would try and install an offensive capability in Cuba," he scoffed.

"There's fifty-odd-thousand Cuban refugees in this country," sneered President Kennedy himself, "all living for the day when we go to war with Cuba. They're the ones putting out this kind of stuff."[9] Exactly 48 hours later U-2 photos on the President's desk revealed those refugee rumors, complete with nuclear warheads, and pointed directly at Bundy, JFK and their entire staff of sagacious Ivy League wizards—to say nothing of Herbert Matthews.

Much of that very good and very hard intelligence had been vouchsafed to Robert Kennedy by Soviet Ambassador Anatoly Dobrynin. The setting was one of those (hush-hush, wink-wink) "back-channel" meetings for which the Soviet ambassador and the U.S. attorney general were to become famous. The irresponsible rumor-mongering from Republican Senators Keating and Goldwater about Russian missiles in Cuba had obviously reached Premier Khrushchev's attention, explained Dobrynin.

But he fully realized (wink-wink) that mid-term elections loomed in the U.S. So he fully expected those rascally Republicans (wink-wink), in light of their poor prospects and eager to affect a reversal, to engage in politics at their sleaziest. Hence their crackpot claims of Soviet missiles in Cuba, accompanied by tens of thousands of fully-armed Soviet troops.

Robert Kennedy assured Dobrynin that the president (wink-wink) was an old hand at this type of thing. He knew full well what the Republicans were up to and saw right through their scam. Soviet Premier Khrushchev need not worry. In the November elections the rascally Republican scare-mongers (wink-wink) would get their comeuppance, and all would return to normal.

In sum: eyewitness reports regarding Soviet missiles from men dodging Soviet patrols and risking death from Soviet-armed firing squads were poo-poohed as unreliably biased. Instead the president of the U.S.—to confirm his "back-channel" scoop from a Soviet ambassador originally appointed by Stalin—sought out a presumably unbiased report regarding Soviet intentions. For this he chose a man whom a Soviet satrap had personally decorated with a medal inscribed, "To Our American Friend Herbert Matthews with Gratitude. Fidel Castro." In addition, the FBI had been monitoring this (presumably unbiased) man for three years. "One can't get much closer to communism without becoming one," J. Edgar Hoover had written Vice President Nixon about Herbert Matthews in July of 1959.[10]

After Carlos Bringuier and his in-laws had secured Eusebio Mujal's exit-visa from Argentina, the labor leader asked that Bringuier discreetly drive him to the airport—and in disguise. "If I take a taxi, Castro's hit-team will get me before I reach the airport," Mujal explained.

"Again I thought Mujal was exaggerating," recalls Bringuier. "'Drama queen' wasn't a term used in those days, but that's pretty much what I thought at the time. Regardless, we followed all his instructions and got him safely to his flight to Miami.

"Well, a week later I get a call from Lara, the Cuban consul in Argentina," said Bringuier. "'Where's Eusebio Mujal?' asks Lara. 'Have you seen him? Tell him to be careful. Two men from Uruguay were here yesterday looking for him. I overheard their conversation. . . . I know this sounds crazy, but I'm pretty sure I overheard them sounding like they were out to kill him.'"

Cuban consul Lara, let's keep in mind, was in a weird spot at the time. He was a career Cuban foreign-service official. He'd been ambassador to Argentina under the Batista government, so he was still on the job in early 1959. The Comintern's hit-men had apparently been tipped off to Mujal's whereabouts by Castro. And assuming that the Cuban consul in Argentina must be a Castro-regime apparatchik, the hit-men were not as discreet as normal in their conversations.

"Where is Eusebio Mujal?" Fidel Castro shrieked during a speech in Santa Clara, Cuba that very week, almost as if to confirm Mujal's fears. "All I can say is that those who have not yet fallen will soon face the firing squad!"

"*¿Donde Esta Mujal?*" (Where is Mujal?) asked Cuba's Castroite paper of the time, *Prensa Libre*, in a headline some weeks later. "I was back in Cuba by then," recalls Carlos Bringuier. "But I sure wasn't telling."

Successful hit-men also found a warm welcome in Castro's Cuba. In 1961, promptly upon completing his prison sentence in Mexico, Trotsky's ax-murderer Ramon Mercader found his way to Cuba, where he became a bosom-buddy of his longtime fan Che Guevara, then serving as Cuba's minister of industries. In that capacity Che anointed Ramon Mercader as Cuba's inspector of prisons. Quite fittingly, in 1961, Castro's prisons held about the same number of political prisoners per capita as Mercader's boss (and Che's idol) Stalin's had held in 1936. But "Cuba is now a happy island," assured *The New York Times*' Herbert Matthews.

Granted, in this age of "Occupy" movements where union officials march behind Communist Party placards and shoulder to shoulder with their card-carrying bearers, the notion of labor leaders on a Communist Party hit-list sounds odd. But three or four decades ago this was common practice, as Eusebio Mujal's American friend and associate George Meany would have willingly and gruffly explained.

CHAPTER 8

Papa Hemingway Admires Death in the Cuban Afternoon

Herbert Matthews was "the only person absolutely qualified to write about Cuba," according to his friend and frequent host in Cuba, Ernest "Papa" Hemingway.[1]

As for the famous novelist—according to KGB defector Alexander Vassiliev, "the 42-year-old Hemingway was recruited by the KGB under the cover name 'Argo' in 1941, and cooperated with Soviet agents whom he met in Havana and London." This comes from a book published in 2009 by Yale University Press (not exactly a branch of the John Birch Society).

"Castro's revolution," Hemingway wrote in 1960, "is very pure and beautiful. I'm encouraged by it. The Cuban people now have a decent chance for the first time." Papa's sometime friend John Dos Passos said Hemingway "had one of the shrewdest heads for unmasking political pretensions I've ever run into."[2]

"Cuban mothers, let me assure you that I will solve all Cuba's problems without spilling a drop of blood." Fidel Castro broadcast that promise into a phalanx of microphones upon entering Havana on January 8, 1959. As the jubilant crowd erupted with joy, Castro continued: "Cuban mothers, let me assure you that because of me you will never have to cry."

Indeed, Hemingway saw behind these pretensions of love, charity and humanism—quite literally.

Some background: as commander of Havana's La Cabana prison and execution yard in the early months of the revolution, Che Guevara often coached his firing squads in person, then rushed up to shatter the skull of the convulsed man (or boy) by firing the *coup de grace* himself. When other duties tore him away from his beloved execution-yard, Che consoled himself by viewing the slaughter. His second-story office in La Cabana had a section of wall torn out to better view his darling firing squads at work, often in the company of distinguished friends. Havana resident Ernest Hemingway was one of these.

Accounts of "Papa" Hemingway's presence at these massacres comes courtesy of Hemingway's own friend, the late George Plimpton (not exactly a right-wing Cuban exile) who worked as editor of *The Paris Review* (not exactly a McCarthyite scandal-sheet).

In 1958 George Plimpton interviewed Hemingway in Cuba for one of *The Paris Review's* most famous pieces. They became friends, and the following year Hemingway again invited Plimpton down to his Finca Vigia just outside Havana. During the 1990's, an editor at *The Paris Review* related how this highbrow publication passed on an option to serialize the manuscript that became Che Guevara's *Motorcycle Diaries*—and revealed "Papa's" unwitting role in the rejection.

"I took the paper-clipped excerpt upstairs to the Boss [Plimpton]," writes James Scott Linville, "flopped down in the chair to the side of his desk . . . and said I had something strange and good. As I started to tell him about it, his smile faded. I stopped my pitch and said, 'Boss, what's the matter?'"

"James, I'm sorry," Linville recalls Plimpton replying. A sad look came over him and he said, "Years ago, after we'd done the interview, Papa invited me down again to Cuba. It was right after the revolution. 'There's something you should see,'" Hemingway told Plimpton while preparing a shaker of drinks for the outing.

Linville carried on, paraphrasing Plimpton's account. "They got in the car with a few others and drove some way out of town.

They got out, set up chairs and took out the drinks, as if they were going to watch the sunset. Soon a truck arrived. This, explained George, was what they'd been waiting for. It came, as Hemingway knew, the same time each day. It stopped and some men with guns got out of it. In the back were a couple of dozen others who were tied up. Prisoners.

"The men with guns hustled the others out of the back of the truck, and lined them up. Then they shot them. They put the bodies back into the truck.

"I said to George something to the effect of, 'Oh, my God.'

"Then I said, 'I don't believe you.' I'm not sure why I didn't.

"'Did you ever write about this?'" Linville asked his boss Plimpton.

"'No.'

"'Why not?'

"'He looked uncomfortable and shrugged.

"'In the 20 years I knew George, it was the only time he refused to look at a piece of writing," continues Linville. "It was unusual for George to talk about politics. . . . But still I didn't quite believe him. Quite simply, I'd never heard a word about such executions," concludes Linville.[3]

And there's the money quote.

Over the years *The Paris Review* has featured the works of literary luminaries William Faulkner, Jack Kerouac, V. S. Naipaul, Tom Wolfe, Vladimir Nabokov and Philip Roth, among many others. In the words of one critic, the magazine is "one of the single most persistent acts of cultural conservation in the history of the world." So up until the mid-1990's the ultra-educated editor of a magazine catering to the ultra-educated had no idea that Castro's regime had executed people. And he learned about a few of those executions only by a fluke.

"A writer without a sense of justice and of injustice would be better off editing the yearbook of a school for exceptional children than writing novels," said Hemingway in that very *Paris Review* interview with George Plimpton. "The most essential gift for a good writer is a built-in, shockproof, shit detector. This is the writer's radar and all great writers have had it."

So was Hemingway duped by Castroism? Did his shit-detector malfunction? Or was it on high alert? Few people, after all, had such access to Castroism's crime scenes. And the KGB, while certainly appreciating the work of dupes and useful idiots, was not known to sign them on (openly).

The Cuba Archive estimates that by the end of that year 2,000 Cubans had been murdered in the manner Ernest Hemingway loved to watch from his picnic chair while sipping *mojitos*. Significantly, both Hemingway and Plimpton passed on writing about any of those deaths in the afternoon—and morning and midnight. Augusto Pinochet's regime, needless to add, would never have gotten off so easily.

I guess "left-wing death squads" just doesn't have the same ring to it as the other Latin American type, so often and reflexively condemned by literati. That the Cuba Archive Project has already documented (by name) almost triple the number of murdered and "disappeared" by Castro and Che Guevara's death-squads as the estimate of those disappeared by Pinochet's just doesn't register among the enlightened. George Plimpton's deputy editor provided the perfect example. It's worth quoting him again: "I didn't quite believe him. Quite simply, I'd never heard a word about such executions."

According to the internationally acclaimed *Black Book of Communism*, 16,000 executions took place 90 miles from U.S. shores, while Cuba swarmed with foreign reporters and Hollywood producers.

But in Linville's defense, and assuming he relied on the mainstream media for news and history, where would he have heard of them?

ENTER I.F. STONE

By 1964, with the egg on his face crusting into a thick layer, even *The New York Times* began rejecting Herbert Matthews's Cuba articles, whereupon I.F. Stone stepped up to the plate, citing Matthews's "outstanding history of reporting" on Cuba. "Report on Cuba The New York Times Was Afraid to Print," he titled a Matthews article of February 1964 in his *I.F. Stone's Weekly*. "Fidel Castro is one of the most extraordinary men of our age," the article starts. "The U.S. has paid heavily for a shocking underestimation of his intelligence and abilities."

Declassified Soviet documents expose I.F Stone as a full-fledged KGB agent from 1936 to 1939 and a desultory "agent of influence" for the rest of his life. This was again shown by declassified KGB documents in a book published by Yale University Press, not exactly a propaganda arm for J. Edgar Hoover's FBI.

Does anyone else notice some commonalities among Herbert Matthews's friends and champions?

CHAPTER 9

Castro's "Revolution of Youth" —Imprisoning the Young

"Castro's is a revolution of youth." (Herbert Matthews)[1] The notion of Castro's Cuba as a stiflingly Stalinist nation never quite caught on among the enlightened. Instead the island often inspires hazy visions of a vast commune, rock-fest or Occupy encampment, studded with free health clinics and with Wavy Gravy handing out love-beads at the entrance. The regime was founded by beatniks, after all. In 1960 Jean-Paul Sartre hailed Cuba's Stalinist rulers as *"les enfants au pouvoir"* (the children in power). A few months earlier Fidel Castro spoke at Harvard on the same bill as Beat poet Allen Ginsberg. And ever since then, long-haired Che Guevara has reigned worldwide as top icon of youthful rebellion.

"They saw in him," writes Camelot court scribe Arthur Schlesinger, Jr., "the hipster who in the era of the Organization Man had joyfully defied the system. . . . ."[2]

In fact the brain-shackled robot Fidel Castro and Che Guevara tried to create with their firing squads, forced-labor camps and Stalinist indoctrination makes the Eisenhower era's Organization Man look like a combination of Jimi Hendrix and Jack Kerouac.

"Youth must refrain from ungrateful questioning of govern-mental mandates!" declared Che Guevara in a famous speech in 1961. "The very spirit of rebellion is reprehensible," commanded this icon of flower-children. "Instead the young must dedicate themselves to study, work and military service."[3]

Youth, wrote Guevara, "should learn to think and act as a mass." Those who chose their own path (as in growing long hair and listening to Yankee-imperialist rock 'n' roll) were denounced as worthless delinquents and herded into forced-labor camps at Soviet bayonet-point. In a famous speech, Che even vowed "to make individualism disappear from Cuba! It is criminal to think of individuals," he raved.[4]

And if the Eisenhower era's Organization Man often brought some of his work home, the Castroites sought to outdo him a thousand-fold. "Our revolutionaries," Che Guevara wrote in his "Man and Socialism in Cuba," "have children who with their first faltering words do not learn to call their father; wives who must be part of the general sacrifice necessary to carry the revolution to its destination. Their circle of friends is strictly limited to the circle of revolutionary companions. There is no life outside the revolution. A father who devotes himself to the revolution cannot be distracted by the thought of what his child needs, of his worn shoes, of the basic necessities which his family may lack."

Castro, said Camelot scribe Arthur Schlesinger, Jr., had "summoned a dozen friends and overturned a government of wicked old men."

THE YOUNG AND THE FEARLESS

"I'm going back to Cuba to kill Che Guevara!" snarled Jose Castano (then 17) to fellow paratrooper Manel Menendez (then 23). These youths were then in Guatemala, training as members of Brigade 2506 for what came to be known as the Bay of Pigs invasion.[5]

Che Guevara had personally tortured and murdered Jose's father two years earlier. Needless to add, Jose Castano, Sr. had been completely defenseless at the time. To Jose's 16-year-old son, Che Guevara—twice his age at the time—was a very wicked old man.

Herbert Matthews had declared that "Castro's is a revolution of youth" at around the time Jose, Manel and hundreds of other Cuban youths were training to overthrow Castro. "If a label must be given he is a pre-scientific Utopian socialist, not a Marxist."

The average age of the thousands of men murdered by firing squad during this overturning of wicked old men was probably about 25. During a two-week period in August 1964, 477 men were murdered by Castro's firing squads. Not a single victim had been affiliated with the wicked Batista regime. Most, in fact, had fought it. Many, perhaps most, of the murdered men were younger than Castro and Che by a decade and had been early members of Castro's own rebel army and government.[6]

Carlos Machado was 15 years old in 1963 when a volley from Castro's firing squad shattered his body. His twin brother and father crumpled beside Carlos from the same volley and tumbled into the same mass grave. Felicito Acosta, Lorenzo Espino, Justo Garcia Jr., Efrain Brizuelas and Jesus Carrillo were all 16 when they died by Soviet-armed firing squad in the same area. Lorentino Pelaez Jr., Tito Sardinas and Juan Blanco were 17. Emeterio Rodriguez and Ruben Acosta were 15. Antonio Ruiz Acosta and Luis Gonzalez were each 14 when the Castroite volley tumbled them into a mass grave.[7]

These Cuban teenagers (along with thousands of others) had joined their fathers, uncles and cousins to resist the plans of Soviet advisors three and four times their age to steal their families' small farms and build a Stalinist *kolkhoz*.

Jose Ramon Cruz was four years old when Castro and Che marched into Havana in 1959. As a teenager he took to writing mildly ribald graffiti on some of the walks of his home town of Camaguey. Unfortunately his brand of humor was completely lost on Castro's Stasi-tutored police, who repeatedly jailed and beat him. In 1971 Jose organized a public protest against his revolutionary treatment. Castro's police quickly showed up, and this time they shot him to death. The beloved teenagers' funeral was a crowded, noisy event that required Castro's Soviet T-34 and Stalin tanks to rumble into the area, quell the hooliganism and restore order. A mini-Budapest in the tropics.

Among Jose Castano and Manel Menendez's band of brothers in Brigade 2506 during the Bay of Pigs invasion was 16-year-old Felipe Rodon, who on April 17th, 1961 grabbed his 57 mm cannon and ran to face point-blank one of Castro's Soviet tanks on the bloody Bay of Pigs beachhead. At 10 yards Felipe fired at the clanking monster and it exploded, but the momentum kept it going and the Soviet tank, sent to Cuba by the fat and wicked old men in the Kremlin, rolled over little Felipe.

Gilberto Hernandez was 17 when a round from a Czech burp-gun put out his eye on that same beachead. Castro troops were swarming in but he held his ground, firing furiously with his recoilless rifle for another hour until the Soviet-trained Castroites finally surrounded him and killed him with a shower of grenades.

When he hit the beach at the Bay of Pigs, Jose Antonio San Roman, the commander of Brigade 2506, was 27 years old. His second-in-command, Erneido Oliva, was 27. The political delegate of the exiles' provisional government, Manuel Artime, was 28.

Among the leaders of the anti-Castro Cuban underground of the time were Rogelio Gonzalez, Alberto Tapia, and Virgilio Campaneria. None was older than 26 in 1961 when murdered by Soviet-armed firing squads. Seventeen other college kids were murdered by Castro and Che's firing squads that week in early 1961. Far from belonging to Batista's "wicked old men," all these youngsters had fought against the Batista regime. In utter vain will you search for any mention of this by *The New York Times* or the media in general.

As for foreign commentators on the Cuban revolution, Jean-Paul Sartre, Arthur Schlesinger, Jr., et al., weren't merely wrong; they were smugly propounding the very opposite of the truth.

Cuban "children" were in positions of power all right, but as armed opponents of Fidel Castro and Che Guevara. These youngsters were also paying for their bravery with their lives—and by the thousands. The ones captured stood tall, proud, defiant and silent through ghastly torture by Castro's secret police, then being tutored by wicked old men from the Kremlin (KGB). But the Cuban kids went to their deaths before Castro's firing squads while defiantly yelling "Down with Communism!"

"The defiant yells of 'Down with Communism!' made the walls of La Cabana prison tremble," recalls an eyewitness to these firing-squad massacres, Armando Valladares, who suffered 22 torture-filled years in Castro's prisons and was later appointed by Ronald Reagan as U.S. ambassador to the UN Human Rights Commission. Valladares himself was 21 when jailed for the counter-revolutionary crime of refusing to display a pro-Castro sign on his desk. During Cuba's "reign of terror"—Batista's dictatorial rule, according to Herbert Matthews—such a crime would have elicited mere chuckles from those wicked old men.

For the above crime, and in a secret trial, Castro's judicial apparatchiks gave Valladares a 30-year prison sentence. Before, during and after this trial the Castro regime jailed tens of thousands of political prisoners for crimes similar to that of Valladares. For planting bombs in public places—and during an open trial crammed with international observers—an independent judiciary gave the same sentence, 30 years, to Nelson Mandela. The segregationist regime of South Africa was often suspended from the UN for its human-rights violations. Castro's regime, on the other hand, went on to chair the UN Human Rights commission.

Felix Rodriguez was 17 when he first volunteered to fight the wicked old men (almost twice his age) who had taken over Cuba in 1959 with the help of the wicked older men in the Kremlin. As a 19-year-old member of Brigade 2506, Felix infiltrated Communist Cuba weeks before the Bay of Pigs invasion, organizing underground freedom-fighters, planning for the sabotage of key roads and bridges, staying a step ahead of the Castro's secret police and their KGB handlers and coaches, as 58-year-old Herbert Matthews shilled for them in the U.S. media. Almost half of his comrades in the infiltration teams (all in their early 20's) died in front of firing squads, after torture. Nineteen-year-old Felix Rodriguez knew the odds. He volunteered anyway.

After the Best and Brightest had stabbed the Bay of Pigs freedom-fighters in the back, Rodriguez again foiled the Communist dragnet by slipping into the Venezuelan embassy and escaping a year later to Florida. After the Best and Brightest stabbed them again and twisted the blade with the Kennedy-Khrushchev swindle that supposedly solved the Missile Crisis, Rodriguez, along with hundreds of his Brigade 2506 brothers, enlisted in the U.S. Army.

Later, as a CIA operative, Rodriguez played the key role in tracking down and capturing Che Guevara in Bolivia and was the last to question him. "Finally," at age 26, "I was face to face with the assassin of thousands of my countrymen, of hundreds of my patriot friends," recalls Rodriguez. His captive Che Guevara was almost 40 at the time; in Felix's eyes he was among the wickedest of the old men who had converted his homeland into a joyless, stifling police state and satrapy of the even older men in the Kremlin.

But remove the wispy beard and beret from Che Guevara and you've got Jim Morrison of The Doors. In 1959, Raul Castro with his blond ponytail was a ringer for Joe Walsh circa "Hotel California." Yank the cowboy hat from Camilo Cienfuegos's head and you've got the Grateful Dead's Jerry Garcia. Put a green army cap on Cream's drummer Ginger Baker, darken his thin beard a bit, and there's Fidel Castro himself.

So these Cuban Stalinists were on the cutting edge of fashion. They pre-empted the Haight-Ashbury look by a decade. In any picture with them, Nikita Khrushchev looks as far out of place as the frumpy Ed Sullivan introducing the psychedelic Jefferson Airplane on his stage. But in fact the fat, bald, boorish Butcher of

Budapest was the main patron, bankroller and soul-mate of these young, hirsute, hard-core Cuban Bolsheviks.

And woe to Castro's subjects who attempted the "Heepee" look and lifestyle when it really kicked in a few years later!

"These youths walk around with their transistor radios listening to imperialist music!" raved Fidel Castro as he denounced rock 'n' roll in a 1968 speech. "They corrupt the morals of young girls and destroy posters of Che! What do they think? That this is a bourgeois liberal regime? No! There's nothing liberal in us! We are collectivists! We are communists! There will be no Prague Spring here!"[8]

Imagine long-haired youths destroying images of Che Guevara! It's easy when you are, unlike Occupy demonstrators, actually forced to live under Che Guevara. The impulse then becomes irresistible.

USEFUL IDIOTS FROM WOODSTOCK NATION

Not that stupid old men like Jean-Paul Sartre, Arthur Schlesinger, Jr. and Bob Beckel are alone in hailing the youthful idealism of a Stalinist regime that jailed tens of thousands of Cuban youths for the crime of growing long hair and listening to "Yankee heepee" rock music.

In fact many of the very "Yankee heepees" whose music was criminalized by Fidel Castro themselves hail the KGB-mentored jailing of their fans. This hailing often takes the form of composing songs in honor of the regime that jailed young Cubans who were caught listening to their own music smuggled into Cuba.

When in 1979 Fidel Castro invited Stephen Stills to perform in Cuba, the famous Woodstocker could hardly contain his elation. The fervent champion of human rights, civil rights and free speech—indeed, CSNY's last tour in 2010 was entitled "The Free-Speech Tour"—not only took up the offer to perform at this

"Havana Jam" but also composed a song in Castro's honor, entitled "Cuba al Fin!"

Jazz-master Paquito D'Rivera, still living in Cuba at the time, recalled watching Stills on stage at Havana's Karl Marx theatre lovingly crooning the song to the families of Castro's Stalinist *nomenklatura* as if Havana Jam were a personal performance for the Soviet satrap himself.[9] Within blocks of this cheeky "jam"—which also included fervent human-rights activists Kris Kristofferson and Billy Joel—Cuban youths, black and white, languished in dungeons as they suffered prison sentences longer than Nelson Mandela's. Their crime was the commission of free speech.

"They invited me because they knew I was politically astute,"[10] gloated Stephen Stills about the acumen and good taste of his Cuban hosts, who to this day jail Cuban youths for the crime of saying "Down with Fidel!"

"There's a man with a gun over there, tellin' me I gotta beware," wrote Stepen Stills in his 1967 hit, "For What it's Worth." You know what, Stephen Stills? Cuban youths have something to tell you regarding that scenario. If only you'd deigned to part company from your Stalinist hosts in Havana and asked around.

"Paranoia strikes deep, into your life it will creep. It starts when you're always afraid, Step out of line, the men come and take you away." Your lyrics, Mr. Stills—and they describe to a T your hosts in Havana, who took away Cubans at a higher rate than Stalin took away Russians or Hitler took away Germans.

"Young people speaking their minds, And getting so much resistance from behind . . . ." Quite so, Mr. Stills. Cuban youngsters were getting it from the people right behind your stage – from the Stalinists who were sponsoring you, who were brown-nosing with you, while they were jailing and torturing young people for the crime of listening to your music.

"You have to give them due respect because they have a unique form of socialism that's very significant in the scheme of world history," Stills declared in explaining his Cuba visit.[11]

Oh, it's unique all right, Mr. Stills. Can you think of another 20ᵗʰ-century regime that jailed and tortured youths *en masse* for the crime of growing long hair and craving rock music?

Famous Woodstocker Carlos Santana also glorifies the regime that criminalized his music and imprisoned his fans. At the 2005 Oscars the famed guitarist, on hand to perform the theme song for *Motorcycle Diaries*, stopped for the photographers, smiled deliriously and flung his jacket open.

Ta-DA! There it was: Carlos's elegantly embroidered Che Guevara t-shirt. Carlos's face as the flashbulbs popped said it all. "I'm so cool!" he might have beamed. "I'm so hip! I'm so sharp! I'm so politically astute—like my buddy Stephen Stills!"

Indeed, as if hipness, sharpness and political astuteness meant proudly advertising the emblem of a regime that criminalized your music and lifestyle.

Judy Collins, though not physically present at Yasgur's farm on August 15, 1969, certainly merits mention here. The Spanish-sounding gibberish that closes out "Judy Blue Eyes" is Stills employing a *faux* Cuban accent, singing: "How beautiful it would be to bring me to Cuba, the queen of the Caribbean. I only want to visit you there, how sad that I can't go, Oh va, oh va, va!"

Well, exactly ten years later Stills fulfilled his wish, and as a personal guest of the beautiful island's owner and warden.

Upon Che Guevara's death, the bereaved "Sweet Judy Blue Eyes" herself sought solace in songwriting, composing a lovely ballad entitled "Che." "You have it in your hands to own your life, to own your land" goes the chorus which represents Che himself consoling Bolivian *campesinos* who mourn their savior's death.

Attempting to own their own lives and land is precisely what got thousands of Cuban country-folk massacred by Che Guevara's firing squads. America's millionaire songstress might have mourned Che's death, but it was Bolivian *campesinos* who helped track him down and kill him.

"Only through the total eradication of private property will we create the new man," instructed Che Guevara. "Youth must refrain from ungrateful questioning of governmental mandates. Instead they must dedicate themselves to study, work and military service. The very spirit of rebellion is reprehensible!" thundered this idol of the "do-your-own-thing" Bohemians.

Not to be outdone by Judy Collins, famous Rhodes Scholar Kris Kristofferson composed a song entitled "Mal Sacate," wherein he laments: "You have stolen all the land that you can steal, and you killed so many heroes."

A perfect tribute to his Havana Jam hosts, you might think?

Instead Kristofferson was lambasting Stalinism's enemies, the men who fought Che Guevara. The very next stanza mentions the "murdered heroes," among whom we find none other than—Che Guevara!

Judy Collins and Kris Kristofferson obviously share the same "political astuteness" with their friend and soulmate Stephen Stills. So let's excuse them for confusing Fidel Castro with Country Joe McDonald and Che Guevara with Wavy Gravy.

Former "Pretenders" singer Chrissie Hynde's latest album is entitled *Fidelity!* in honor of Fidel Castro. She and her lover had recently visited Cuba and "saw pictures of Fidel Castro everywhere!" she explained.

Imagine that!

Champion of Cuban Stalinism (and segregation) Chrissie Hynde was a noisy opponent of South African segregation. You'll find the identical "incongruity" in Castro fans from Charles Rangel to Maxine Waters, from Danny Glover to Jack Nicholson, from Sidney Pollack to Steven Spielberg, from Francis Ford Coppola to Norman Jewison, from Ry Cooder to Bonnie Raitt.

Speaking of Bonnie Raitt, she composed a song in honor of Fidel Castro entitled "Cuba Is Way Too Cool!" and performed it in his very fiefdom in March 1999 during a star-studded musical extravaganza entitled "Music Bridges Over Troubled Waters."

In brief, the only regime in recent history to criminalize rock music and jail its fans for the crime of being its fans has songs composed in its honor by rock musicians Bonnie Raitt, Stephen Stills, Judy Collins, Kris Kristofferson and Chrissie Hynde. Not to be outdone, native New Yorker and civil-rights activist Carole King sang a personal and heartfelt "You've Got a Friend" to the man who boasts of craving to nuke New York and who jailed the longest-suffering black political prisoners in modern history.

The testimony of a Cuban rocker-wannabe might clarify matters: "In Cuba freedom is nonexistent," the rock guitarist told Mexico's *Proceso* magazine. "The regime demands submission. It persecutes all hippies, homosexuals, poets and free thinkers. It employs total repression against them."[12]

The Cuban rocker quoted above divulged the truth only because he'd managed to escape the nation-prison that Bonnie Raitt, Chrissie Hynde, Jimmy Buffett, Andy Summers, etc. all herald. That escapee's name is Canek Sanchez Guevara—Ernesto "Che" Guevara's very grandson. The regime co-founded by his grandfather jailed and tortured Canek for the crime of trying to play rock music.

CHAPTER 10

Jon Stewart to Don Fidel: Thank You, Godfather

*"I mean everybody who saw **Godfather II** knows what it was like when Castro took over!"* (Chris Matthews, "Hardball, The Place for Politics," MSNBC, October 20, 2011)

*"All I know about pre-Castro Cuba I learned from **Godfather II!**"* (Jon Stewart, July 23, 2008)

The media love to dwell on how a few U.S. mobsters once bribed a few Cuban politicians to allow a few casinos in Havana. To hear them tell it: in an economy that was overwhelmingly Cuban-owned, export- and manufacturing-oriented, and provided Cubans per capita with an income higher than most Europeans, the 13th-lowest infant mortality on earth, and attracted a flood of (primarily first-world) immigrants, this tiny sideline—the casino business—made Cuba a hopelessly wretched place screaming for a communist revolution. So don't bother us with any boring statistics, you Cuban-exile revanchists!

For almost forty years the primary—and perhaps *exclusive*—educational text on Cuba for liberals was a screenplay by fiction-writer Mario Puzo and winemaker Francis Ford Coppola.

Bestselling author T.J. English, in collaboration with Castro-regime apparatchiks, then expanded on this educational franchise. *Havana Nocturne: How the Mob Owned Cuba, and Lost it to the Revolution,* he entitled the "New York Times Bestseller" that enchanted and enlightened Comedy Central's Jon Stewart, also known as the primary news and educational source for Americans under 40.

"Well-researched . . . knowledgeable . . . Briskly paced and well-sourced, *Havana Nocturne* has the air of a thriller with the bonus of being true," rhapsodized Tom Miller of *The Washington Post* about the book.

"Thoroughly and impressively researched," attested *The Miami Herald.*

"Bringing together long-buried historical information with English's own research in Havana . . . *Havana Nocturne* takes readers back to Cuba in the years when it was a veritable devil's playground for mob leaders," glows the PR notice from publisher William Morrow.

"The roots of this epic antipathy [between the U.S. and Castro] can be traced in part to the influx of mobsters and the plundering of Havana that took place in the late 1940's and 50's . . . This book is nothing less than The Rosetta Stone, the key to understanding the Cuban Revolution," the author modestly claims.

During this interview the legendarily edgy and iconoclastic Jon Stewart royally blew his chance to revel in a nonstop snark-fest against the (genuine) establishment. Instead:

"I *love* this book!" Stewart gushed upon greeting the author on his "Daily Show." "This is the true story of Cuba—a fascinating book!" continued the Peabody Award-winner, barely containing himself.

As a service to "The Daily Show's" producers I prepared a script—based on fully-documented information—for Stewart's interview with T.J. English that seemed ideal for enhancing the

Peabody Award-winner's acclaim for deflating blowhards and smashing pious platitudes with snarky truth. Here it goes.

Welcome to the show, Mr. English, and thanks for coming. First off, it appears that the primary source for your book, cited no fewer than 72 times in quotes and footnotes, is an official of Castro's totalitarian regime named Enrique Cirules.

In fact, *Senor* Cirules is an official of Cuba's La Casa de las Americas, which publishes and promotes the Castro regime's propaganda in books and articles under the guise of art. In 1983 a high-ranking Cuban Intelligence officer named Jesus Perez Mendez defected to the U.S. and spilled his guts to the FBI. Among his gut-spillings we encounter the following: "The Cuban DGI (Castro's KGB-trained spy agency) controls Casa de las Americas." We were hoping to have Mr. Perez-Mendes on tonight to contribute his views on the veracity of your book's claims, Mr. English, but were thwarted upon discovering that he lives under FBI protection for fear of being assassinated by the folks who hosted you in Cuba and collaborated with you in writing the book.[1]

Mr. English, in your book's acknowledgements you describe this Castroite apparatchik Enrique Cirules as a "Cuban author." Wouldn't this be like describing Julius Streicher as a "German author"?

Instead, minutes into the interview and in response to another *Godfather*-ite cliché by the smug T.J. English, Stewart—this winner of the Television Critics Association award for "Outstanding Achievement in News and Information"—gushes: "Wow! So the mob actually *built* Cuba's economy! So it was actually *worse* than shown in *Godfather II!*"

To continue with my script for "The Daily Show:" Mr. English, let's look at statistics published by scholars who live in a free country without fearing torture-chambers and firing squads for telling the truth. The following items were culled from the Organization of American States, from the UN Statistical yearbook and from the Cuban government before it was totalitarian. We'll compare these against the claims made by the Castro-regime apparatchik who constitutes the primary source for your *non*-fiction bestseller.

In 1955, for instance, Cuba contained a grand total of three gambling casinos. The biggest was at the Tropicana Club and featured ten gambling tables and 30 slot machines. The Hotel Nacional featured seven roulette wheels and 21 slot machines.[2]

By contrast, in 1955 the Riviera Casino in Las Vegas featured 20 tables and 116 slot machines. This means that in 1955 one Las Vegas casino had more gambling action than all of Cuba.

We also ran some numbers, Mr. Author of the Rosetta Stone on the Cuban Revolution. For instance, according to the Las Vegas Convention and Visitors Authority the typical tourist spends five days in their city and spends an average of $580 ($75 in 1957 dollars) on gambling, the main motive for 90 per cent of visitors.

Your own book acknowledges that Cuba's casinos were patronized almost exclusively by tourists. Well, throughout the 1950's Cuba averaged 180,000 tourists a year.[3] For the sake of this show's time-constraints, we decided to be very generous and ignore Cuba's beaches, fishing, dining, palm-studded country-side, old-world architecture, sightseeing etc., etc. We said: let's assume all those tourists—men, women, adolescents, children—did nothing in Cuba but gamble, and at the Las Vegas rate.

Well, our calculator revealed an extremely generous total of $13.5 million for Cuba's gambling industry annually. But in 1957 Cuba's gross domestic product was $2.7 billion, and Cuba's foreign receipts were $752 million.[4] Mr. English, could you explain how the beneficiaries of that miniscule fraction of Cuba's income came to own the entire nation of Cuba and to "infiltrate its levers of power from top to bottom," as your impressively-researched book claims? "U.S. mobsters," you write, "concerned themselves with controlling casinos, banks, political leaders and the gross national product of the island."

More comical still, your book claims that: "Every Monday at noon, a [mobster Meyer] Lansky-appointed bagman was allowed into the presidential palace through a side door. He carried with him a satchel filled with cash, part of a monthly payment of $1.28 million that was to be delivered to the president. Batista never met the courier. He used a relative as an intermediary."

So, Mr. English, are you claiming that mob chief Meyer Lansky was slipping Batista more than the combined annual gross from every casino in Cuba, including those unaffiliated with Meyer Lansky?

Author Tom Miller, who writes for *The New York Times*, *The Washington Post* and *National Geographic* among many other prestigious publications, hailed your book as "well-sourced," "well-researched" and "knowledgeable."

We note that Mr. Miller is granted visas by the totalitarian Cuban regime for the asking and currently leads National Geographic "people-to-people" tours of Cuba at a cost of $5,095 per person. These junkets are run in partnership with the Castro regime. Just thought we'd bring this up.

Several books have been written on Meyer Lansky and mob operations in Cuba: Robert Lacey's *Little Man: Meyer Lansky and the Gangster Life*, Scott M. Deitche's *The Silent Don: The Criminal World of Santo Trafficante Jr.*, and Eduardo Saenz Rovner's *The Cuban Connection: Drug Trafficking, Smuggling, and Gambling from the 1920s to the Revolution*. Not one of the major findings in these exhaustively-researched books, by authors who relied on primary sources outside the Castro regime, corresponds with any of yours.

Cuban historian Juan Antonio Blanco—who was acquainted with Enrique Cirules in Cuba but who now teaches at Florida International University—went so far as to follow some of your footnotes to Cirules's works. He then followed Cirules's footnotes, many of which sourced documents in the U.S. Blanco found all to be utterly bogus. The FBI files on Meyer Lanksy, for instance, were three feet high. And there was no mention in them of the Meyer Lansky-Batista money launderer named Amadeo Barletta. Something else caught our eye. We were also wondering, Mr.

English, given that gambling was perfectly legal in 1950's Cuba, just what was the point of laundering the proceeds?

Also, Mr. English, according to a U.S. Department of Commerce analysis from 1956, Cuba was "the most heavily capitalized country in Latin America."[5] Is it your assertion, Mr. English, that a few slot-machines and bartender tips accounted for that capitalization?

Another interesting statistic, Mr. Impressive Researcher: in 1953, more Cubans vacationed in the U.S. than Americans vacationed in Cuba.[6] How could the wretched and brutalized residents of that plundered and impoverished nation, as you depict it, have possibly pulled that off?

Mr. English, you wrote in the book's introduction as follows: "The country's most precious resources—sugar, oil, forestry, agriculture, refineries, financial institutions, and public utilities— were all up for sale. . . . Foreign capital washed over the island. . . . Such was the extent of American interest in Cuba that this island, roughly the size of the state of Tennessee, ranked in third place among the nations of the world receiving U.S. investments. The financial largesse that flooded Cuba could have been used to address the country's festering social problems. Hunger, illiteracy, subhuman housing, a high infant-mortality rate, and the dispossession of small farmers had been facts of life in Cuba throughout the island's turbulent history."

But in fact, Mr. English, in 1958, out of Cuba's 161 sugar mills, only 40 were U.S.-owned. And according to the U.S. Chamber of Commerce, in 1958 U.S. investments in Cuba accounted for only 14 per cent of Cuba's GNP, and U.S.-owned companies employed only seven per cent of Cuba's work-force.[7]

By contrast, in 2011 13 per cent of the U.S. manufacturing work-force was employed by foreign-owned plants. So here we have the same liberals who bewail U.S. exploitation and humiliation of pre-Castro Cubans, rejoicing over this greater exploitation and humiliation of Americans today. In fact, here's the liberal-in-chief himself in June 2011:

"The United States consistently receives more foreign direct investment than any other country in the world," President Barack Obama said in a statement. "By voting with their balance-sheets, businesses from abroad have clearly stated that the United States is one of the best places in the world to invest.'"[8]

But in the case of businesses from abroad voting with their balance sheets for pre-Castro Cuba, liberals decry it as a blot on Cuba's honor and a national humiliation for Cubans. Why the double standard?

Now let's take pre-Castro Cuba's festering social problems as you list them *ad seriatim:*

1.) Hunger—According to the UN's Statistical Yearbook, in 1958 Cubans consumed 81 pounds of meat annually, making them the third-highest protein consumers in Latin America. That year the UN's Food and Agriculture Organization also ranked Cuba per capita as the biggest exporter of food products in Latin America. In marked contrast, starting in 1962 the Castro regime started rationing food to its subjects to the tune of two ounces of meat, three ounces of rice, 6.5 ounces of starch and one ounce of beans daily. In marked contrast to these rations, back in 1842 the Spanish king had royally decreed daily rations of eight ounces of meat, four ounces of rice, 16 ounces of starch and four ounces of beans for all slaves in the Spanish colony of Cuba.[9]

This means, Mr. English, that Cuban slaves ate better than the subjects of the regime that essentially co-wrote your book.

On to the next of these festering social problems:

2.) High infant mortality—in 1958, Cuba's infant mortality was the 13th-lowest—not in Latin America, Mr. English, not even in the hemisphere, but in the world. And Cubans per capita had more doctors and dentists than the U.S.[10]

3.) Subhuman housing—Cuba's per-capita income in 1958 was higher than half of Europe's. "One feature of the Cuban social structure is a large middle class," starts a UNESCO study of Cuba from 1957. "Cuban workers are more unionized (proportional to the population) than U.S. workers. The average wage for an 8-hour day in Cuba in 1957 is higher than for workers in Belgium, Denmark, France and Germany. According to the Geneva-based International Labor Organization, the average daily wage for an agricultural worker was also among the highest in the world, higher than in France, Belgium, Denmark, or West Germany. Cuban labor receives 66.6 per cent of gross national income. In the U.S. the figure is 70 per cent, in Switzerland 64 per cent."[11]

4.) Dispossession of small farmers—Cuba's agricultural wages in 1958 were higher than those in half of Europe. And far from huge *latifundia* hogging the Cuban countryside, the average Cuban farm in 1958 was smaller than the average in the U.S.[12]

5.) Illiteracy—In a mere 50 years since a war of independence that cost Cuba almost a fifth of her population, Cuba managed almost 80 per cent literacy and budgeted more for public education (23 per cent of national expenses) than any Latin American country. Better still, Cubans were not just literate but also educated; they were allowed to read George Orwell and Thomas Jefferson along with the arresting wisdom and sparkling prose of Che Guevara.[13]

When no *New York Times* reporter, CNN correspondent or Ivy League scholar is within hearing-range, Communists can be extremely frank with each other.

Early in the Cuban revolution, for instance, Czech economist Radoslav Selucky visited Cuba and was rudely awakened. "We thought Cuba was underdeveloped except for a few sugar refineries," he wrote when he got home to Prague. "This is false. Almost a quarter of Cuba's labor force was employed in industry where the salaries were equal to those in the U.S."[14]

Now here's Che Guevara himself in 1961, after returning with his Cuban underlings from a lengthy tour of Eastern Europe. "We're not going to say we only saw marvels in those countries," admitted Che, who undoubtedly had heard much scoffing and snickering from his Cuban subalterns during the trip. "Naturally, for a 20th-century Cuban with all the luxuries to which imperialism has accustomed him, much of what he saw [in Eastern Europe] struck him as belonging to uncivilized nations."[15]

In 1958 a Mexican (Marxist) professor and United Nations operative visited Cuba and reported: "Cuba has a tremendous advantage in national integration over other Latin American countries because of a largely homogeneous white Spanish immigrant base. Cuba's smaller Negro population is also culturally integrated. Those feudal modes of labor that exist in the rest of Latin America don't exist in Cuba. The Cuban *campesino* does not resemble the one in the rest of Latin America who is tied to the land, and is profoundly tradition-bound and opposed to innovations which would link him to a market economy. The Cuban *campesino*, in all respects, is a modern man. They have an educational level and a familiarity with modern methods unseen in the rest of Latin America."[16]

The above are hard facts, Mr. English. Your book was written mostly in Cuba with the collaboration of Castro's KGB-founded-and-tutored regime. "Most people cooperated with me for one simple reason," you write. "They wanted to see this story finally told free of propaganda and misrepresentation." But in your acknowledgements you profusely thank Enrique Cirules, an apparatchik of the DGI-run *Casa de las Americas*, and William Galvez, who is among the highest-ranking *comandantes* in Castro's military.

Mr. English, Jon Stewart and his audience are one thing—but do you take all potential readers for complete idiots?

PROSTITUTION THEN AND NOW

Cuban prostitution also figures big in the T.J. English-Castroite collaboration—pre-Castro prostitution, needless to say. In 1961 the Castroites rounded up what they determined were all the prostitutes in Cuba and herded them into re-education camps to learn more seemly professions—like joining Castro's militia. The total number of women rounded up in this "brothel of the

Americas," as the liberal mantra has called it for over half a century, was about 14,000 (out of a population of 6.7 million Cubans).[17]

But a study by the *American Journal of Nursing* estimates 50,000 prostitutes in New York City alone. With New York City and Cuba having roughly comparable population, that means more than three times the number of prostitutes in New York.

For many folks who grew up in pre-Castro Cuba, an amateur film by Canadian Andrew Lindy entitled "The Cuba Prostitution Documentary" proved more heartbreaking than anything they'd seen on their homeland to that date. Lindy is a winner of the Canadian National Magazine Award; he has no obvious axe to grind. After a visit to Cuba as a tourist in 2011, he observed: "Prostitution is rampant." Indeed, during his entire stay Lindy was hard-pressed to find a single Cuban woman or girl who wouldn't offer sex for pay of some sort. And half the males he encountered were at least part-time pimps.

Fortunately for the sake of truth, Lindy visited Cuba as a tourist. Had he gone officially as a documentarian, his work would be as useless for determining the truth about Castroite Cuba as that of Steven Soderbergh, Oliver Stone, Sidney Pollack, NPR, ABC, NBC, CBS, etc.; or that of Harvard, Yale, Columbia or Berkeley professors. In brief, his work does not fall into the category of 98 per cent of what is published and shown about Cuba outside of Cuba.

Andrew Lindy did not enjoy the advice, expertise or hospitality of KGB-trained apparatchiks.

Upon reading T.J. English's book, many residents of pre-Castro Cuba noticed the discrepancies between the book and what they'd seen. They decided to defy Groucho Marx by believing their eyes instead of an Irish-American author who had visited Cuba 30 years after the events and conjured them in conjunction with Castro-regime officials.

But it turned out that instead of merely citing an apparatchik of Castro's DGI-controlled *Casa de Las Americas,* the bestselling author—whose book enchanted and illuminated Jon Stewart, dazzled the MSM with its "impressive research," and was optioned for a film—this author, Mr. T.J. English, actually transcribed the Communist propaganda screeds of this Castro-regime apparatchik word for word. To wit:

"I have no intention of talking to Mr. T.J. English," harrumphed the book's dedicatee, Enrique Cirules himself, in Castro's (literally) captive media (March 16, 2010). "Instead, I'm offering figures, data and clear evidence of his plagiarism. In his book *Havana Nocturne* (2008) T.J. English did not quote my work; instead, 72 times he mentioned the name of Cirules in an attempt to justify plagiarizing more than 260 pages from the novels *El imperio de La Habana* and *La vida secreta de Meyer Lansky*."[18] Major portions of English's "true" and "thoroughly and impressively researched" book, as hailed by the MSM, were apparently transcribed word-for-word from a *novel* conjured by a Castro-regime apparatchik.

So this chapter started with a novel (*The Godfather*) as the main educational source for liberals on Cuba. And it ends with the torch being passed to another book (*Havana Nocturne*) essentially transcribed from another novel 40 years later.

BLACKS IN CUBA, THEN AND NOW

Fidel Castro overthrew a Cuban government in which the president of the senate, the minister of agriculture, the chief of the army and most crucially the head of state were black. (Fulgencio Batista was a mulatto grandson of slaves born in a palm-roofed shack in the Cuban countryside.) These blacks had all served in a nation 72 per cent white, by the way. Fulgencio Batista had been Cuba's legally-elected president from 1940 to 1944. In 1952, his presidency resulted from a lamentably illegal if nearly bloodless and mostly unopposed coup.[19]

Not that you'll learn any of this from the liberals' exclusive educational source on pre-Castro Cuba: the *Godfather II* movie.

Today the prison population in Stalinist-apartheid Cuba is 90 per cent black, while only nine per cent of the ruling Stalinist party is black. Many of Cuba's most prominent dissidents are black.

In fact, while a smitten Jesse Jackson yelled "Viva Che! Viva Fidel!" alongside the latter at the University of Havana in 1984—with the Reverend Jeremiah Wright, among Jackson's entourage, clapping wildly from the sidelines—the world's longest-suffering black political prisoner, Eusebio Penalver, languished in a torture-chamber within walking distance of the celebration.

"N*gger!" taunted his Castroite jailers between tortures. "We pulled you down from the trees and cut off your tail!" Eusebio Penalver suffered longer in Castro's prisons than Nelson Mandela in apartheid South Africa's.[20]

Shortly after a smitten Congressional Black Caucus visited with Raul Castro in December 2009 and returned hailing him as "one of the most amazing human beings we've ever met,"[21] the black human-rights activist Orlando Zapata Tamayo was beaten coma-tose by his Castroite jailers and left with a life-threatening fractured skull and subdural hematoma. A year later, Zapata was dead after a lengthy hunger strike. *Samizdats* smuggled out of Cuba contain eyewitness reports that Zapata's jailers, while gleefully kicking and bludgeoning him, yelled: "Worthless n*gger! Worthless peasant!"

Shortly before a smitten Charlie Rangel engulfed Fidel Castro in a mighty bear-hug in Harlem's Abyssinian Baptist Church, as the smitten audience shook the rafters with bellows of "Viva Fidel!" black human-rights activist and doctor Oscar Elias Biscet was grabbed by Castro's KGB-trained police, thrown into a dungeon, kicked, spat upon and burned with cigarette-stubs. Biscet was given a 25-year sentence in 1999 but released from Castro's torture-chambers in March 2011. Essentially his crimes involved reciting the works of Dr. Martin Luther King, Jr. and the UN Declaration of Human Rights in a Cuban public square, while carrying the Cuban flag upside down. This "crime" was greatly compounded by

Dr. Biscet's specifically denouncing the Castro regime's policy of forced abortions.

"Here in this dark box where they make me live, I will be resisting until freedom for my people is gained," Biscet had declared in the vain hope that any of the "news"-agencies' "press" bureaus permitted by his torturer would report the plight of Cuba's political prisoners.

"My dad explained to me he is in prison for a cause, the cause is human rights, rights for Cubans. Also for the right of that child which hasn't even been born yet," declared Dr. Biscet's daughter Winnie, who lives in the U.S.

This latter crime goes a long way towards explaining why you've probably never heard of Dr. Oscar Biscet in the MSM. Yet in November 2007 President Bush awarded Dr. Biscet the Presidential Medal of Freedom. The award was presented to Dr. Biscet's son and daughter, who reside in freedom in the U.S. The ceremony was virtually blacked out by the media.

Penalver, Zapata, Biscet and thousands upon thousands of other Cubans were convicted in secret, by the regime's hack judges, in a court system copied from Stalin. They suffered their sentences 90 miles from the U.S., with press bureaus including CNN, NPR, ABC, CBS, NBC, AP and Reuters within walking distance or a short cab-ride of their cells.

Chances are you're familiar with the injustices against Nelson Mandela but have never heard the names of the Cuban political prisoners, much less the details of their suffering.

CHAPTER 11

Not Your Father's Hit-Men: Gangsters in Cuba Today

"When the Castro revolution prevailed, mobsters, who once had the run of Havana, became outcasts," writes *The Washington Post's* Tom Miller in his paean to the T.J.- English-Castro-regime co-production, *Havana Nocturne*. Both Miller and English forget to add how Castro subsequently rolled out the red carpet for much wealthier and more murderous mobsters to set up shop in Havana. The Castroites' partnership with Colombia's cocaine cowboys made Meyer Lansky's deal with Batista look like a nickel-and-dime gratuity. And the murder tally from the Mexican drug cartel Los Zetas, who partner with Cuban officials in the Yucatan, equals about one St Valentine's Day Massacre every ten hours for five years.

"We lived like kings in Cuba," revealed Medellin cartel bosses Carlos Lehder and Alejandro Bernal during their trials in the 80's and 90's. "Fidel made sure nobody bothered us."[1]

Also, there's no mention by T.J. English as to how the Castroite *nomenklatura*, in cahoots with Colombia's cocaine cowboys throughout the 70's and 80's, made multiple times the measly $13 million per year.

In 1996 a federal prosecutor in south Florida told *The Miami Herald:* "The case we have against Fidel and Raul Castro right now is much stronger than the one we had against Manuel Noriega in

1988." Four grand juries at the time had disclosed Cuba's role in drug-smuggling into the U.S. The Clinton administration, hell-bent on cozying up to Castro, refused to press ahead with the case against the Castro brothers' dope-trafficking.[2]

The chumminess between Castro and the world's richest, most murderous criminal organizations was showcased in 1981 when the Colombian Communist terrorist group M-19 kidnapped the daughter of one of Colombia's most powerful cocaine *capos*, Fabio Ochoa. Balking at paying any ransom, the enraged Ochoa called together 200 other drug bosses from the Medellin area and explained that a showdown with this commie riff-raff was long overdue.[3] So let's settle this thing once and for all, he reasoned—much as Alejandro Sosa settled things with the uppity "little monkey" Tony Montana in the movie *Scarface*. "You wanna go to war! You wanna go to war! OK, I *take* you to war!"—as Scarface yelled shortly before the movie's gory end.

The fuse was burning down to such a war in Colombia when peacemaker Fidel Castro proffered his good offices. He brought together the two gangs of murderers and the problem was resolved amicably and without bloodshed (for each other) if expensively. The communist terrorists would start getting a cut of the cocaine-smuggling action for various services rendered to the cartel.[4]

Castro, after all, had started partnering with drug-smugglers almost as soon as he landed in Cuba from Mexico in December 1956. The marijuana planters and dealers in Cuba's remote Sierra Maestra were also enemies of Batista's police and army. An alliance between them and the Castroite guerrillas made perfect sense, especially in view of Castro's protection and promotion by the U.S. media, State Department and CIA. To these ragamuffin dope-smugglers, a partnership with Fidel Castro meant political protection, respectability and cachet similar to what the partnership with Don Corleone lent the sleazier Tattaglia and Barzini.

"Me and my staff were all Fidelistas," boasted Robert Reynolds, the CIA's Caribbean Desk Chief from 1957 to 1960.[5] "Everyone in the CIA and everyone at State were pro-Castro, except [Republican] Ambassador Earl T. Smith, boasted Robert Weicha, CIA operative in Santiago de Cuba between 1957 and 1959.[6]

"Various agencies of the United States directly and indirectly aided the overthrow of the Batista government and brought into power Fidel Castro," said Ambassador Smith, who served from 1957 to 1959.[7]

Castro rebels were often provided sanctuary by the U.S. embassy in Havana and at Guantanamo Naval base, where they had also established a spy network for smuggling out arms. "Our cells in Guantanamo were very effective," writes Cuban General Demetrio Montseny in his memoirs. "We had an intelligence network inside the base. In one memorable action in early 1958, we stole one dozen 61-mm mortars, a 30 caliber machine gun, and 12 Garand m-1's."

The fruits of the Castro-brokered partnership between the cocaine cartel and M-19 burst into the news on November 6, 1985 when M-19 gunmen stormed the Colombian Supreme Court and murdered twelve, or half, of Colombia's 24 Supreme Court justices. They also burned the U.S. extradition files on cartel boss Pablo Escobar.[8]

"See?" Fidel Castro must have beamed. "I told you this would work out. A rollicking win-win!"

In 1984 Colombian drug lord Pablo Escobar and his drug-smuggling cohort Manuel Noriega, who facilitated his shipments' layovers in Panana, had a falling-out over storage and transportation fees. It was Fidel Castro again who prevailed upon both parties to kiss and make up. They mediated and resolved the matter in no time. Castro's coziness with both parties again patched up the criminal partnership. Castro's own fiefdom, after all, was beginning to surpass Panama as a transit-point for Colombian cocaine. "The ideological sympathies [anti-Americanism] between my brother and Fidel Castro really came out when Pablo would travel to Cuba and visit with Fidel Castro," said Pablo Escobar's sister

Alba during a recent radio interview in Miami.[9]

In 1982 indicted swindler and drug-smuggler Robert Vesco holed up in Havana's Marina Hemingway. Cuban intelligence defector Manuel De Buenza reported seeing him often aboard Fidel Castro's yacht, the Yarama, always accompanied by Castro himself. Vesco died in Cuba on November 2007.

On December 6, 1998, Colombian police seized seven-and-a-half tons of cocaine in the port city of Cartagena and discovered they were bound for Cuba, the pit-stop at the time for much of the cocaine bound for the U.S. The beaming Colombians proudly informed U.S. diplomats of the big bust. That it implicated Fidel Castro, the U.S.'s most implacable enemy, must have struck the Colombian police as particularly gratifying.

But the deluded Colombians did not know that the Clinton administration was deep into courting Cuba at the time. So instead of trumpeting the Colombian coke bust the U.S. State Department pressured the Colombians into hushing up the bust's Cuba connection.

Upon learning the details of this cover-up, Congressman Dan Burton, then serving as Chairman of the House Government Reform and Oversight Committee, fired off a letter to Secretary of State Madeleine Albright: "Sources close to the American embassy in Bogota have informed me that officials at the U.S. Embassy solicited silence from the Colombian National Police regarding a seven-and-a-half-ton cocaine seizure, destined for Cuba, because it could hurt our budding relationship with the Western Hemisphere's only surviving dictator. It is only logical to conclude the reason there has been no official reaction from the State Department on the seizure is that State did not want the air of coddling a ruthless dictator to be muddied by allegations of drug trafficking." Congressman Burton never received a reply.

Needless to add, any similar cover-up, especially one involving such a trashing of the "Good Neighbor Policy" and such "Yankee bullying" of a Latin neighbor, would have normally delighted the media and liberals in general. Those Colombian police officials, the poor saps, were sure that by risking their lives in this case they were being exemplary "good neighbors."

That was one Colombian bust involving seven tons of cocaine bound for Cuba, by the way. One ton of cocaine has a wholesale price of about $10 million. Recall that the (generously) estimated combined gross for all Cuban casinos in 1958 was about $13 million per year in the dollars of the time. And you're telling us, Mr. T.J. English, that organized crime "lost" Cuba to the Castro revolution?

NOT YOUR FATHER'S MOBSTERS

On Mother's Day 2012 police near Monterrey, Mexico found the bodies of 43 men and six women along a highway. The bodies were headless and so badly hacked up that for most of them identification proved impossible. Two weeks earlier, 23 bodies had been displayed just across the U.S. border. Fourteen were decapitated and nine others—all badly battered and disfigured—hanged by the necks from an overpass. Fifty thousand people have been killed in Mexico's drug wars in the past six years.[10]

No director could credibly create a *Godfather*, *Scarface* or *Goodfellas* from the Mexican cartels. No brutal-but-likeable Tony Montanas or Mikey Corleones here. Steven Soderbergh's *Traffic* best captured the blanket sleaze, treachery and horror of the (mostly for now) Mexican drug wars.

"To a great extent," Los Zetas "are the ones who have caused this spiral of violence in recent years," according to Jorge Chabat, a Mexican expert on organized crime. The Zetas are dedicated to "kidnapping, extortion, people-trafficking, collecting protection money, and murdering people," while the Sinaloa cartel "is more traditional. They kill their rivals, but there is no evidence that they are involved in other types of crimes," added Chabat.[11]

"These Zetas want to be known as the meanest, most sadistic criminal organization in at least the Americas if not the world," explains Professor George Grayson of the Foreign Policy Research Institute. In December 2009, just across the Rio Grande from McCallen, Texas in Reynosa, Mexican cops found not human bodies but portions of bodies: severed heads, torsos and limbs, all badly mutilated and lying on a tarmac in splashes of drying blood. "See. Hear. Shut up, if you want to stay alive," read a note written in blood on a crude billboard nearby.[12]

In 2010 near Tamaulipas, just across the border from Texas' Zapata County, Mexican police unearthed a mass grave containing the bodies of 58 men and 14 women. Most of the victims were not Mexicans but Central American migrants with no apparent links to the drug trade. They either refused to join the Zetas as couriers or refused to pay ransom for passage through their *plaza* (turf).[13] You'd never guess it from the media, much less the Congressional Hispanic Caucus, much less Mexican officials, but Central Americans caught sneaking into Mexico greatly envy the treatment of Mexicans caught sneaking into the U.S. The shelters that house these hapless Central Americans in southern Mexico, according to the Rev. Alejandro Solalinde who ministers in one, have been infiltrated by Zetas, who mingle with the detainees to determine which are headed to the U.S. More importantly, the Zetas want to know which of these detainees have relatives in the U.S. These migrants then became valuable for kidnapping. Practice shows that their U.S.-based relatives are most cooperative with ransom for their kidnapped and tortured family-members.[14]

More alarming to their mobster rivals, in 2010 the Zetas broke the "golden rule." While driving from their temporary office at the U.S. Immigration and Customs Enforcement office in Mexico City to a meeting in Monterrey, two U.S. ICE agents were ambushed and shot. One died and the other was badly wounded. "This always brings down too much heat," lamented a Zeta rival.

Unlike the mobsters who helped build a very few casinos in Havana, the Zetas recognize no "Untouchables." The severed heads of Mexico's Eliot Nesses often rot on pikes in the sun while their disemboweled bodies hang from bridges alongside those of the cartel's snitches, rivals, and recalcitrant ransom-payers. *"Plata o plomo"* ("silver or lead"), Los Zetas cheekily call their "offers you can't refuse" in extortion.

Felipe Calderon hadn't been sworn in as Mexican president for a week before he sent 40,000 federal troops to the Mexico-U.S. border. To give him credit, he didn't promise a rose garden; "the conflict will intensify before it is brought under control," he admitted at the time. Perhaps partly to blame for the intensification is the fact that most of Los Zetas' officer corps are deserters from elite units of the Mexican armed forces.

But this is no lateral career-move. The pay is much better on the Zetas' side, as even some Mexican doctors have noticed. The Gulf cartel now employs doctors to supervise their torture and amputation sessions. An overzealous interrogation often leads to a victim dying too soon, and thus rendered useless. But under a doctor's supervision the questioning can be expertly prolonged and the desired answers patiently extracted.

"Many of Mexico's existing drug cartels will kill their enemies and snitches, but not go out of their way to do it. The Zetas look forward to inflicting fear on their targets." So says Professor George Grayson.[15]

In 2009 retired Mexican general Enrique Tello Quinones was appointed to crack down on the rampant drug-trafficking by Los Zetas in the Cancun area of the Mexican state of Quintana Roo, which is also home to about seven thousand Cubans. These aren't exiles, however. They enjoy a form of dual nationality and can travel back and forth perfectly legally. Quinones had been on the job for all of a week when he and three associates were kidnapped, tortured and murdered. Some say he was closing in on the cartel's political protection.[16]

Among those arrested for the murder was a Cuban named Boris Del Valle, nephew of Cuba's former and long-time minister of the interior Sergio del Valle. Boris is also a relative of Fidel

Castro's common-law wife, Dalia Del Valle. "El Boris," as he was also known, had worked for decades as a Cuban G-2 (military intelligence) officer. No doubt his KGB-trained dad had helped his son's impressive career-trajectory. At the time of his arrest Boris was serving officially as the security-assessor for Cancun's mayor, Gregorio Sanchez, who himself was arrested the following year and charged with a string of crimes including money-laundering and trafficking in drugs and illegal immigrants—all in cahoots with Los Zetas.[17]

Sanchez was running for governor of Mexico's state of Quintana Roo (which includes Cancun and the Caribbean "Mexican Riviera") at the time of his arrest. Among his campaign pledges was to root out drug-related corruption. His security-assessor's arrest a year earlier had greatly "shocked" him.

Also interesting, Gregorio Sanchez is married to a Cuban woman named Niurka Saliva, daughter of one of Cuba's top intelligence (Ministry of the Interior) officials. According to police sources, Boris Del Valle worked closely with the Sanchez couple; he was the hands-on operative for the smuggling of drugs and humans into the U.S. with help from Los Zetas and a sophisticated visa-counterfeiting operation that had all the earmarks of Cuban DGI technology.[18]

In brief, according to some of Mexico's most diligent investigative reporters, Fidel Castro's minion "El Boris" had set up his own police and military fiefdom in the Cancun area working hand-in-glove with Los Zetas. He also imported hundreds of fellow Castroite functionaries to staff his smuggling operation. Most of these Cuban agents entered Mexico under the guise of "cultural exchanges," also a major initiative of the Obama State Department with Cuba.[19]

At the time of Sanchez's arrest, Mexican investigative reporter Raymundo Riva Palaci ran an article in Mexico's prestigious *El Financiero* newspaper entitled, "Cuban Intelligence's Penetration" of Cancun.

In June 2010 the Mexican news organization SIPSE ran an investigative report saying: "The Cuban Mafia seeks to use our state as a trampoline [into the U.S.] for illegals."

And here, perhaps, we see why Fidel Castro loudly joined the liberal rants against Arizona's SB 1070. "A brutal violation of human rights!" is how Governor Brewer's law was denounced by the Stalinist dictator.

Governor Brewer's law probably stung the Castro regime hard—and right where it hurts most. The drug and human contraband—including Cubans, Russians, Chinese and perhaps Al-Qaeda-affiliated Somali terrorists—from their little Mexican fiefdom and way-station, courtesy of Gregorio Sanchez, his Castroite wife, his Castroite "security-assessor" and Los Zetas, were mostly bound for the U.S., with Arizona a probable entry-point.

Connecting a few dots regarding the above-mentioned human contraband: on June 4, 2010 the *New York Daily News* reported that "Anthony Joseph Tracy, 35, was set free after pleading guilty to human-smuggling charges. . . . Tracy, a former informant to two U.S. intelligence agencies, was collared at JFK Airport last January. He copped to helping 272 Somalis illegally enter the U.S. from Kenya though *Cuba*. Tracy allegedly helped the Somalis *get travel visas to Cuba*. After traveling from Kenya to Dubai to Moscow to Cuba, they then went to South America before *entering the United States through the border in Mexico.*" (emphasis mine)

PIPELINE FOR TERRORISTS?

The Border Patrol calls them OTMs (Other Than Mexicans) and The Department of Homeland Security, SIAs (Special Interest Aliens) . These are people from "Special Interest Nations" (Iraq, Iran, Somalia, Sudan, Somalia, Pakistan) caught trying to enter the U.S. from Mexico.

In 2007 National Intelligence Director Mike McConnell confirmed to the *El Paso Times* that terrorists were definitely using the Mexican border to enter the U.S. "Coming up through the Mexican border is a path," he said. "Now are they doing it in great numbers? No. Because we're finding them and we're identifying them and we've got watch lists and we're keeping them at bay. There are numerous situations where people are alive today because we caught them [the terrorists]."

Testifying before a congressional committee in 2006, FBI Director Robert Mueller confirmed that some Hezbollah terrorists had crossed into the U.S. from Mexico. Then, for obvious security reasons, he clammed up. A year later Mueller told reporters that "we have had indications that leaders of other terrorist groups may be contemplating … having persons come across assuming identities of others, and trying to get across the border. There is intelligence that indicates there have been discussions on that."

"Mexican drug cartels, including the Zetas, have infiltrated 276 U.S. cities and represent the nation's most serious organized-crime threat;"[20] this according to the U.S. Department of Homeland Security, which somehow also declares our border "safe and secure."

In 2009 the U.S. DEA launched Operation Xcellerator, billed as a "nationwide takedown" of Mexican drug-traffickers. Taken down were more than 750 members of the Sinaloa cartel. The arrests were made from sea to shining sea, with many in Washington, D.C. itself, not far from DEA headquarters. In the process the DEA also seized 13 tons of cocaine, eight tons of marijuana, a ton of methamphetamine 149 motor vehicles, three planes, three boats and 169 weapons. On the Mexican side, the cartel's arsenal included rocket-propelled grenades, shoulder-mounted missiles and attack helicopters.

These types of weapons didn't come courtesy of Eric Holder's "Fast and Furious."

"Several reports, citing U.S. law-enforcement and intelligence sources, document that Hezbollah operatives have provided weapons and explosives training to drug-trafficking organizations that operate along the U.S. border with Mexico"—this according to testimony by Roger Noriega, former U.S. ambassador to the OAS, to the House Committee on Homeland Security's Subcommittee on Counter-terrorism and Intelligence on July 7, 2011. "But the U.S. and Mexican governments have declined to share information publicly on these cases." Continued ambassador Noriega: "Our inquiries to at least one Mexican official about a specific arrest of a suspected Hezbollah operative in Mexico in June 2010 were met with the response, 'Don't ask about that.'"

"If our government and responsible partners in Latin America fail to act," Noriega added, "I believe there will be an attack on U.S. personnel, installations or interests in the Americas as soon as Hezbollah operatives believe that they are capable of such an operation without implicating their Iranian sponsors in the crime."

The arrest of a Hezbollah member tasked with setting up a cell in Tijuana was confirmed in a memo from the Tucson Police Department in April 2010. "Many experts believe Hezbollah and drug cartels have worked together for decades." wrote U.S. Rep. Sue Myrick (R-NC) to the U.S. Department of Homeland Security. "Hezbollah operates almost like a Mafia family in Northern Mexico, often demanding protection money and 'taxes' from local inhabitants." She also noted that lately gang tattoos of many prisoners in Arizona jails are written in Farsi.

According to Sheriff "Sigi" Gonzalez of Zapata county, Texas, the practice of beheading enemies is relatively new to the Mexican gangs and ma have been inspired by Middle Eastern terrorists traveling through Central America and Mexico.

Perhaps related to this issue, in September 2011 the Italian daily *Corriere della Sera* reported that Hezbollah was setting up a base of operations in Cuba in order "to extend its ability to reach Israeli targets in Latin America." According to the Tel Aviv daily *Yedioth Ahronoth*, three members of Hezbollah had already arrived in Cuba to set up the cell, which will allegedly "include 23 operatives, hand-picked by Talal Hamia, a senior member tasked with heading the covert operation." The clandestine terror operation was reportedly called The Caribbean Case, and was mainly a base for logistics purposes, including "intelligence collection, networking *and document forgery.*"[21] (my emphasis)

For years the KGB and East German Stasi (Cuba's intelligence and police mentors) were the recognized experts in document-forgery. As mentioned, "El Boris'" operation in Cancun also specialized in document-forgery.

Meanwhile, as of 2012, deaths in this Mexican civil war surpass those on all sides in Afghanistan. More than 50,000 people have been killed since 2006 in Mexico's drug wars, mostly at the hands of Zetas. "The Zetas have obviously assumed the role of being the #1 organization responsible for the majority of the homicides, the narcotic-related homicides, the beheadings, the kidnappings, the extortions that take place in Mexico," according to Ralph Reyes, the U.S. Drug Enforcement Agency's chief for Mexico and Central America. They're "the most technologically advanced, sophisticated and dangerous cartel operating in Mexico."[22]

Indeed, from the KGB to the Medellin cartel to the FARC to Los Zetas, the Castro regime has picked its partners in crime with a penchant for extreme terror. Yet every media mention of Cuba and organized crime still refers exclusively to Meyer Lanksy, Batista and a few slot machines.

COMING TO A NEIGHBORHOOD NEAR YOU

Some perspective: Castro's guerrilla war, plus the urban insurgency against Batista in Cuba that saw the U.S. State Department issue travel warnings and evacuate Americans from the island, cost a grand total of 898 Cuban casualties on both sides, including all collateral damage.

When this writer secured the first U.S. interview with Honduran interim president Roberto Micheletti in July 2009, the U.S. State Department was issuing travel warnings on Honduras and American Airlines had cancelled all flights to Tegucigalpa. An utterly bloodless and scrupulously constitutional coup had triggered these jitters among U.S. officialdom.

But the wholesale slaughter along our Mexican border triggers nothing of the sort. In March 2011, Janet Napolitano, standing on the very Bridge of the Americas that joins El Paso, Texas with Juarez, Mexico (where over three thousand people were murdered last year, far surpassing the murder rate of Mogadishu or Baghdad), attempted to allay any and all jitters. With cameras rolling and surrounded by mikes, the chief of Homeland Security clarified that, although "there is a perception that the border is worse now than it ever has been, security along the U.S.-Mexican border is better now than it ever has been. The so-called spillover violence is not yet a serious issue."[23]

This perception generally issues from Americans who currently live and work along that border, instead of in Washington D.C. "Mexican drug gangs literally control parts of Arizona," says Sheriff Paul Babeu of Pinal County, Arizona. "This is going on here in Arizona—30 miles from the fifth-largest city in the United States. And these gangs are armed with radios, optics and night-vision goggles as good as anything we have. We are outgunned, we are outmanned and we don't have the resources here locally to fight this. President Obama's promise of 1,200 troops spread out among four border states will fall short. What is truly needed is 3,000 soldiers for Arizona alone."[24]

In March 2010 the same U.S. State Department that seems so complacent regarding our border with Mexico forced U.S. government employees at six border-area U.S. consulates to evacuate their families for safety's sake. The six consulates are in the border cities of Tijuana, Nogales, Juarez, Nuevo Laredo, Monterrey and Matamoros.

The State Department evacuation order was prompted by the murders of Lesley Enriquez, 35, a U.S. consulate employee in Juarez, and her husband Arthur Redelfs, 34, a prison guard. The couple, driving their vehicle (sporting Texas license-plates) home to El Paso, were chased through the streets of Juarez by another vehicle and finally cornered when they crashed into a sreetlight pole and murdered in a hail of automatic fire behind Juarez' City Hall. When local cops opened the bullet-riddled car they found the murdered couple's three-month-old daughter in her baby chair on the back seat, bawling but unharmed.

If the border is secure, the U.S. Department of Homeland Security forgot to tell the U.S. Bureau of Land Management. "Warning! You are Entering Active Drug and Human Smuggling Area!" declare signs recently posted along a stretch of Interstate 8 east of Phoenix, more than 100 miles north of the "secure" Mexican border. "Danger in this Area of Encountering Armed Criminals and Smuggling Vehicles Traveling at High Rates of Speed!"

A Pinal County sheriff's deputy expertly ducked some shots aimed at him in the area but others weren't as fortunate. "There's been some homicides recently with some of the smugglers," explained Kathy Pedrick from the U.S. Bureau of Land Management about the warning signs.

Gilbert Meehl of the BLM explains that "those who pull off the road [Interstate 8] from another state to take their picture with a cactus and they travel down one of these roads, there's no telling what they can run into." The signs also warn people to stay away from trash, clothing, backpacks, abandoned vehicles, or "anyone looking suspicious." And to call 911 upon any hint of trouble with any of the aforementioned objects or personages.[25]

According to Texas sheriff Sigifredo "Sigi" Gonzalez, "Those of us who live and work along the border know they're already here. Our own country needs to stop them at the border. We know they're coming, we just don't want to admit it. Instead, we continue to say the border is more secure than ever, when we all know that is absolutely not true."[26]

By "they" Sheriff Gonzalez refers primarily to Castro's partners, the Zetas. As mentioned, much of the Zetas' so-called ingenuity refers to the frequency and gusto with which these mobsters employ the traditionally low-key measure of last resort among mobsters: the hit.

Amazingly, the same U.S. Homeland Security Department that declares the border "safe and secure" admits that Mexican drug cartels, including the Zetas, have infiltrated 276 U.S. cities and represent the nation's "most serious organized-crime threat."[27]

In August 2008, police in Columbiana, Alabama, found five bodies with their throats slit, and surrounded by the paraphernalia of electric torture. An FBI investigation determined that the victims owed a debt of $400,000 to the Zetas. A month earlier, a stakeout by Atlanta cops had ended in a furious firefight with a Zeta gunman who thought he'd be picking up a $2 million kidnap ransom at the setup. Upon discovering the ruse the Mexican mobster went into Tony-Montana-at-the-end-of-*Scarface* mode. But he was the only one killed in the fusillade.[28]

In September 2008, students at Tijuana's Valentin Gomez Farias Elementary School were presented with twelve mutilated bodies lined up prominently near this elementary school's entrance. "The victims were naked, or partially dressed, and all of them had been tortured," reads the story in *The New York Times*. "Most had their tongues cut out. This was a message sent directly to children, something for them to think about as they consider their future lives in the community: Don't talk too much. 'It was a warning, and it means what it means,' said the head teacher, Miguel Angel Gonzalez Tovar."[29]

Granted, there are few areas to "sleep with the fishes" in the northern Mexican deserts. But on top of eschewing the traditional mobster chivalry, these Mexican cartels would never send a simple dead fish as notice. After their victims die—often more horribly than Luca Brasi—they make sure to spread not only the news, not only the proof, but also the gruesome details of the murder.

A recent report lays out the symbolism of the gang's violence in stark detail. "If a tongue is cut out it means the victim has talked too much. A person who has given up any information on a cartel, no matter how minuscule, has his finger cut off and put into his mouth upon his death. This is because a traitor is known as a "dedo"—a finger. . . . If you are castrated it means that either you have slept with a cartel member's woman or you have, in the case of a government official, police or the military, become too boastful about battling the cartels. Severed arms mean you stole from your consignment of illegal goods or skimmed profits. Severed legs mean that you tried to walk away from the cartel.

Decapitation, however, is something altogether different. It is a statement of raw power, a warning to all, like the public executions of old."[30]

Disappearing an enemy in the traditional manner of Latin America's "dirty wars" would defeat the purpose of this dirtiest of wars now being waged on our very southern border.

Though most of the Mexican mob's drugs are U.S.-bound, the major border cities have lately become major markets themselves. Tijuana and Juarez have an estimated 20,000 drug retailers each. In consequence, rehab centers are sprouting. And ever alert to their market base, the cartels have started terrorizing the rehab centers. Last year hit-men entered the Barrio Azul rehab center in Juarez and randomly machine-gunned a dozen patients and staff to death, making sure their deed was well-publicized. Customer retention, at least for now, is sought differently on the U.S. side. Imagine Al Capone's St. Valentine Day's massacre, not against his rum-running rivals but against an AA meeting.

"While it gets harder for us to infiltrate them," explains special agent Butch Barrett of Douglas, Arizona, "they will use relatives and friends to infiltrate us. There's going to be a situation where you have [an American in law enforcement whose] cousins are across the border. And he's going to get a call saying, 'Hey, we'd like you to join the customs service and do as you're told'—let this car through or turn a blind eye there. And that's going to be said by your cousin on the other side, and it's going to be an offer you can't refuse. And that's happened, because I know it has."[31] Helping buttress agent Barrett's case: Transparency International estimates that Mexicans paid $2.75 billion in bribes to police and other officials last year. Ninety-five per cent of violent crimes in Mexico go unsolved. Perhaps related to this, Fidel Castro's vice-nephew "El Boris" Del Valle was released from jail last year.

Our "vital energy interests," some say, explain our media-government obsession with Mideast events but in fact Mexico is our second-biggest source of oil—bigger than Saudi Arabia, ten times bigger than Kuwait, where America certainly perceived a vital interest in 1990. Nowadays the official state-sponsor-of-terrorism that came closest to nuking the U.S. and sits 90 miles from U.S. shores has partnered with a criminal cartel that virtually rules over portions of America's second-biggest source of oil up to our very borders; it terrorizes much of Mexico and has cells in 276 U.S. cities.

You'd really think this issue would garner more interest. Among the few to show interest is Rep. Michael McCaul, Texas Republican, who recently introduced legislation to designate six Mexican cartels, including the Zetas, as "foreign terrorist organizations" or FTO's on the official U.S. list. And why not? Since 1982 the U.S. State Department has listed their partner, Cuba, as a state sponsor of terrorism, alongside Iran, Syria and Sudan.

"They won't just cut off your ear. They'll cut off your head and think nothing of it. They enjoy killing—they want to terrorize communities," says professor Grayson. "They've gone down Mexico's east coast and they have virtually taken over Guatemala, which is a failed state, and they have penetrated deeply into El Salvador and Honduras."[32]

CHAPTER 12

How Barack Obama Tried to Lose Honduras to the Dictators

Cocaine isn't produced in Mexico. The heart of cocaine production lies in Colombia. Instead our southern neighbor serves as the jugular for the drug's flow into the U.S.; 90 per cent of the flow, according to the DEA. Central America, including Honduras, also provides several way-stations. The same DEA report estimates that this storage, courier and security service nets the Mexican cartels $323 billion a year, an amount equal to a third of Canada's GDP.

That $323 billion also exceeds the combined GDP's of Colombia and three of the six Central American nations. But it's an old story that middlemen make all the money.

A DEA report attributes half of the world's cocaine supply to Colombia's FARC ("Revolutionary Armed Forces of Colombia"), the largest, oldest and most murderous terrorist group in our hemisphere, whose death-toll dwarfs that of al-Qaeda and the Taliban combined and includes many murdered U.S. citizens. This same FARC is in debt to Fidel Castro for its immense fame and fortune. "Thanks to Fidel Castro," boasted the late FARC commander Tirofijo in a 2002 interview, "we are now a powerful army, not a hit-and-run band."[1]

A report from Colombia's military intelligence DAS, obtained by the Colombian newspaper *El Espectador*, revealed that the FARC maintains a major office in Havana. The report also described a recent visit by FARC officers Hermes Aguilera and Olga Marin to Cuba for some brainstorming with Castro's DGI (the Cuban CIA). The report mentions that this very Olga Marin "receives a $5,000 monthly stipend through the Cuban bank-account of a Venezuelan government office."[2]

Hardly known is that one of the most important U.S. military bases in the Western Hemisphere is in Palmerola, Honduras. But for the so-called coup of June 2009 that removed Manuel Zelaya from the presidency of Honduras, the U.S. might have lost this vital base to Zelaya's drug-running friends. The so-called coup was at once denounced by the Obama State Department.

"That Obama doesn't know what he's doing!" snapped Honduran foreign minister Enrique Ortez on July 4. "He doesn't know anything about anything!" continued Ortez. "He probably can't even find Tegucigalpa on a map."[3]

As Hondurans saw it, the action labeled as a "coup" by Obama's administration was a democratic uprising to uphold the constitution and thwart the creation of a client narco-state for the Chavez-Castro axis. In late June 2009, after Manuel "Mel" Zelaya's relentless trashing of Honduras's democratic constitution, that nation's Supreme Court voted unanimously to oust the serial outlaw from the presidency. The Honduran legislature voted 125-5 to do the same. The five contrarian legislators belonged to Honduras's Communist party, long known as dutiful water-carriers for Papa Fidel.

The Obama State Department promptly fell in line with the five card-carrying Communists. "We don't recognize Roberto Micheletti as the president of Honduras," declared State Department spokesman Ian Kelly in June 2009. "We recognize Manuel Zelaya."

The Honduran minister, Enrique Ortez, knew full well what had been at stake. On the day before his legal ouster, Zelaya had led a Chavez-funded mob to break into an army barracks and steal ballots for an illegal referendum. Ortez also knew the meticulously legal procedure his countrymen had followed and was quite understandably, if also quite undiplomatically, blowing his cool at the U.S.

The Honduran constitution mandated that the nation's president of Congress, Roberto Micheletti, replace Zelaya. One of President Micheletti's first official acts was to fire minister Ortez for his insulting comments regarding the U.S. president. Not that Honduras' *de jure* president didn't know full well how his nation's legal machinery had functioned in the nick of time to save both his nation's and the U.S.'s interests by ousting Zelaya.[4]

The Obama State Department showed its gratitude by cutting millions in aid for Honduras, cutting visa services for her citizens and by yanking President Micheletti's own U.S. visa. Today it's easier for a Cuban DGI agent to travel to Washington than for a Honduran textile-salesman to visit New Orleans for a convention. Indeed, Roberto Micheletti was denied a U.S. visa to testify at a U.S. House Committee on Foreign Affairs hearing in June 2011.

By contrast, in May 2012 Raul Castro's daughter Mariela was issued not only a U.S. visa but a security detail from the State Department's Bureau of Diplomatic Security (at an estimated cost to U.S. taxpayers of $50,000) for a U.S. visit. This apparatchik of the only regime in the Western Hemisphere to herd thousands of men and boys into forced labor camps under Soviet bayonet for the crime of fluttering their eyelashes, flapping their hands and talking with a lisp was granted a U.S. visa and security entourage in order to lecture Americans on "Gay Rights." The venue for Stalinist Cuba's first daughter to lecture Americans on freedom and civil rights was a panel on "sexual diversity" at a conference organized by the Latin American Studies Association in San Francisco, May 23-27, 2012.

From San Francisco this official for the only regime in the Western Hemisphere to fuel bonfires with Orwell's *Animal Farm*, and to jail librarians for stocking it, traveled to the New York Public Library where she lectured Americans on artistic freedom and the evils of censorship.

When Cuban-American legislators including Senator Marco Rubio, House Committee on Foreign affairs chairman Ileana

Ros-Lehtinen and Congressmen David Rivera and Mario Diaz-Balart protested this State Department feting of Raul Castro's daughter, *The Washington Post* quickly rushed to the Stalinist regime's defense. In an editorial the paper sniffed at "the absurd outcry from Cuban-American politicians, including members of Congress, bent out of shape that a visa was granted to Mariela Castro, the daughter of Cuban president Raul Castro and an advocate of gay and transgender rights. What are they so frightened of?"[5]

The least laudatory term that can be found in the pages of *The Washington Post* for Al Sharpton, for instance, is "flamboyant." There is no record in that paper's pages of any "absurdity" or "getting bent out of shape" by this fine figure of an agitator.

Actually few Cuba-watchers were surprised by the editorial. *The Washington Post* boasts a long history of affection for the Castro regime. Cliff Kincaid of Accuracy in Media was an eyewitness to this warm relationship. Here we'll turn over the floor to him:

"When Laurence Stern, the national news editor of *The Washington Post*, passed away in 1979, Reed [Irvine, founder of Accuracy in Media] asked me to attend and observe his memorial service. I was astounded when a man identified as Teofilo Acosta was introduced and told the service: 'I'm from Cuba. I am Marxist-Leninist. I am human. Larry Stern was my friend, one of my best friends. I loved him.' Acosta was publicly known as a first secretary in the Cuban Interests Section that has been set up inside the Czech Embassy in Washington. In reality, he was a Cuban intelligence agent."

Kincaid then saw executive editor Ben Bradlee warmly greet the Cuban DGI officer and repeatedly call him by his first name. The *London Daily Telegraph* of September 3, 1979 quoted Teofilo Acosta boasting of "having a number of U.S. senators and congressmen in my pocket."[6]

To say nothing of U.S. editors and reporters.

If only President Micheletti had sent Manuel Zelaya to the firing squad, along with every Honduran who looked at him cross-eyed, then perhaps the U.S. State Department and media would treat him with the same deference they extend to Stalinist Cuba's First Daughter.

CNN SPINS HONDURAS

During a week-long visit to Honduras immediately following Zelaya's ouster, this writer found himself amidst hundreds of thousands of Hondurans demonstrating in the streets. Just the type of thing to get the media cameras rolling and the mikes shoved in front of demonstrators' faces, wouldn't you think?

Hah! These demonstrations by hundreds of thousands in the Honduran capital of Tegucigalpa supported Zelaya's ouster, you see. So there was no sign of the international mainstream media. A very common placard carried by the Honduran demonstrators read, "*CNN, Why Don't You Show This!*" Others read, "*CNN—The Chavez News Network.*" Surely American Tea Partiers recognize the sentiment.

In fact, up until this demonstration CNN had been running regular reports from Honduras by their local reporter, Krupskaia Alis. The blackout on the pro-Micheletti demonstrations was explained to me by Honduran officials. Ms. Alis, you see, had been an official of the Daniel Ortega's Sandinista regime and was still married to a Sandinista official. But you will search CNN in utter vain for a clue to Ms. Alis's political affiliations.

Now when it came to Mariela Castro's U.S. visit in 2012 CNN was on full alert; Christiane Amanpour smiled her way through a lengthy interview with Raul Castro's daughter. While the diehard Communist denounced U.S. lawmakers of Cuban heritage as "Mafiosi" and Cuban dissidents as "liars, crooks and mercenaries," Amanpour flashed cutesy family pics of the Castro family in the background.

As it happened, concurrent with the Mariela-CNN lovefest a black Cuban dissident named Jorge Luis Garcia Perez was testifying about Castroite murder, torture and repression to a U.S. Senate subcommittee via teleconference. For his peaceful dissidence the regime represented by Mariela Castro had condemned Garcia Perez to the same term in Castro's dungeons as Nelson Mandela had gotten in South Africa's for planting bombs. You might think Garcia Perez's testimony was newsworthy?

Hah! Not a single U.S. network carried the Cuban dissident's testimony. And right after his testimony he was arrested by Mariela Castro's dad's KGB-trained police, beaten comatose and again tossed in a jail cell.[7] When Ann Coulter was asked on ABC's "The View" if she had ever seen two women having sex, she replied: "Not since Katie Couric interviewed Hillary Clinton." Christiane Amanpour's interview of Mariela Castro came close to such a spectacle—while a black victim of Mariela's lily-white family regime was being beaten and jailed for the crime of speaking truth to power.

"We were convinced that Zelaya was scheming to turn your military base in Palmerola over to Chavez," Honduran interim President Roberto Micheletti told this writer in June 2009. "We started getting suspicious when suddenly in mid-2008, and seemingly out of the blue, Zelaya declared that Honduras desperately needed another international airport.

"'What?' we legislators asked ourselves, while looking at each other wide-eyed. Honduras' airports are perfectly adequate for our needs, and everyone knew that.

"'That U.S. base in Palmerola would make a great location for that airport,' Zelaya continued. 'And Venezuela has promised to finance the project.'

"'Whoops!' we all said. Then we started inquiring more closely, and got to the bottom of this scheme. Zelaya, we finally concluded, planned to boot out the U.S. military and convert this base, essentially, into a way-station for Chavez-FARC drug shipments to the U.S."

During the last 18 months of Zelaya's term, 14 Venezuelan-registered planes crashed in Honduras. All carried cocaine or traces of the substance. During Micheletti's interim presidency not one such plane was discovered. Note: those were only planes that crashed. Imagine the overall traffic Zelaya was facilitating through Honduras for his sugar-daddy Hugo Chavez and his drug-running partners, the FARC.

Given a free hand to investigate by Micheletti, Honduran authorities quickly discovered nine clandestine airstrips in remote portions of the nation. "I've always been a friend and great admirer of the United States," Micheletti stressed to this writer. "No legally elected president of Honduras will give the U.S. base in Honduras to Hugo Chavez, who is so closely allied with the soon-to-be nuclear-armed Iranian regime."

As mandated by the Honduran constitution, Roberto Micheletti resigned his interim presidency in January 2010—ceding his office to a political rival who had won it in a regularly-scheduled election.

CHAPTER 13

Keep Your Pants On, Stephen Colbert. Che Wasn't That Hot

*"Learn some history! The movie is **Che**. Go! Learn!"* (Stephen Colbert while hosting *Che* leading man and producer Benicio Del Toro, July 1, 2009)

"A great piece of work. This movie is based on history. It went to the source. If you own the poster and t-shirt you owe it to yourself to go learn about the man." (MSNBC's Willie Geist while hosting Benicio Del Toro, January 6, 2009)

"I still have my Che Guevara poster. Che Guevara was a freedom fighter." (Bob Beckel, Fox News, September 5, 2011)

While accepting the "best actor" award at the Cannes Film Festival for his role as Che Guevara in Steven Soderbergh's movie *Che*, Benicio Del Toro gushed: "I'd like to dedicate this to the man himself, Che Guevara!" As the crowd erupted in a thunderous ovation, he continued: "I wouldn't be here without Che Guevara, and through all the awards the movie gets you'll have to pay your respects to the man!" In a flurry of subsequent interviews in Europe, Del Toro equated Che Guevara with Jesus

Christ and again told a Spanish interviewer, "Ideologically I feel very close to Che." [1]

"Dammit, this guy is cool" is the title of an interview with Del Toro in The Guardian. As a teen, he said, "I hear of this guy, and he's got a cool name. Che Guevara!" Years later, doing film-work in Mexico, "I went to a library and I was looking at books, and I came across a picture . . . . I thought, 'Dammit, this guy is cool-looking!'" [2]

Right here Benicio Del Toro, who fulfilled an obvious fantasy by starring as Che Guevara in the four-and-a-half-hour movie he also co-produced, probably revealed the inspiration (and daunting intellectual exertion) of most Che fans worldwide, including Beckel and Colbert. It wasn't enough that Stephen Soderbergh and Benicio Del Toro produced what even The New York Times recognized as an "epic hagiography" of the Stalinist who co-founded a regime that jailed political prisoners at a higher rate than Stalin during the Great Terror; murdered more Cubans than Hitler murdered Germans during the Night of Long Knives; craved to incite a worldwide nuclear war; and in the process converted a nation with a higher per-capita income than half of Europe into a pesthole that repels Haitians.

No, this wasn't enough for them. In addition, upon the hagiography's screening by the American Film Institute at Grauman's Chinese Theater in 2008, the families of the thousands of Che Guevara's murder victims were gratuitously and cheekily insulted. "Che Guevara is a hugely controversial figure," laughed Lou Diamond Phillips, who played the role of Bolivian Communist party leader Mario Monje. The cameras in front of Grauman's then turned to "Che" himself, Benicio Del Toro, who snickered along with Phillips, "I don't know how this film is gonna go over in Miami"—then smirked with co-star Joaquim de Almeida while cackles from the cast erupted in the background.

And all this in Hollywood, the world capital of sensitivity-training, where an offhand quip about a black or a gay, about slavery or lynching can end a career; where "bullying" can take the form of prolonged eye-contact or a sneer; but where, apparently, public laughter and open ridicule of at the grief of thousands of Cuban-Americans, whose loved ones were murdered, passes for humor.

Miami, as you might guess, is home to most of the wives, mothers, daughters, sons and brothers of the thousands of defense-less men—and boys and even some women—murdered by the regime Che Guevara co-founded.

Most of the Cubans Che murdered, he murdered because he claimed they were affiliated with the U.S. ("Batista, America's Boy," "CIA mercenaries," etc.) In fact probably 90 per cent of the men, boys and women his regime murdered had no affiliation whatsoever with Batista. The vast majority had actually fought *against* the Batista regime—but as non-communists.

So actually the thousands of murdered and tortured Cubans were more a form of collateral damage as Che Guevara craved to get his cowardly hands on his true hate-obsession: Americans, the very people crowding Grauman's, snickering and cackling.

"The U.S. is the great enemy of mankind!" raved the terrorist whom Soderbergh and Del Toro glorified and who got a standing ovation in Hollywood with both Robert Redford's *The Motorcycle Diaries* and Soderbergh's *Che.* "Against those hyenas [Americans] there is no option but extermination! The [American] imperialist enemy must feel like a hunted animal wherever he moves. Thus we'll destroy him! We must keep our hatred [against the U.S.] alive and fan it to paroxysm! If the [Soviet] nuclear missiles had remained [in Cuba] we would have fired them against the heart of the U.S., including New York City."

As usual, most of the people Che Guevara craved to incinerate viewed protests against the Che movie as a quaint and silly obsession by hyper-sensitive, loudmouthed and even ungrateful Cuban-Americans. The film's reception in Castro's Cuba was vastly different from the one in Miami—but similar to the one in Hollywood.

"THUMBS UP IN CUBA"

"'Che' film gets thumbs up in Cuba," ran the headline from CNN's Havana Bureau on December 8. 2009. Benicio Del Toro was in the Cuban capital at the Havana Film Festival that week, presenting the movie he co-produced. "Che the movie met Che the myth in Cuba this weekend," started the CNN report, "and the lengthy biopic of the Argentinean revolutionary won acclaim from among those who know his story best."

Indeed, but the acclaim came because "those who know his story best"—Castro and his Stalinist henchmen, the film's chief mentors and veritable co-producers—saw that their directives had been followed slavishly; that Che's actual story was completely absent from the movie. This, of course, seemed lost on CNN, the first network to be bestowed a Havana bureau by the film's co-producers.

Del Toro and Soderbergh's movie provides no hint of any of the above, while proving that the Castro regime has lost none of its touch at co-opting the foreign media and Hollywood. "This is Cuban history," gushed Del Toro at his Havana press conference. "There's an audience in here that that could be the biggest critics and the most knowledgeable critics of the historical accuracy of the film."

Yes, but if any these dared criticize the historical accuracy of the film they'd likely find themselves in a Cuban jail-cell or torture-chamber. The difference is often academic.

As seems mandatory when any scholar, author or documentarian researches Cuban history, only the propaganda ministry of a Stalinist regime qualifies as a reliable source.

Che was billed as the highlight of the 2009 Havana Film Festival. The Stalinist regime rolled out the red carpet for their honored guest and A+ pupil, Benicio Del Toro. "It's a privilege to be here!" gushed Del Toro to his Castroite hosts. "I'm grateful that the Cuban people can see this movie!"[3]

And why shouldn't Castro's subjects be allowed to view this movie? Weren't Stalin's subjects allowed to watch *The Battleship Potemkin*? Weren't Hitler's subjects allowed to watch Leni Riefenstahl's *Triumph of the Will*? Both were produced at the direction of the propaganda ministries of totalitarian regimes—as was Soderbergh's and Del Toro's *Che*.

The screenplay was based on Che Guevara's diaries as published by Cuba's propaganda ministry with the foreword written by Fidel Castro himself. The film includes several Communist Cuban actors; the other Latin American actors spent months in Havana being prepped by for their roles by official Cubans.

A proclamation from Castro's own press dated December 7, 2008 actually boasts of their role. "Actor Benicio Del Toro presented the film [at Havana's Karl Marx Theater] as he thanked the Cuban Film Institute for its assistance during the shooting of the film, *which was the result of a seven-year research work in Cuba*." (emphasis added) The Cuban Film Institute (ICAIC) is an arm of Cuba's KGB-founded propaganda ministry, as revealed by Cuban defector Jesus Perez Mendez.[4]

An obsession among all involved with making the 271-minute *Che* hagiography was said to be "historical accuracy." Steven Soderbergh made certain his new movie, *Che*, about the life of revolutionary Ernesto 'Che' Guevara, couldn't be attacked — at least on a factual level. "I didn't mind someone saying, 'Well, your take on him, I don't really like', or 'You've left these things out and included these things'. That's fine," Soderbergh said. "What I didn't want was for somebody to be able to look at a scene and say, 'That never happened.'"[5]

Well, Mr Soderbergh and CNN, pull up a chair.

HISTORICAL ACCURACY

Let's forget the film's omissions, namely, the only successes in Che's life: the mass murders of defenseless men and boys. Let's instead focus on this shoot-'em-up war movie's battle scenes, with their attendant dialogues, and compare them to the historical record as published outside Cuba.

For starters, the only guerrilla war on Cuban soil during the 20th century was fought not *by* Fidel and Che, but *against* Fidel and Che.

After the glorious victory, some of the Castroite guerrillas explained the harrowing battlefield exploits so expertly dramatized by Soderbergh to Paul Bethel, who served as U.S. press attaché in Cuba's U.S. Embassy in 1959. Paul Bethel: "Che Guevara's column shuffled right into the U.S. agricultural experimental station in Camaguey where I worked. Guevara asked manager Joe McGuire to have a man take a package to Batista's military commander in the city. The package contained $100,000 with a note. Guevara's men moved through the province almost within sight of uninterested Batista troops."[6]

According to Bethel, the U.S. embassy had been highly skeptical about all the battlefield bloodshed and heroics reported in *The New York Times* and investigated. They ran down every reliable lead and eyewitness account of what *The New York Times* called a "bloody civil war with thousands dead in single battles."

They found that in the Cuban countryside, in those two years of ferocious battles, the total casualties for both sides actually ran to 182. The famous "Battle of Santa Clara," which Soderbergh depicts as a Caribbean Stalingrad, claimed about nine casualties total—for *both* sides.

He's lauded as the century's most celebrated guerrilla fighter but he barely fought in anything properly describable as a guerrilla war. "The guerrilla war in Cuba was notable for the marked lack of military skills or offensive spirit in the soldiers of either side." That's not a Cuban exile with an axe to grind. It's military historian Arthur Campbell in his authoritative *Guerrillas: A History and Analysis.* "The Fidelistas were completely lacking in the basic military arts or in any experience of fighting."

"In all essentials Castro's battle for Cuba was a public relations campaign, fought in New York and Washington." That's no right-wing Miami Cuban; it's British historian Paul Johnson, who initially sympathized with the Castro-Che regime.

Yet Soderbergh and Del Toro, obsessively wary of lapsing into the slightest historical inaccuracy, relied on the Castro regime as their principal source—and made a shoot-'em-up war movie!

In one scene, amidst the thunder of bombs and hail of bullets, Che laments how the U.S. is intervening on Batista's side. In fact: at the very time of Che's lament as depicted in this obsessively accurate movie, the Batista regime was under a U.S. arms embargo.

On a visit to Cuba in 2001 for a "scholarly summit" with Fidel and Raul Castro, Robert Reynolds—who served as the CIA's Caribbean desk's specialist on the Cuban revolution from 1957 to 1960—clarified the U.S. diplomatic stance of the time: "My staff and I were all Fidelistas," he boasted to his beaming hosts.

Reynolds's colleague Robert Weicha concurred. In the late 1950's, Weicha had served as CIA chief in Santiago, Cuba—the city nearest the Iwo Jima-like exploits depicted in this movie. "Everyone in the CIA and everyone at State was pro-Castro, except Ambassador Earl T. Smith," he said.

Weicha's was a hands-on type of Fidelismo. In the fall of 1957, he and a partner, U.S. consul Park Wollam, smuggled into Cuba and delivered to soldiers in Castro's July 26 Movement the state-of-the-art transmitters that became Castro and Che's "Radio Rebelde" or "Rebel Radio." From these mics—shown in the movie, right before the scene of Che's "U.S. intervention for Batista" lament—the Castroites broadcast their guerrilla victories island-wide, along with their plans to liberate, uplift and democratize Cuba.[7]

That Che's famous Radio Rebelde was CIA-issue probably went unmentioned by Soderbergh's Cuban co-producers. Somehow this would not mesh well with the film's message.

Soderbergh's movie also shows Che Guevara steely-eyed and snarling with defiance during his capture. Only seconds before, Che's very M-2 carbine had been blasted from his hands and rendered useless by a fascist machine-gun burst! Then the bravely grimacing Guevara jerked out his pistol and blasted his very last bullets at the approaching hordes of CIA-lackey soldiers.

In the theater, viewers gape at the spectacle. Eyes mist and lips tremble at Soderbergh and Del Toro's impeccable depiction of such undaunted pluck and valor. OK, but just where did Soderbergh and Del Toro—utterly obsessed with historical accuracy—obtain this version of Che's capture?

Soderbergh's scriptwriters transcribed this account of Che's capture exactly as penned by Fidel Castro. Ah, but when it came to the script for his film *Erin Brockovich*, Soderbergh balked at anything and everything issuing from Pacific Gas & Electric Company as completely biased and unreliable. No such scruples applied against the propaganda ministry of a Stalinist dictatorship. Why, the man who mentored Soderbergh's film for impeccable historical honesty is also on record for the following testaments:

"Let me be very clear—very clear—I am not a communist! And communists have absolutely no influence in my nation!" (Fidel Castro, April 1959)

"Political power does not interest me in the least! And I will *never* assume such power!" (Fidel Castro, April 1959)[8]

But as evidenced by Steven Soderbergh's films, the author of these proclamations deserves to have *his* version of Che's capture transcribed on the silver screen as gospel. Fidel Castro, you see, wrote the forward to *Che's Diaries* wherein this Davy Crockett-at-the-Alamo version of events appears.

All accounts of Che's capture, by the Bolivian soldiers who actually captured him, reveal major discrepancies between Soderbergh and Del Toro's Fidel Castro-mentored film and historical truth. In fact, on his second-to-last day alive, Che Guevara ordered his guerrilla charges to give no quarter, to fight to the last breath and to the last bullet. With his men doing exactly that, Che, with a trifling flesh-wound to the leg—depicted by Soderbergh as ghastlier than the one to Burt Reynolds's character in *Deliverance*—snuck away from the firefight, crawled towards the Bolivian soldiers doing the firing, spotted two of them at a distance, then stood up and yelled: "Don't Shoot! I'm Che! I'm worth more to you alive than dead!"[9]

His Bolivian captors record that they took from Che a *fully-loaded* PPK 9mm pistol. And the damaged carbine was an M-1—not the M-2 his diary said he was carrying. The damaged M-1 carbine probably belonged to the hapless guerrilla charge, "Willy," whom Che dragged along to his doom. But it was only after his obviously voluntary capture that Che went into full Eddie-Haskell-greeting-June-Cleaver mode. "What's your name, young man?!" Che quickly asked one of his captors. "Why, what a lovely name for a Bolivian soldier!"

"So what will they do with me?" Che, desperate to ingratiate himself, asked Bolivian captain Gary Prado. "I don't suppose you will kill me. I'm surely more valuable alive. . . . And you, Captain Prado!" Che commended his captor. "You are a very special person! . . . I have been talking to some of your men. They think *very highly* of you, captain! ... Now, could you please find out what they plan to do with me?"[10]

From then on, Che Guevara's Eddie Haskell-isms only get more uproarious. But somehow none of these found their way into Soderbergh's film.

Soderbergh and Benicio Del Toro actually had an intriguing and immensely amusing theme, if only they'd known how to plumb it. Soderbergh hails Guevara as "one of the most fascinating lives in the last century." Almost all who actually interacted with Ernesto

Guevara—and are now free to express their views without fear of firing squads or torture-chambers—know that The Big Question regarding Ernesto, the most genuinely fascinating aspect of his life, is this:

How did such a dreadful bore, incurable doofus, sadist and epic idiot attain such iconic status?

The answer is that this psychotic and thoroughly unimposing vagrant named Ernesto Guevara had the magnificent fortune of linking up with modern history's foremost PR man, Fidel Castro. For going on half a century now, Fidel has had the mainstream media anxiously scurrying to his every beck and call, eating out of his hand like trained pigeons. Had Ernesto Guevara De La Serna y Lynch not linked up with Raul and Fidel Castro in Mexico City that fateful summer of 1955, everything points to Ernesto continuing his life of a traveling hobo, panhandling, mooching off women, staying in flophouses and scribbling unreadable poetry.

SNUBBING THOSE WHO KNOW

Many who interacted with Che Guevara at close range now live outside Stalinist Cuba, primarily in south Florida, and could have provided accounts of Che's story without fear of torture-chambers if they deviated from the Castroite party line.

But Cuban-American Felix Rodriguez, the CIA operative who played a key role in capturing Che, was pointedly snubbed by the film's producers. "They called and asked for an interview, and though I agreed, they never followed through," he told this writer.

Dariel Alarcon, who was on the other side, also was snubbed by Soderbergh. As an illiterate 17-year-old-Cuban hillbilly, he joined Che's guerrilla band in 1957, then remained among Che's closest adjutants until the very end. Alarcon was part of Che's guerrilla group in Bolivia who shot it out with the Bolivian Rangers advised by Felix Rodriguez.

Unlike Che Guevara, however, Alarcon never surrendered to the Bolivian Rangers. In the same firefight where Che snuck away and surrendered with a full clip in his pistol, Alarcon fought to his last bullet and then escaped. He and four others then fought and snuck their way through the Andes to Chile, where then-senator Salvador Allende helped them make their way back to Cuba.

Now here's a feat of genuine guerrilla ingenuity, and one genuinely admirable regardless of the cause Alarcon then served.

Safely back in Cuba, Alarcon was tasked by Fidel Castro with assassinating Felix Rodriguez. It fit a pattern. Bolivian officers involved in Che's capture were being picked off. A peasant who had helped the Bolivian army set up an ambush was murdered. Bolivia's president at the time of Che's capture, Rene Barrientos, died 18 months later in a mysterious helicopter crash.

The week after Guevara's capture, on October 8, 1967, Fidel Castro had indeed put a price on Felix Rodriguez's head, as he had on all the of the Bolivian army officers Felix assisted.

Eight years later, in May 1975, General Joaquin Zenteno, a Bolivian officer who had worked with Rodriguez and was now Bolivia's ambassador to France, was murdered on a Paris street. When Felix Rodriguez picked up the phone a few days afterward, he heard the words, "You're next," then a click.[11]

"When you get to Miami," Cuban political prisoner Roberto Martin-Perez heard from one of his jailers the day of his release in 1987, "tell your friend Felix Rodriguez his days are numbered. It's one of *el comandante* Castro's top priorities." Roberto Martin-Perez had been childhood friends with Felix Rodriguez and spent 28 years in Castro's dungeons and torture-chambers. He was arrested in August 1959 at age 22.[12]

But Rodriguez always managed to elude Alarcon. Now here again was a fascinating subplot, if not an entire movie, for Soderbergh. Alas, this genuine *guerrilla*—the title of part two of Soderbergh's hagiography is entitled "Guerrilla"—defected from

Castro's regime in 1997 and today lives in Paris. Many movie producers would say, "Ah, perfect!"

"Lets' see—both Felix Rodriguez and Dariel Alarcon are intimately tied to the Che Guevara story; both were alternately cat-and-mouse with each other as part of this narrative; both have fascinating first-person accounts of war and international intrigue; and both live in free countries. So both could be easily located and both could speak at length without fear of censorship about Che Guevara's military exploits, which constitute the entirety of our film."

Hah! That was exactly the rub. That's the very last thing Steven Soderbergh and Benicio Del Toro's co-producers—the Castro regime—would allow. So it never came to pass, though both Rodriguez and Alarcon had been initially contacted and made to believe their stories would be part of the film. More interesting still, guerrilla hunter and hit-target Rodriguez and guerrilla and hit-man Alarcon have since become friends and socialize often.

But don't look for their fascinating story anywhere. It doesn't fit the Hollywood narrative, nor that of PBS, NPR, ABC, CBS, NBC, the History Channel, A&E, and so on. All of these have been granted Havana bureaus and/or frequent Cuban visas. All would probably need the Castro regime's approval first. So forget it.

Little known—because it makes Che Guevara look like the monumental bungler he was—is how Dariel Alarcon and four others from his guerrilla band fought their way out of the Bolivian army ambush; then found their way across some of the world's wildest terrain all the way over to Chile, and finally escaped back to Cuba. As mentioned, here's material for a genuinely exciting and intriguing Hollywood movie all by itself.

Only one hitch: Everyone with half a brain would quickly conclude how this (by any measure) genuinely proficient guerrilla action was finally made possible: namely, that these five were finally rid of the blundering leadership of an incurable jackass named Che Guevara, who seemed unable to apply a compass-reading to a map.

Under Che's leadership the guerrilla band had been split; they walked in circles and actually engaged in firefights against each other, each thinking the other was the Bolivian enemy!

Free from such brilliant command after Che's whimpering surrender, they pulled off a genuinely skillful fighting retreat across two countries and some of the world's tallest mountains.

According to Soviet-bloc intelligence defector Ion Pacepa, the Che Guevara myth was a KGB creation; the words were "Operation Che" and the photo was that ultra-famous portrait of *"Guerrillero Heroico,"* the Heroic Guerrilla, taken by Alexander Korda, a Cuban intelligence officer. To that recipe, add Fidel Castro's vast media savvy and contacts, and you cook up some history.[13]

Would the Castro regime dare pop this bubble? The question answers itself.

Alas, having Fidel Castro as your PR man has its drawbacks since, as former colleagues all attest, "Fidel only praises the dead." So prior to whipping up the legend of Che Guevara, Fidel sent him to "sleep with the fishes." Too bad Soderbergh and Del Toro didn't interview the former CIA officers who revealed to this author how Castro himself, via the Bolivian Communist party's Mario Monje, constantly fed info to the CIA on Che's whereabouts in Bolivia. They might also have added drama by including Fidel's directive to Monje regarding Che and his merry band. "Not even an aspirin," instructed Cuba's Maximum Leader to his Bolivian comrade— meaning that Bolivia's Communists were not to assist Che in any way—"not even an aspirin" if Che complained of a headache.

Recall that Lou Diamond Phillips played the Monje role in Soderbergh's movie. Imagine how this intrigue and treachery would have spiced up the plot. Woody Allen or Quentin Tarantino might have rolled up their sleeves and made this material interesting—if not the character himself, then perhaps whatever malfunction in his brain-synapses might animate his fans. But utterly starstruck by their subject and slavishly compliant to Fidel Castro's script and casting-calls, Del Toro and Soderbergh let all the fascinating plots and subplots fly right over their heads—to the immense gratification of their Cuban co-producers.

"And I'll tell you another thing that shows me a little bit more about Castro," said frequent Cuba visitor and Castro fan Jesse Ventura during a March 2010 interview with Christopher Stipp. "The main downtown building in Havana has this huge flat wall and it has got a huge portrait on it. It's not Castro. It's Che Guevara. The biggest photograph in downtown Havana was a mural of Che. Now if Castro was such an egomaniac and all this, wouldn't he put himself up there instead of Che?"

For a man with Ventura's (mostly self-vaunted) street-smarts, Fidel Castro's blandishments of (the dead) Che Guevara should be a cinch to plumb. Didn't Don Barzini send the biggest and fanciest flowers to Don Corleone's funeral?

Now, on to Cuba's genuine guerrilla war, the one fought from 1960 to 1966 and—it cannot be repeated often enough—*against* the Fidel-Che regime. Farm collectivization was no more voluntary in Cuba than in the Ukraine. And Cuba's kulaks had guns, a few at first anyway. At the time, Cuba's enraged *campesinos* had risen in arms by the thousands as Castro and Che started stealing their land to build Soviet *kolkhozes,* and murdering all who resisted. Alarmed by the savage insurgency, Castro and Che sent a special emissary named Flavio Bravo whimpering to their sugar-daddy Khrushchev. "We are on a crusade against kulaks like you were in 1930," whimpered this old-guard Cuban Communist party member.

In short order, Soviet military advisors, still flush from their success against their own *campesinos* in the Ukrainian Holocaust, were rushed to Cuba.[14]

This anti-Stalinist rebellion, 90 miles from U.S. shores, involved ten times the number of rebels, ten times the casualties and more than twice the amount of time as the puerile skirmish against Batista; but it found no intrepid U.S. reporters anywhere near Cuba's hills. What came to be known as The Bay of Pigs invasion was originally planned as a link-up with the Cuban resistance of the time, which was more numerous per capita than the French resistance before D-Day, though you'd never know it from any media outlet.

Had these rebels gotten a fraction of the aid the Afghan Mujahedeen got, the Viet Cong got—indeed, that George Washington's rebels got from the French—had these Cuban rebels gotten any help, those Latin American Bandits named Fidel Castro and Che Guevara would merit less textbook and Wiki space today than Pancho Villa. And Miami's jukeboxes today would carry more Faith Hill than Gloria Estefan.

TAKE ANOTHER LITTLE PIECE OF MY WALL, BABY

In 1955 Fidel Castro and his wealthy Cuban backers of the time hired a Cuban Korean war veteran named Miguel Sanchez to train his guerrilla band in Mexico for their invasion of Cuba to topple Batista. None of the trainees had the slightest combat experience so their extra-curricular curiosity on the matter did not surprise or annoy Sanchez.

But one of the trainees struck Sanchez as curioser and curioser than the others about the act of killing. "How many men have you killed?" he constantly asked Sanchez. "What does it feel like to kill a man?"

"Look, Ernesto," Sanchez would tell the younger man, who did not yet have the moniker, 'Che.' "It was a war. I was in combat. It wasn't a personal thing. Most soldiers don't make it a personal thing. You aim at an enemy uniform and pull the trigger. That's it."

"But did you ever come upon a wounded enemy and kill him with the *coup de grace*?" A wide-eyed Ernesto Guevara would continue. "What did it feel like? I want to know what it feels like."

"It became obvious to me that the man who would shortly become known as 'Che' wanted to kill for the sake of the act itself," says Sanchez, "instead of—as in the case of most others, and this includes Fidel and Raul Castro—as a means to an end. That end for Castro, of course, was absolute power. . . . His power lust fueled his killing, and it didn't seem to affect him one way or the other. With Ernesto Guevara it struck me as a different motivation, a different lust."[15]

"On Sundays in Mexico I would often dine with Guevara and his Peruvian wife, a great cook," recalls Sanchez. "Ernesto was a voracious reader and loved poetry. I'll never forget his favorite poem, 'Despair' by Jose de Espronceda: 'I love a sullen-eyed gravedigger crushing skulls with his shovel! I would love to light the flames of a holocaust which spreads devouring flames that pile up dead and roast an old man until he crackles, What pleasure! What Pleasure!'

"Ernesto Guevara would close his eyes dreamily and recite it from memory during all of my visits, even at the dinner table," recalled Sanchez.[16]

Che Guevara's favorite poem continues: "I love to see bombs falling from the sky and lying still and silent then bursting, vomiting fire and leaving dead everywhere!"

"Crazy with fury I will stain my rifle red while slaughtering any enemy that falls in my hands!" writes Ernesto "Che" Guevara in his own diaries that later become known as "Motorcycle." "My nostrils dilate while savoring the acrid odor of gunpowder and blood." Robert Redford somehow overlooked this part of Che's *Motorcycle Diaries.*

"He went into convulsions for a while and was finally still," gloats Che Guevara in his diaries later known as *Reminiscences of the Cuban Revolutionary War.* He was lovingly describing the death-agonies of a bound Cuban peasant he had just shot in the temple with his pistol. "Now his belongings were mine." (Here, unwittingly, Che Guevara gives us communism in a nutshell: cowardly murder and theft.)

A study by the late Armando M. Lago of the Cuba Archive, which is documenting all deaths from the Cuban revolution, found that during the entire year of 1957 Che Guevara's guerrilla band suffered a total of 35 combat casualties. But 47 so-called deserters and informers were executed (murdered) during that year in the manner lovingly described by Che in his diaries.

On April 18, 1961 freedom-fighter Manel Menendez para-chuted into the inferno of Soviet firepower known as the Bay of Pigs and ripped into the Communists to his very last bullet, like his entire band of freedom-fighting brothers who inflicted casualties of 20-to-1 against their Soviet-led and -armed enemies.

Castro rules today primarily for one reason: The knights of Camelot cut off the bullet-supply to Manel and his freedom-fighting band of brothers. During dinner with this author many years later, Manel described Che's visit. "We'd all run out of ammo and been captured and herded into an enclosure," he recalls. "And so here comes Che, strutting and sneering as usual. He strutted up and looked around with that famous sneer of his. Then he started snickering. Many of us were wounded, but one of our guys faced him down and said, 'Well I guess you'll send us all to the *paredon* [firing wall] now, right, Che?'

"No," Che snapped. "No *paredon*. We're gonna hang all of you, slowly! The firing squad's too good for you."

"I was standing close to Che at the time," recalls Menendez, "and got a closeup of his face when he was talking. It was plain from the way his eyes lit up that the man was sick, mentally ill, a bona-fide sadist. Sure, most military commanders or wartime leaders—Patton, Chesty Puller, Winston Churchill, whatever—bad-mouth and taunt enemy soldiers. But that's during combat, to get the troops fired up for the kill, etc. Here, the combat was over. We were uniformed adversaries, but completely disarmed."

A Basque priest named Javier Arzuaga landed the traumatic duty of comforting many of Che's murder victims. The Spanish priest happened to preside over the Havana parish that included the city's La Cabana Fortress which Che, with his firing squads, converted into Cuba's murder-central in January 1959. During his painful rounds father Arzuaga was shocked to find a 16-year-old boy named Ariel Lima among the condemned war-criminals. The priest described the boy as totally dazed, unaware of his surroundings, with his teeth constantly chattering. The other prisoners, though mostly certain of their fate, pleaded with Father Arzuaga to talk to somebody, *anybody*—even Che himself—about the kid. How could this boy possibly have been sentenced to death by firing squad by one of Che Guevara's revolutionary tribunals?

Father Arzuaga managed to get an audience with Che where he pleaded the boy's case. "So what's the big deal?" Che snapped at the priest. "What's was so special about the boy?"

"He's only 16 for heaven's sake," responded the priest. "Besides, any mistake or injustice on the revolution's part, it's also politically unwise," he tried to explain to the smirking Guevara. "What will the world think when they learn that the revolution is shooting 16-year-old boys as war criminals?"

"Quickly I realized my pleas were pointless," recalls the priest. "The harder I pleaded for his compassion, the wider and crueler became Che's famous sneer."

"Fine. We'll take it up at the Tribunal of Appeals," Che said while dismissing the priest.

Came the appeals hearing and the death sentence was confirmed mechanically. In fact, Che added that the boy would be shot *that very night*. As they left the hearing, "Che was walking with his usual entourage when he noticed me," recalls Father Arzuaga. "He smiled cynically and waved hello. I kept watching him as he walked back to his office, when I saw a distraught woman run in front of Che and throw herself on the ground."

"That's Ariel Lima's mother," one of his men told Che, who looked down at her.

"'Woman,' he sneered at her, 'go see *that* guy.' And Che turned and pointed at me," Father Arzuaga recalled. "*Padre* Javier Arzuaga is a master at consoling people," Che chuckled. "Then he looked over at me, smiling widely. 'She's all yours, *padre*.'"

"I walked over and helped the devastated women from the ground," said the priest. "'Put yourself in God's hands, *senora*,'" I told her. "'Try and rise above this tragedy. God will help you learn to live without your son.'"

"That night Ariel Lima was still in a totally dazed condition as they tied him to the execution stake," wrote Father Arzuaga, "totally unaware he was about to be murdered."

"*Fuego!*" And the volley shattered Ariel's quivering little body. Che was probably watching from his window, as was his custom. Che's second-story office in La Cabana had a section of wall torn out so he could watch his darling firing squads at work.

"From that moment on I hated Che Guevara," said the priest.[17]

The man featured in the above anecdotes (plucked from thousands of others as sickening), who relished the murder of the defenseless and who craved to ignite a worldwide nuclear war, became the international icon of flower-children and peace creeps. Who but Fidel Castro could have pulled off such a public relations con-job? As he stressed as early as 1955: "Propaganda is vital. Propaganda is the heart of our struggle."

The Red Terror had come to Cuba. "Do not search for evidence," Cheka chief Felix Dzerzhinsky's top lieutenant Martin Latsis instructed his hangmen in the Ukraine. "Simply ask him to what class he belongs, what are his origins, education, and profession. Those are the questions that should decide the fate of the accused."[18]

Che Guevara often cheekily signed his early correspondence as "Stalin II."

REQUIEM FOR A FLACK

An AP story from 2003 reported that on his visit to Cuba Steven Spielberg met with Cuban Jews, "who had dwindled from 15,000 before the revolution to 1,300 afterward."

This dwindling, by the way, took place mainly over a three-year period, from about 1959 to 1962. In light of this, some people might get the impression that the dwindling might have had something to do with the imposition of Communism.

In other words, what Czar Nicholas failed to accomplish with 20 years of pogroms, President Castro pulled off in two years of his rule. He drove a higher percentage of Jews out of Cuba than Czar Nicholas drove from Russia and even Hafez Assad drove out of Syria. None of this prevents Shoah Foundation founder Stephen Spielberg from gushing about his dinner with Fidel Castro in 2003 as "the eight most important hours of my life."[19]

In the interest of full disclosure: upon my publicizing this quote, Mr. Stephen Rivers, the Hollywood agent who had arranged Spielberg's trip to Castro's fiefdom, promptly notified me that Spielberg had uttered nothing of the sort. Therefore, he said, I should retract the statement from my writings.

Rivers, an independent and powerful publicist formerly with Creative Artists Agency, explained to me that Castro's own media had concocted the Spielberg quote from thin air. So there was absolutely no truth to it.

To the high-rolling Mr. Rivers I replied: "Well, what you're telling me actually makes my point better than any quote issuing from Spielberg."

Indeed, my writings document that Fidel Castro is a master propagandist and that his KGB/Stasi-trained secret services specialize in obtaining many such statements from many such luminaries, voluntarily or often as a result of various forms of persuasion, i.e., blackmail.

So the proper and logical course of action, if Mr. Spielberg had indeed been swindled, would have been for Mr. Spielberg or his agent to make Fidel Castro's treachery known publicly. After all, Mr. Spielberg supposedly was the aggrieved party here, and the damage (from what Mr. Rivers was telling me) had been inflicted maliciously by the secret services of a Stalinist regime.

But there is no record that Mr. Rivers, Mr. Spielberg or any of their spokespersons ever clarified this issue publicly; which didn't surprise me then, and surprised me even less after Mr. Rivers's June 2010 passing.

The late Mr. Stephen Rivers, who once worked as Tom Hayden's press secretary and Jane Fonda's agent, had also arranged Cuban trips for Oliver Stone, Michael Moore, Benicio Del Toro, Robert Redford's Sundance Institute and Stephen Soderbergh, among many others who sought the invaluable collaboration of Castro's propaganda ministry for their films. Essentially Rivers was Hollywood's "go-to" guy when planning a visit to Fidel Castro's fiefdom, a meeting with his communist functionaries, or even a coveted audience with the mass-murderer himself, as generously bequeathed to Spielberg.

Despite the notorious U.S. embargo against Cuba that we keep hearing and reading about in the media, and despite Cuba's meticulous vetting of any applicant for a visa, Stephen Rivers managed to visit Castro's island fiefdom more than two dozen times over the course of a few years. When Mr. Stephen Rivers passed away, his friends and clients poured forth the eulogies:

"Stephen Rivers was a man committed to the truth," wrote Oliver Stone, "wanting the best for the United States, and digging away at the hypocrisy of so much of our political and media leadership. . . . I will miss him deeply."[20]

But the most effusive eulogy was published in *The Huffington Post* by Margarita Alarcon.

THE HUFFINGTON POST AND DADDY'S LITTLE GIRL

"Stephen had been for the better part of the last years of his life an exemplary 'Bridge' between Cuba and the United States, but he didn't just bridge Cuba and the US culturally, he also was very aware of the need for sovereignty and independence from imperial powers," Miss Alarcon wrote. "When he gave a gift it wasn't just a gesture of friendship it was always a gesture of *solidarity with a cause*. . . . May he rest in peace and may he know that I feel safe because I know *he is on my side*." (emphases mine) [21]

In other *Huffington Post* articles Margarita Alarcon denounced Senator Marco Rubio, Rep. Ileana Ros-Lehtinen (chairwoman of the House Committee on Foreign Affairs), Rep. Mario Diaz-Balart and former U.S. president George W. Bush, all as "silly and insane."

"Margarita Alarcon is a Havana-based media analyst," innocuously informs *The Huffington Post* about one of their feature writers.

Margarita Alarcon is also a "Havana-based" columnist for Castro's regime-run press, an official of Cuba's *Casa de las Americas*, and the daughter of one of Fidel Castro's longest-serving and most faithful ministers. Margarita's father, Ricardo Alarcon, has functioned as Castro's foreign minister, ambassador to the UN, and most recently as the president of Cuba's "Parliament." In 1983 a high-ranking Cuban intelligence officer named Jesus Perez Mendez defected to the U.S. and revealed to the FBI that the Cuban DGI controls the *Casa de las Americas*.[22]

Let's say that Rupert Murdoch's newspaper, *The New York Post*, had published comments by Mahmoud Ahmadinejad's daughter, denouncing several U.S. legislators and a former U.S. president as "silly and insane"—and then innocently described this apparatchik for a sovereign terror-sponsor as a "columnist" and "Teheran-based news analyst." Might the disclosure of her employment and pedigree merit media mention?

But for this very task, *The Huffington Post* deploys the daughter of the president of a terrorist-sponsor's parliament. Nobody bats an eye—mostly, of course, because few people know the details. In 2000, during a major crackdown by the Bush administration against Cuban spying, Margarita's father was denied a U.S. visa.

So shameless and relentless has been Ricardo Alarcon's

ass-kissing over the decades that Margarita's father is often named a likely heir to Cuba's Stalinist throne.

Unsurprisingly, Senator Marco Rubio, the son of Cuban refugees, heads the list of legislators denounced in *The Huffington Post* by the loyal daughter of Fidel Castro's most slavish cabin-boy. Margarita Alarcon's columns usually appear just to the left of Fidel and Raul Castro's official pronouncements. So in running her articles, *The Huffington Post* is essentially transcribing a Stalinist regime's propaganda for the benefit of unsuspecting American readers.

From Margarita's *Huffington Post* bio we do learn that "raised in New York City, Margarita has spent most of her adult life in Cuba. She has been traveling to the United States since her return home in the early 1980s."

"Awwww, well isn't that nice," might react the typical *Huffington Post* reader. "She's a world traveler, probably with a backpack, eager to expand her cultural horizons, like so much of her generation. . . . Awwww."

In fact, her raising in New York occurred during her father's lengthy stint as Fidel Castro's ambassador to the UN. "Virtually every member of Cuba's UN mission is an intelligence agent," revealed Alcibiades Hidalgo, who defected to the U.S. in 2002 after serving as Raul Castro's chief of staff and Cuba's ambassador to the UN. In 2003, 14 of those UN-stationed Cuban spies were rooted out and booted from the U.S.

Interestingly, *The Huffington Post's* bio on Margarita Alarcon discloses that "she has not been back [to the U.S.] since 2003."

No reason to single out *The Huffington Post*, however. CBS has also run Margarita Alarcon's articles, describing her innocuously as a writer for Havana's *Casa de las Americas*. Castro's intelligence services are widely touted as among the world's best. So Margarita Alarcon is probably good at her job. But *The Huffington Post* and CBS (those noisy proponents of full disclosure by Republicans) could be more forthcoming about what that job is.

CHAPTER 14

Sickos! The Cuban Health-Care Hoax, Directed by Michael Moore

"Medical care was once for the privileged few. Today it is available to every Cuban and it is free. . . . Health and education are the revolution's great success stories." (Peter Jennings, "World News Tonight," April 3, 1989)

"Castro has brought great health-care to his country." (Barbara Walters, ABC, October 11, 2002)

"Frankly, to be a poor child in Cuba may in many instances be better than being a poor child in Miami, and I'm not going to condemn their lifestyle so gratuitously." (*Newsweek's* Eleanor Clift on "The McLaughlin Group," April 8, 2000)

"One of Cuba's greatest prides is its health care-system. And, according to the World Health Organization, the country has much to boast about." (PBS's Ray Suarez reporting from Havana, December 22, 2010)

"Cuba could serve as a model for health-care reform in the United States." (Morgan Neill, CNN, August 2009)

For more than a quarter-century, we have struggled unsuccessfully to guarantee the basic right of universal health care for our people .

. . but Cuba has superb systems of health-care and universal education."
(Jimmy Carter, University of Havana, May 14, 2002)

The voice on the phone sounded frantic, which surprised me. It was George Utset, pioneer Cuban-American blogger and a normally composed fellow. "ABC sold us out," he sputtered. "We got the videos out and everything was going perfectly. But the regime got word about them somehow. Now it looks like ABC wimped out."

Years earlier the Castro regime had bestowed on ABC a coveted Havana bureau, its only bureau in Latin America outside of Mexico City. Most importantly, ABC employs Fidel Castro's most famous and frequent interviewer, Barbara Walters.

"I asked them to give us [the 9/11 workers featured in *Sicko*] the same care they give their own Cuban citizens," assures Michael Moore in his film. "No more, no less. And that's exactly what they did." Cubans watching it felt like retching. And some resolved that this outrageous lie would not stand. Hence the secret videos, the original pledge from ABC, and the desperate call from George.

The videos that so agitated my friend George had been snuck out of Cuba via the diplomatic pouch of an East European embassy to Mexico, and had then made their way to Miami where George held them at the time of his call. "Many Cubans took great risks to make them and get them out," he reminded me. "Now it looks like it was all for nothing."

As a reminder, the Cuban constitution prohibits private ownership of media or any independent exercise of journalism. Speech, print or video issuing from the island is perfectly permissible—so long as it "conforms to the aims of a socialist society." "Enemy propaganda" and "unauthorized news" meet with severe penalties.

Michael Moore's *Sicko* not only made Castro's cut but was shown free throughout Cuba, as had been Moore's *Farenheit 9/11*. This obvious partnership with the Castro regime enraged many

Cuban dissidents and provoked the smuggled videos held by George Utset, about which he was calling me.

But amazingly, Michael Moore's parroting of Castro's claims in *Sicko* gagged even some in the mainstream U.S. media. An ABC producer had earlier been shocked by pictures smuggled out of *genuine* Cuban hospitals and posted on George Utset's website, therealcuba.com. When he saw *Sicko* he was revolted by Moore's shameless propagandizing. The revolted party (who requested that I not use his name here) is no "right-winger" or Cuban exile. He's simply someone who takes his profession seriously.

So he decided to counter *Sicko* by using ABC's Havana bureau to interview Cuban dissidents. These would then reveal the actual conditions in Cuba's hospitals on an ABC special. When this producer ran the idea by ABC's Havana bureau the folks there shuffled nervously, but reluctantly agreed. First, however, they'd naturally have to ask the Castro regime's permission for such an interview.

The permission was not granted. Can you believe that? Thwarted by their own Havana bureau, the ABC producer enlisted some allies within the network. They resolved to get their hands on any evidence regarding genuine conditions in Cuba's hospitals, and produce a blockbuster report about a topic much in the news at the time.

For this they went to George Utset, whose website and pictures had originally impressed them. George now turned to contacts inside Cuba. The evidence was to come from the very belly of the beast, in the form of smuggled videos. Michael Moore's reputation inside Cuba greatly helped the clandestine project. In September 2005 Fidel Castro had hailed Michael Moore as "that outstanding American!" while *Fahrenheit 9-11* was repeatedly featured on Cuba's state TV. Castro's subjects were as appalled by Moore as their oppressors were enamored. Then *Sicko* confirmed the worst.

The American millionaire "documentarist" struck many Cubans as a simple accomplice to their oppression—one of many. Worse, the Castroite propaganda in *Sicko* was obviously reaching millions worldwide. So, imagining that the truth could reach millions of Americans via ABC's "20/20," Cubans risked their lives by using hidden cameras to film conditions in Cuban hospitals—but only those hospitals that were genuinely Cuban, meaning that they served Cubans.

Ninety-nine percent of Cubans have no more experience with a hospital like the one featured in *Sicko* than Michael Moore has with a Soloflex. Most Cubans view a hospital like the one featured in *Sicko* the way teenage boys used to view *Playboy* magazine or husbands view a Victoria's Secret catalog: "Wow! If only . . . !"

But getting the truth out isn't easy. In 1997 Cuban doctor Dr. Dessy Mendoza was on the phone with a Miami radio-station reporting an outbreak of Dengue fever in eastern Cuba, near Guantanamo, when Castro's police stormed his house and arrested him. He was charged and sentenced for "spreading enemy propaganda." The Cubans who collaborated with Michael Moore are obviously immune to this charge.

"Self-censorship is a very common practice," wrote Spanish TV correspondent Vicente Botin about the daily habits of foreign correspondents in Cuba. "No one on the island can write the truth of what happens there." The regime is suspected by most foreign correspondents of "electronically monitoring their phones, cars and homes," and keeping close tabs on their "political ideas, their preferences, their tendencies and above all their weaknesses like drugs, sex, alcohol."[1]

Lapses in this self-censorship are quickly addressed. In March 2007 Gary Marx of *The Chicago Tribune*, Stephen Gibbs of the BBC, and Cesar Gonzalez-Calero, of the Mexican newspaper *El Universal*, were all booted from Cuba. The regime cited their "lack of objectivity." They got off easy.

In September 2011 Spanish filmmaker Sebastian Martinez was arrested by Castro's police and sentenced to seven years in prison. Martinez had produced a film on Cuban child prostitution. But he managed it without the regime guidance and help so valued by Stephen Soderbergh, Benicio Del Toro, Michael Moore, Robert Redford, Oliver Stone, etc. The Castroites learned of Martinez's documentary only when it ran on Spanish television. On his very next visit to Cuba they nabbed Martinez and threw him in the KGB-designed prison complex named Villa Marista.

Robert Redford, on the other hand, before releasing *The Motorcycle Diaries,* held a private screening in Havana for Fidel Castro and Che's widow Aleida. Redford got an appreciative go-ahead from both. On his frequent subsequent visits to Cuba, this fervent Hollywood proponent of artistic freedom has always found himself feted by the Stalinist regime that has jailed and exiled more writers and filmmakers than any in the Western Hemisphere.

Cuba's "Law of National Dignity" mandates jail sentences of three to ten years for "anyone who, in a direct or indirect form, collaborates with the enemy's media." And as you might guess, the definition proves quite broad and elastic. Joke-maker Chevy Chase didn't seem to be joking when he gushed that "Socialism works. I think Cuba proves it."[2] But this working Cuban socialism means that Cubans who chose Chevy's (or Jon Stewart's, Bill Maher's, Kathy Griffin's, Whoopi Goldberg's, etc.) line of work are either unemployed or rotting in Cuban jails. The prison sentences for criticizing or ridiculing not only the Cuban president but any member of the Council of State or National Assembly can reach three years. And unlike apartheid South Africa or Pinochet's Chile, for instance, Cuba puts its prisons strictly off-limits to inspection by any international organization like the Red Cross or Amnesty International.

Cuba's Law of National Dignity also provides jail sentences for "anyone who, in a direct or indirect form, collaborates with the enemy's media." You'll note that whenever CNN, ABC, PBS or NBC interviews a Cuban man-on-the-street, the interviewee has always "requested that we not use his last name." Outside of regime apparatchiks and pampered tourists, the "Law of National Dignity" has made Cuba a nation of first names, at least as reported by the media.

SICKO SICKENS CUBAN DISSIDENTS

The Cuban hospitals showcased by Michael Moore exclusively serve rich foreigners and high Communist party officials. Watching Moore reading from Castro's cue-cards by claiming these hospitals served average Cubans, knowing this propaganda would be spread worldwide and swallowed by many if not most, was more than many Cubans could stomach.

So, at enormous risk, two hours of shocking, often revolting, footage was obtained with tiny hidden cameras and smuggled out of Cuba by diplomatic pouch. The man who assumed most of this risk was Cuban dissident Dr. Darsi Ferrer, himself a medical doctor, who also talked on camera, narrating many of the video's revelations. Dr Ferrer worked in the real Cuban hospitals daily, witnessing the truth. More important, he wasn't cowed from revealing this truth to America and the world.

Alas, with the videos finally in their hands, ABC started getting cold feet. The "20/20" segment kept getting smaller and smaller. The impending explosion made a Havana press bureau seem that much more precious, especially to ABC whose Havana staff, as mentioned, had already whimpered their objections to the health-care exposé. They were unaware of the smuggled videos but many of their colleagues stateside apparently "felt their pain." They knew such a show would not make their Cuban hosts happy.

So more cutting and more paring ensued. On September 12, 2007 "20/20" ended up running a tiny segment on the matter, barely five minutes long and with almost none of the smuggled video footage.

Even so, viewer response was thunderous. "20/20" was deluged with congratulatory e-mails. ABC announced a follow-up show. The Cuban regime followed up also. The Cuban Communist party's central committee called a meeting to discuss the issue, then called in ABC's Havana bureau for talking-to.

Bottom line: John Stossel's follow-up shows on *Sicko* included no mention of Cuba's health-care.

Enter Fox News, and Sean Hannity in particular. After hanging up with George Utset I got on the phone with Fox News and notified them of the smuggled videos. They immediately requested a look. Two days later Hannity's producers were busy editing, translating and subtitling. On October 10, 2007 they ran huge segments of the smuggled videos. Fox viewers saw naked patients covered with flies while lying on hospital beds consisting of a bare mattress. They saw hospital buildings that would be condemned by the health board of any U.S. municipality. They saw and heard Dr. Darsi Ferrer along with other Cubans who described their inability to obtain something as basic as aspirins.

Greed was the motif of Michael Moore's *Sicko*. Among the highlights of the smuggled videos, Fox viewers saw Cubans being told by regime officials that aspirins and other medicines just might be available to them—but only if they paid in U.S. dollars, not the Cuban pesos they held out in desperation.

Dr. Julio Cesar Alfonso, a Cuban doctor who defected in 1999 after working within Cuba's health-care system for years, reminded America of something that should have been blatantly obvious: "The treatment Moore and the rescue workers receive in the film [*Sicko*] was done specifically for them, because the regime knew it would make great propaganda."[3]

Dr. Alfonso had barely finished his interview with *The Miami Herald* when some entity called "Havana Hospital" launched a website. "After being featured in the Cannes Film Festival-honored film *Sicko*, we are now open for medical *tourism* to Cuba," says the site. "We welcome you with peace and goodwill without any concern towards politics or propaganda. We are very good surgeons ready to help." Among the featured bargains: "Breast augmentation/implants for only $1,500 (through the belly button procedure)."

So Michael Moore, champion of the poor, greatly boosted the boob-job business for Castro's Cuba among Cannes Film Festival-goers.

As eagerly expected by Michael Moore's Cuban collaborators, *Sicko's* screening was the signal for their other propaganda assets to chime in. "Cuba has developed the world's first meningitis-B vaccine, which is available in Third World countries but not in Europe or the United States due to U.S. sanctions," reported Anthony Boadle from Reuters' Havana Bureau shortly after *Sicko's* release.

Of this 27-word sentence, exactly 14 words are true. This vaccine is not available in the U.S. and Europe, but hardly because of sanctions. In fact, in 1999, Bill Clinton's Treasury Department granted the pharmaceutical giant, SmithKline Beecham, a license to market the Cuban vaccine in a joint venture with Castro's medical ministry—pending FDA approval.

And why not? Castro's minister of public health himself, Carlos Dotres, had hailed the vaccine as "the only effective one in the world." Highly impressed, Bill Clinton's FDA chief, Dr. Carl Frasch, said it could annually prevent 1,000-2,000 cases of the dreaded disease in the U.S.; 110 members of Congress promptly signed a special letter to Secretary of State Madeline Albright, beseeching her to allow this breach of the diabolical embargo "if only to protect the lives of America's children!"[4]

That was 12 years ago. As this book goes to press no effective vaccine against meningitis B exists. The reason the vaccine is not available today in the U.S. and Europe is simply that—like so many other Castroite concoctions and proclamations dutifully trumpeted by news agencies who earn Havana bureaus—the vaccine is a farce and its sale a swindle. And, at least in this case, most civilized countries refuse to help perpetrate the swindle on their citizens.

Some countries found out the hard way. "Brazil has wasted

$300 million on a Cuban vaccine that is completely ineffective," wrote Dr. Isaias Raw, director of Sao Paolo's prestigious Butantan Institute, specializing in biotechnology.

A 1999 study by Brazil's Center for Epidemiological Research seconded Dr. Raw: "The studies conducted on the use of the Cuban vaccine in children under four years old—the major risk-group for meningitis B—showed no evidence that the vaccine protected them against the disease. This vaccine should not be recommended."[5]

The current medical literature as of 2012 flatly asserts that despite countless attempts, no effective vaccine against meningitis B has yet been developed.

Sadly for Michael Moore's Cuban handlers, the medical establishment remains infested with men and women who stubbornly cling to their professional ethics. Enlisting their full cooperation presents challenges much more daunting than enlisting the cooperation of news-agencies panting for a Havana bureau, or of a portly filmmaker obsessed with vilifying his country.

THE VICTIMS OF "DOCTOR DIPLOMACY"

A few years back Castro launched his "doctor diplomacy," wherein he started sending Cuban doctors to heathen lands (while their spouses and children were kept hostage in Cuba) to heal the sick and raise the dead. This was coupled with free treatment of poor foreigners from the Caribbean and Latin American nations in Cuban hospitals. The scheme has gotten no end of gushy reviews in the mainstream media.

Some reviews from the non-major media might help with perspective. Here's one from the Jamaican newspaper, *The Gleaner*, entitled "Eye Surgery Hopes Dashed; Patients Suffer Complications After Cuba": "The survey included 200 patients [Jamaicans who traveled to Cuba for eye surgery], and of that group, 49 patients—nearly a quarter—experienced post-surgery complications. According to Dr. Albert Lue, Head of Ophthalmology in Jamaica's Kingston Public Hospital, the complications causing the patients' impaired vision was corneal damage and damage to the iris due to poor surgical technique."

Brazil also got a bird's-eye view of Cuba's vaunted "doctor diplomacy." An April 2005 story from Agence France-Presse entitled "96 Cuban Doctors Expelled from Brazil" reported: "Federal Judge Marcelo Bernal ruled in favor of a demand by the Brazilian state of Tocantins' Regional Council on Medicine that Cuban doctors be prohibited from practicing in their state." Based on the results they'd achieved with Tocantins' residents, the judge referred to the Cuban doctors as "witch-doctors and shamans. We cannot accept doctors who have not proven that they are doctors."

According to a report by the Association of American Physicians and Surgeons, more than 75 per cent of "doctors" with Cuban "medical degrees" flunk the exam given by the Educational Commission for Foreign Medical Graduates for licensing in the U.S.

Most Cuba-certified doctors even flunk the commission's exam for certification as physician assistants, making them unfit even as nurses in the U.S. None of this is meant to disparage the hapless men and women who were simply cursed by fate to be born under a Stalinist tyranny, who took it upon themselves to overcome that curse and who today enjoy the blessings of liberty while employed in other fields. These are simply facts which Michael Moore's Cuban case-officers are desperate to hide.

A PBS report from Havana makes this assertion: "One of Cuba's greatest prides is its health-care system. And, according to the World Health Organization, the country has much to boast about. There are twice as many doctors per person in Cuba as in the United States. In fact, it's the highest doctor-patient ratio in the world. How can one of the poorest countries in the Western Hemisphere provide free care and achieve such impressive health outcomes?"

Maybe because PBS is basing this impression on claims by a Castro-regime apparatchik—and not a low-level one.

Marzo Fernandez, an economist who until defecting in 1996 served as secretary-general of Castro's ministry of nutrition, was somehow overlooked by PBS for its special report. He elaborates on some impressive health outcomes also overlooked by PBS and its Cuban handlers.

"The average height of Cubans has decreased by eight centimeters in the past 25 years," he reported on Miami television in October 2010. "For the first time in Cuban history, thousands of microcephalic children [abnormally small heads in proportion to their bodies] due to protein [primarily milk] deficiencies have been found in the eastern provinces."

RECEIVING IS BELIEVING

In 1996 Katherine Hirschfield, an Oklahoma University doctoral candidate, undertook a study of Cuba's vaunted health-care—but as a participant rather than as a regime-escorted scholar. Her plan was to live for a year with a Cuban family in Cuba's second-largest city of Santiago. From this embedded position she would "observe the ways Cubans behaved with respect to health and disease in their everyday lives . . . and also observe the workings of family-doctor clinics in the area."

As she explained it: "From the local community and the clinics I would finally I would draw a series of case-studies that best exemplified the social and cultural dynamics of Cuba's health care."[6]

Typical of scholarly studies that include a visit to Cuba, Hirschfield's study comes with this admission: "My project was intended to document and highlight Cuba's *achievements* in Social Medicine." (Hence her lightning-quick visa clearance.)

Shortly after settling in with her Cuban hosts, Hirschfeld found her immediate neighborhood full of Cubans suffering from

Dengue fever. She kept hearing of nearby areas in a similar condition. But upon every enquiry to the Castroite authorities (which included most of the doctors in the area) she was told that Dengue, though rampant during the unspeakable Batista era (when in fact it was virtually unknown), had been eradicated by the glorious revolution shortly upon its triumph. She was imagining things. This American woman was obviously hysterical. Cuba's Ministry of Truth had spoken.

Recall how, in *Invasion of the Body Snatchers*, Dr. Bennell and a few folks who had caught on to the pod-people epidemic tried warning the townspeople, only to be accused of lying or falling victim to an "epidemic of mass hysteria."

Soon Hirschfield herself caught Dengue fever and was ushered into a crowded, filthy clinic, swarming with mosquitoes and guarded by soldiers. The crowding testified to the obvious epidemic of Dengue fever then ravaging eastern Cuba and denied by authorities; while the soldiers told of the regime's craving to keep the epidemic secret.

Many of the infected Cubans were unable to walk; so the walking-wounded among the patients, including Hirschfield, were helping the disabled ones. No nurses were in evidence, no doctor was provided to Hirschfeld, and no medication was offered. "One day they finally did do a blood draw," writes Hirschfield. "But they sterilized my arm with rum because there was no disinfectant."

Infected herself, and in a hospital crammed to suffocation with Cubans suffering horribly from the disease, Katherine Hirschfeld took a cue from Groucho Marx and decided to believe her eyes rather than Castro's Ministry of Truth.

Then she tried phoning her family from Cuba to inform them of her plight; but Soviet-armed soldiers prevented the call. Recall how, in *Invasion of the Body Snatchers*, Bennell tries to place a long-distance call to get word out about the pod-people but the local operator nixes the call.

"The experience left me skeptical of official Cuban government communiqués regarding health care," says (the obviously understated) Dr. Hirschfeld.

Hirschfeld said she "feared the intense politicization of certain sectors of the [Cuban] exile leadership." She said she "had also noted several dismissive and disparaging comments about Cuban exiles." Hence, she "feared this would lead mainstream academics to dismiss my research." Withal, she published her findings in a book entitled *Health, Politics, and Revolution in Cuba Since 1898.*[7]

She has not been allowed into Cuba since that publication. Michael Moore, needless to add, faces no such ban.

A PLUG FROM CNN

Shortly before the Dengue epidemic CNN was granted its coveted Havana bureau, the first allowed to a U.S. network. Bureau chief Lucia Newman assured viewers: "CNN will be given total freedom to do what we want and to work without censorship."[8]

Hard-hitting stories immediately followed. At the height of the epidemic CNN featured Fidel's office in its "Cool Digs" segment of CNN's "Newsstand." "When was the last time you saw a cup full of pencils on the boss's desk?" asked perky CNN anchor Steven Frazier. "And they do get used—look at how worn down the erasers are! Years ago, our host worked as an attorney, defending poor people. . . . He's Fidel Castro, Cuba's leader since 1959!"

"No dubious campaign spending here [in Cuba]." So reported Lucia Newman during the height of the Dengue epidemic, which coincided with some bogus elections. "No mudslinging—a system President Castro boasts is the most democratic and most honest in the world!"[9]

Though two more epidemics have been reported by the Cuban *samizdat* press since 1997, CNN (along with NBC, CBS and ABC) has never seen fit to mention outbreaks of Dengue fever in Cuba.

Instead, in August 2009, CNN's report on Cuba's healthcare by Morgan Neill boasted on Castro's behalf: "Cuba's infant-mortality rates . . . are the lowest in the hemisphere, in line with those of Canada."

"Amazing!" probably gasped the typical CNN viewer. And indeed, according to UN figures, Cuba's current infant-mortality rate places the country 33rd from the top in worldwide ranking, directly above the U.S.

What CNN left out of its report was that, according to those same UN figures, Cuba in 1958 ranked 13th from the top, worldwide. This meant that pre-Castro Cuba had the 13th-lowest infant-mortality rate in the world. This put her not only at the top of Latin America but atop most of Western Europe, ahead of France, Belgium, West Germany, Israel, Japan, Austria, Italy, Spain and Portugal. Today all of these countries leave Communist Cuba in the dust, with much lower infant-mortality rates.

And even plummeting from 13th (under capitalism) to 33rd (under Communism), Cuba's "impressive" infant-mortality rate is kept artificially low by, among other things, a truly appalling abortion rate of 0.71 abortions per live birth. This is the hemisphere's highest, by far. Any Cuban pregnancy that even hints at trouble gets terminated.

DOCTORING INFANT-MORTALITY RATES

The UN's World Health Organization has a fetish for infant-mortality figures, regarding them as the be-all and end-all of a nation's health index. And Castro, whose fiefdom was awarded a prestigious UNESCO award in 2000, reports carefully doctored—if not utterly bogus—figures on Cuba's infant-mortality rate to the WHO. Michael Moore's *Sicko* relies on these UN figures exclusively.

In April 2001 Dr. Juan Felipe Garcia of Jacksonville, FL interviewed several doctors who had recently defected from Cuba. "The official Cuban infant-mortality figure is a farce," asserts Dr. Garcia. "Cuban pediatricians constantly falsify figures for the regime. If an infant dies during the first year the doctors often report the baby was older. Otherwise such lapses could cost him severe penalties and his job."

A *samizdat* smuggled out of Cuba in January 2003 by Mario Enrique Mayo reported that Dr. Olga Oropeza of Camaguey province was severely reprimanded by her hospital chief, Leonardo Ramirez, for delivering a premature baby. "That could raise this hospital's infant-mortality rate!" Ramirez exclaimed as he berated the terrified woman.

Dr. Julio Alfonso said, "We personally used to perform 70 to 80 abortions a day." Yanet Sanchez, a Cuban exile, said she was simply told to submit to an abortion. "They told me I should end the pregnancy," said Sanchez. "It was my very first pregnancy. I wanted to have the child."[10]

Other defecting doctors have testified that if a child dies a few hours after birth, the child isn't counted as ever having lived. This obviously cranks up Cuba's UN ranking in the all-important infant-mortality sweepstakes.

According to a report by the Association of American Physicians and Surgeons, the mortality-rate of Cuban children aged one to four is 34 per cent higher than the U.S. (11.8 versus 8.8 per 1000). But these figures don't figure into UN-spotlighted infant-mortality rates, you see. So apparently the pressure is not on Cuban doctors (thus far) to doctor these figures.[11]

The Association of American Physicians and Surgeons also reports that the current *maternal* mortality rate in Cuba is almost four times the U.S. rate (33 versus 8.4 per 1000). Peculiar and tragic: how do so many mothers die during childbirth in Cuba? And how do so many one-to-four-year-olds perish, while from birth to one year old (the period during which they qualify in UN statistics as infants) they're perfectly healthy?[12]

This might lead a few people to question Cuba's official infant-mortality figures. But such people would not get a Havana bureau for their network, much less a visa to film a documentary in Fidel Castro's fiefdom.

Upon Fidel Castro's resignation in 2006—and apparently fearful that some of their reporters might actually take that job-title seriously—CNN issued a memo to its employees, as follows.

From: Flexner, Allison
Sent: Tuesday, February 19, 2008 7:46 AM
To: *CNN Superdesk (TBS)
Subject: Castro guidance
Some points on Castro—for adding to our anchor reads/reporting:
* Please note Fidel did bring social reforms to Cuba—namely free education and universal health care, and racial integration.
* Also the Cuban government blames a lot of Cuba's economic problems on the US embargo, and while that has caused some difficulties, the bulk of Cuba's economic problems are due to Cuba's failed economic polices. Some analysts would say the US embargo was a benefit to Castro politically—something to blame problems on . . .
* While despised by some, he is seen as a revolutionary hero, especially with leftists in Latin America, for standing up to the United States.
Any questions, please call the international desk.[13]

Michael Moore, lionized in the MSM for "brazenly speaking truth to power," finds the equivalent of a welcome-mat, honor-guard and 21-gun salute upon his every visit to Castro's press-censored fiefdom. He might also be interested to know that his hosts and co-producers hold the honor as "the world's worst jailer of journalists."

On June 16, 2010 Joel Simon, executive director of the Committee to Protect Journalists, testified to that effect at a hearing on "Press Freedom in the Americas" held by the U.S. House Subcommittee on the Western Hemisphere. Interestingly, not one medium belonging to the press in these Americas saw fit to report on the item. The reason is not far to seek: most of those media possess Castro-issued Cuban visas, or full-fledged Cuban bureaus.

CHAPTER 15

The Cuban "Embargo"
—Are You Kidding?

"The embargo against Cuba is the stupidest law ever passed in the U.S.," claims Jimmy Carter.

Yet President Jimmy Carter imposed more economic sanctions against more nations than any American president in modern history. These sanctions were against Rhodesia, South Africa, Uruguay, Paraguay, Chile, the Shah's Iran and Somoza's Nicaragua. President Carter was extremely selective in imposing his sanctions. Let's give him that. He was careful to punish only U.S. allies.[1]

But hypocrisy is not our issue here. Stupidity is our issue—more specifically, the stupidity (or mendacity) of claiming that the U.S. embargoes all commerce with Cuba, as relentlessly reported by the media. Webster's defines "embargo" as "a government order imposing a trade barrier." As a verb it's defined as "to prevent commerce." So let's consider:

In 1957—when Cuba was a "U.S. economic colony" as we're constantly told by the media—the U.S. exported $347.5 million worth of goods to Cuba.[2]

In 2010—when Cuba was being "strangled by a U.S. economic blockade," as we're constantly told by the media—the U.S. exported $366.5 million to Cuba, a drop from the $720 million of 2008. In fact, for every one of the past 8 years the "Cuba-blockading" U.S.

has exported more goods to Cuba than it did in 1957.[3]

In 1957—when Cuba was a "playground for U.S. tourists" as we're constantly told by the media—263,000 people visited Cuba from the U.S.[4]

In 2011—when Cuba was being "blockaded" by the U.S.—an estimated 400,000 people visited Cuba from the U.S.[5]

In 1958 with Cuba under a "U.S.-backed dictator," with the U.S. "controlling Cuba's economy," etc., the staff of the U.S. embassy in Cuba numbered 87, including Cuban employees.

Today, with supposedly no diplomatic relations between Cuba and the U.S., the staff of the U.S. Interests Section in Havana numbers 351, including Cuban employees.

The U.S. has transacted almost $4 billion in trade with Cuba over the past decade. Up until three years ago the U.S. served as Cuba's biggest food-supplier and fifth-biggest import partner. We've fallen a few notches recently but we're still in the top half.[6] Besides banning some paltry imports from Cuba, nowadays the so-called U.S. embargo mostly stipulates that the Castro regime pay cash up front through a third-party bank for all U.S. medical and agricultural products; no Ex-Im (U.S. taxpayer) financing of such sales. Enacted by the Bush team in 2001, this cash-up-front policy has kept the U.S. taxpayer among the few in the world spared fleecing by Castro.

Here are a few items regarding the so-called embargo studiously side-stepped by much of the media (especially those with Havana bureaus):

Per capita, Cuba qualifies as the world's biggest debtor nation with a foreign debt of close to $50 billion, a credit-rating nudging Somalia's, and an uninterrupted record of defaults.

In 1986 Cuba defaulted on most of her foreign debt to Europe.[7] Seven years ago France's export credit agency, COFACE, cut off Cuba's credit line. Mexico's Bancomex quickly followed suit. The Castro regime had stuck it to French taxpayers for $175 million and to Mexican taxpayers for $365 million. Bancomex was forced to impound Cuban assets in three different countries in an attempt to recoup its losses.

Recently the London-based Economist Intelligence Unit (EIU) ranked Cuba as virtually the world's worst country business-wise. Only Iran and Angola ranked lower. Standard & Poors refuses even to rate Cuba, regarding the economic figures released by the regime as utterly bogus.

Just last year we heard from one of Castro's latest suckers. "The Cuban regime has a long track-record of failing to pay back our loans," lamented South Africa's shadow deputy minister of Trade and Industry, Geordin Hill-Lewis. "In 2010, South Africa had to write off R1.1 billion [about $126 million] in bad Cuban debt, and on Friday we wrote off another R250 million [about $29 million] in bad debt. The time has come for South Africa to invest in strategic partnerships that deliver prosperity for our people."[8]

A Wikileaked cable from December 2010 reported on a breakfast hosted by a U.S. diplomat in Havana with commercial and economic counselors from five of Cuba's largest trading partners—China, Spain, Canada, Brazil and Italy—plus key creditor nations France and Japan. "The diplomats reported continuing problems collecting their Cuban debts, with the Japanese noting that after restructuring all of Cuba's official debt in 2009, Tokyo had not received any payments. . . . Even China admitted to having problems getting paid on time and complained about Cuban requests to extend credit terms from one to four years," the cable said. "France and Canada responded with, 'welcome to the club.'"[9]

One fine morning in February 2009, the Castro brothers woke up and decided to freeze $1 billion that 600 foreign companies kept in Cuban bank-accounts. Another fine morning in April 2012 the Cuban regime arrested the top officers of Britain-based Coral Capital that had invested $75 million in the Castro brothers' fiefdom and was planning four luxurious golf resorts.[10] These hapless (greedy, unprincipled and stupid, actually) businessmen now find themselves with no more recourse to law than the millions of Cubans who had their businesses and savings stolen *en masse* in August 1960 by Castro's gunmen.

After all, Che Guevara, who served as Cuba's finance minister during the initial mass burglaries of Cuban- and U.S.-owned properties, explained the regime's legal guidelines very succinctly in January 1959, when he served as chief hangman. "Judicial evidence is an archaic bourgeois detail. We execute based on revolutionary conviction."

All the nations, whose taxpayers and businessmen get fleeced and/or arrested by Castro, routinely condemn the U.S. embargo of Cuba at the UN. Our UN ambassador usually keeps poker-faced and mum during the vote and related pontifications. What fun Susan Rice is missing!

As they lobby against the Cuba embargo, the U.S. farm lobby and their affiliates are simply craving the same business deal from U.S. officials via the U.S. Export-Import Bank (i.e., U.S. taxpayers) that government elites in France, Mexico, South Africa, Canada, Italy, etc. bestowed on their business cronies and cocktail guests, at the expense of those nations' taxpayers.

FAILURE OR SUCCESS?

"OK, so there's no embargo. But come on, Humberto! Haven't these sanctions, as you call them, been a long-running failure? I mean, the regime's still there!"

On January 21, 1962 at Punta del Este, Uruguay, U.S. Secretary of State Dean Rusk gave a speech to the Organization of American States recommending the members join the U.S. in voting for an economic embargo of Cuba. In this speech there is not a single word, or even an inference, that toppling the Castro regime was the embargo's goal. Indeed, Secretary Rusk went out of his way to stress that this was not the embargo's goal. "The United States objects to Cuba's activities and policies in the international arena, *not its internal system or arrangements."* (emphasis mine)

Actually, few U.S. foreign policy measures in recent history have been as phenomenally successful as our limited sanctions against the Stalinist robber-barons who run Cuba. Firstly, as mentioned, the U.S. taxpayer has been spared the fleecing visited upon many others who reside in nations that eschew "embargoing" Cuba. Secondly, for three decades the Soviet Union pumped the equivalent of almost ten Marshall Plans into Cuba. This cannot have helped the Soviet Union's precarious solvency or lengthened her life-span. Thirdly, as more and more suckers get burned and sour on doing business with Castro, our sanctions (and our example) may indeed start influencing Cuba's internal system.

Until Castro's Soviet sugar-daddy finally expired in 1991, not much was heard from his mainstream-media auxiliaries about a "cruel U.S embargo" or "blockade." The PR campaign went into high gear with Pope John Paul's visit to Cuba in January 1998, when an outfit called Americans for Humanitarian Trade with Cuba kicked off. "Ordinary Cubans are paying a severe price for the ban on U.S. food and the most severe restrictions on the sale of U.S. medical products," mourned the AHTC manifesto. "Forty years of the strongest embargo in our history has resulted in increased misery for the people of Cuba. . . . We can no longer support a policy carried out in our name which causes suffering of the most vulnerable—women, children and the elderly."[11]

On the Board of this AHTC sat David Rockefeller of the Council on Foreign Relations, Dwayne Andreas of Archer Daniels Midland and Frank Carlucci, at the time chairman of the Carlyle Group, the world's biggest private-investment corporation, which is headquartered on Washington, DC's Pennsylvania Avenue itself. Carlyle Group is widely regarded as the most politically-connected corporation in the world. George Soros was among its founders and major investors.

A few years earlier, something called the U.S.-Cuba Trade and Economic Council had burst upon the scene. Lo and behold,

Dwayne Andreas sat on the board. Follow the money-trail and most of these names keep popping up on practically everything associated with easing the Cuban "embargo." Somebody sees dollar-signs, and it's not the U.S. taxpayer. That's exactly the rub with the politically-connected companies that are trying to sell Castro.

When it comes to political influence, liberals denounce Cuban-American lobbyists as singularly unscrupulous, diabolically clever, and awash in ill-gotten lucre—unlike those babes-in-the-woods Dwayne Andreas, David Rockefeller and George Soros.

The anti-"embargo" reasoning seems to go something like this: the Carlyle Group, Archer Daniels Midland and the Council on Foreign Relations, along with congressmen representing the most heavily taxpayer-subsidized sector of the U.S. economy, spend most of their waking hours agonizing over the welfare of the Cuban people and yearning to succor them. The Cuban peoples' cousins, sons, daughters, brothers and sisters in Miami, however, only want to starve and torture their relatives.

Furthermore, after a couple of junkets to Cuba, executives of the above-mentioned corporations and their crony congressmen and lobbyists become endowed with an uncanny clairvoyance. This enables them to divine the whims and motives of Cuba's officials much more accurately than those who lived for years under Cuba's communist system, and often within the system. These latter often had daily contact with Cuba's current officials.

But never mind. They know nothing. They cannot be trusted. Jeff Flake and Charles Rangel are much shrewder judges of Raul Castro's psyche than Alcibiades Hidalgo, Raul Castro's adjutant and chief-of-staff for over a decade, who defected to the U.S. in 2002 and flatly stated: "Ending the travel ban would be a gift to the Castros."[12]

SOME "EMBARGO" HISTORY

"But come on, Humberto. When Castro took office amidst all the euphoria, couldn't we have tried some carrot along with Teddy Roosevelt's Big Stick? It seems that right off the bat we started trying to overthrow him or assassinate him!"

In fact, the U.S. elite's fetish for carrots and "engagement" with Fidel Castro began before he was even in office.

"Me and my staff were all Fidelistas," boasted Robert Reynolds, the CIA's "Caribbean desk's specialist on the Cuban revolution" from 1957 to 1960.

"Everyone in the CIA and everyone at State was pro-Castro, except [Republican] Ambassador Earl Smith," admitted Robert Weicha, CIA operative in Santiago, Cuba.

The overwhelming CIA and State Department infatuation with Castro proved decisive with the Eisenhower administration; and so January 7, 1959 marks a milestone in U.S. diplomatic history. Never before had the State Department extended diplomatic recognition to a Latin American government as quickly as it did on (unelected) Fidel Castro's that day.

Nothing so frantically fast had been bestowed upon "U.S.-backed" Fulgencio Batista (note the obligatory prefix, used in every MSM and scholarly mention of him) seven years earlier. Batista had in fact been punished by a U.S. arms embargo and heavy diplomatic pressure to resign for a year. Batista was subsequently denied exile in the U.S. and not even allowed to set foot in the country that had supposedly backed him.

When U.S. State department officials finally got their man Fidel Castro in office, however, they were the ones stepping and fetching and rolling over and begging. During Castro's first 16 months in power, while he was insulting the U.S. as "a vulture preying on humanity," flooding Cuba with Soviet agents and stealing U.S. properties to tune of millions of dollars weekly, the State Department made more than ten back-channel diplomatic attempts to ascertain the cause of his tantrums and further "engage" him with ever bigger carrots. Argentinean President Arturo Frondizi was the conduit for many of these and recounts their utter futility in his memoirs.[13]

In the summer of 1960, Castro's KGB-trained security forces stormed into more than 1,600 U.S.-owned businesses in Cuba and stole them all at Soviet gunpoint. Two billion dollars were heisted from outraged U.S. businessmen and stockholders. Rubbing his hands in triumphant glee, Fidel Castro boasted at maximum volume to the entire world that he was freeing Cuba from "Yankee economic slavery" and that "he would never repay a penny."

This might be the only official promise Fidel Castro has ever kept.

Not all Americans surrendered their legal and hard-earned property peacefully. Among some who resisted were Bobby Fuller, whose family farm would contribute to a Soviet-style *kolkhoz*, and Howard Anderson, whose profitable Jeep dealership was coveted by Castro's henchmen. Both U.S. citizens were murdered by Castro and Che's firing squads, after torture.

Here are court records from a suit in the 11th Judicial Circuit Court, Miami-Dade County by Katy Fuller, whose father was murdered in 1960 by for resisting the theft of his family farm.

From *The Estate of Robert Otis Fuller vs The Republic of Cuba*, filed May 5, 2002:

"Agents of the Castro Government acting under orders of the Castro Government, led Bobby Fuller to a firing squad where he was shot and killed after being tortured by having his blood drained from his body. Thereafter, his body was thrown into an unmarked mass grave in an unknown location."

Here's another lawsuit against Fidel Castro by the family of U.S. citizen Howard Anderson, who resisted the theft of his filling stations and Jeep dealership by Castro's gunmen in 1960: Anderson v. Republic of Cuba, No. 01-28628 (Miami-Dade Circuit Court, April 13, 2003). "In one final session of torture, Castro's agents drained Howard Anderson's body of blood before sending him to his death at the firing squad."

Two days after his trial, Howard Anderson refused a blindfold, preferring to glare at his executioners. Medically he was probably in shock at the time from the blood-draining. "*Fuego!*" The bullets shattered Howard Anderson's body at dawn on April 19, 1961.

So, however valuable they have proven to American taxpayers, U.S. sanctions against Castro's regime were not originally enacted due to the regime's abysmal credit rating.

In July 1961, JFK's special counsel Richard Goodwin met with Che Guevara in Uruguay and reported back to Kennedy: "Che says that Cuba wants an understanding with the U.S.; the Cubans have no intention of making an alliance with the Soviets. So we should make it clear to Castro that we want to help Cuba."[14] (How Che managed a straight face during this conversation requires a book of its own.)

In response, Soviet nuclear missiles locked and loaded in Cuba a year later—and pointed at Goodwin's and Kennedy's very homes.

In 1975, President Gerald Ford (under Secretary of State Henry Kissinger's influence) allowed foreign branches and subsidiaries of U.S. companies to trade freely with Cuba and persuaded the Organization of American States to lift its sanctions.

In response, Castro started his African invasion and tried to assassinate Ford. You read right. On March 19, the *Los Angeles Times* ran the headline "Cuban Link to Death Plot Probed." Both Republican candidates of the day, President Ford and Ronald Reagan, were to be taken out during the Republican National Convention. The Emiliano Zapata Unit, a Bay Area radical group linked to the Weather Underground, would make the hits.[15]

Jimmy Carter, in a goodwill gesture, lifted U.S. travel sanctions against Cuba and was poised to open full diplomatic relations with Castro.

In response, more thousands of Cuban troops spreading Soviet terror (and poison gas) in Africa, more internal repression, and hundreds of psychopaths, killers, and perverts infiltrated on boats and shoved at the U.S. in the Mariel boatlift.

Ronald Reagan sent Secretary of State Alexander Haig to meet personally in Mexico City with Cuba's Vice President Carlos Rafael Rodriguez to feel him out. Then he sent diplomatic trouble-shooter General Vernon Walters to Havana for a meeting with the Maximum Leader himself.

In response, Cubans took over Nicaragua and practically practically took over Grenada and El Salvador. But unlike Carter, Reagan responded to Castro with pretty salutary results.

In the 90's, President Clinton tried playing nice again by relaxing trade and travel restrictions.

In response, three U.S. citizens and one U.S. resident who flew humanitarian flights over the Florida straits (Brothers to the Rescue) were murdered in cold blood by Castro's MiG's. Castro agent Ana Belen Montes "moled" her way to head of the Defense Intelligence Agency's Cuba division, achieving the deepest and most damaging penetration of the U.S. Defense Department by an enemy agent in modern history.

The Obama administration mimicked President Clinton's Cuba policy, with similar results. "We have seen Raul Castro's comments and we welcome this overture," Secretary of State Hillary Clinton announced in April 2009. "We are taking a very serious look at it. We are continuing to look for productive ways forward, because we view the present [George W. Bush administration] policy as having failed. Engagement is a useful tool to advance our national interests."[16]

Deeds quickly followed words. In executive order after executive order, President Obama abolished Bush's travel and remittance restrictions to Castro's terrorist-sponsoring fiefdom, to the point where the cash-flow from the U.S. to Cuba in 2011-12 was estimated by Senator Marco Rubio's staff at $4 billion a year. While a proud Soviet satrapy, Cuba had received $3-5 billion annually from the Soviets. Some "embargo."

In response, on December 3, 2009, Castro's police arrested Alan Gross, a U.S. citizen working in Cuba under contract with the U.S. Agency for International Development.

Mr. Gross has languished in a Cuban prison cell ever since. His crime was bringing cell-phone and Internet equipment into Castro's fiefdom to help Cuba's tiny Jewish community communicate more freely with the outside world. Pre-Castro Cuba boasted more phones and TV's per capita than most European countries, by the way. Today, Castro's fiefdom has fewer Internet users per capita than Uganda, and fewer cell phones than Papua New Guinea. The Stalinist regime is very vigilant in these matters.[17]

In March 2011, after he had lost almost 100 pounds from his prison ordeal, a Castroite court finally got around to trying Mr. Gross. He was condemned to a prison sentence of 15 years for working for an agency of the U.S. government "that aimed to destroy the revolution through the use of communication systems out of the control of authorities."

And there's the hitch: control of the authorities. Not even Gaddafi's late regime or Hu Jintao's in China seek to control cell-phone and Internet access. Censor? Absolutely. But outright control of all means of communication is a fetish peculiar to communists, a term which no longer applies to the mainland Chinese regime, though it certainly remains despicable and dangerous.

Senator Marco Rubio was among the first to comment on Alan Gross's sentence: "Mr. Gross is simply a humanitarian who was seeking to help the Jewish community in Cuba access the Internet, and he deserves to be freed and reunited with his family at once. With Mr. Gross's sentencing, the Castro regime has effectively demonstrated the hopeless and dangerous naiveté of this administration's policy toward the regime."

Upon CNN's being bestowed its coveted Havana bureau in 1997, CNN bureau chief Lucia Newman (now with Al Jazeera) assured viewers that, "CNN will be given total freedom to do what we want and to work without censorship." Alas, CNN had little to report on the Gross trial except for the verdict. The trial, in perfect keeping with the Stalinist regime's agenda, was closed to all media.

This type of relentless press censorship by the Castro regime proved too much for Al Jazeera's correspondent, who on June 20, 2012 packed up and left Cuba in a huff. "We can't do any work down here!" complained correspondent Moutaz Al Qaissia of Castro's secret police, who constantly tailed him. Al Qaissia said: "They're uncultured—barely know how to read. They're dogs!" Al Qaissia had offered some mild criticism of the reforms in Cuba and was promptly accused of being in the pay of the Yankees.

Apparently the censorship from "dictators" Saddam Hussein, Gaddafi, Assad, etc., proved petty compared to that of "President" Castro. What's this say about the networks that *stay* in Cuba?

From these networks we'll obviously never learn the totality of the evidence against Alan Gross, but some evidence was later leaked by the regime to some sympathetic blogs. From these we learned that Gross had worked with Cuban Freemasons and Cuban Jewish groups. His main contact, Jose Manuel Collera Vento, was in fact the "Grand Master of the Grand Lodge of Cuba."[18]

Collera was also a Cuban intelligence agent. Gross had worked with him since 2004. Before that, Collera had often visited the U.S. on cultural exchanges and was even awarded the Congressional Medal of Freedom by a group of U.S. senators. Alan Gross made a total of seven trips to Cuba and worked with Jewish delegations in the cities of Havana, Santiago and Camaguey. Every head of every Jewish group that he worked with and befriended testified against him in court.

Another moral of this story: any Cuban academic, cultural or religious figure easily traveling to and from Stalinist nation is probably working for the communist regime's intelligence service. This was common knowledge regarding "cultural ambassadors" from Soviet-bloc countries. "Cultural and educational exchanges with foreign countries are our most effective means of propaganda," states a declassified KGB document recently translated by Vladimir Bukovsky.[19]

The U.S. embassy in Cuba (officially euphemized as an "Interests Section") also responded to Mr. Gross's sentence: "He is guilty of nothing more than caring for the Jewish community and the people of Cuba," said the embassy's public-affairs officer, Gloria Berbena, who added that "the Cuba government seeks to criminalize *what most of the world deems normal*—in this case, access to information and technology."[20] (my emphasis)

So Cuba is Communist after all! Did Ms. Barbena think she was being posted to Belgium? In February 2011 pictures were snuck out of Cuba showing the third-highest ranking U.S. diplomat in Cuba, Puerto Rican-born Joaquin Monserratte, partying hardy with Fidel Castro's son Tony along with the son of the vice-chief of Cuba's secret police, Ernesto Milanes. Monserratte also belongs to the Smoker's Club of Cuba, famous for throwing many bacchanals involving the Castroite elite. Maybe if our diplomatic officers spent less time partying with Cuba's *nomenklatura,* they'd learn how someone like Alan Gross might be subject to arrest.

Based on the reporting by networks and press-agencies that have been bestowed Havana bureaus, an Obama-appointed diplomat can be forgiven for forgetting this; but Castro's is a Stalinist regime. Given our modern college textbooks, this diplomat can be forgiven for never knowing it; but such regimes are rigidly totalitarian. Based on modern public education this diplomat can be forgiven not knowing what totalitarian means; but it means total state control of every facet of a people's life.

"When it is a question of annihilating the enemy," pronounced Stalin's chief prosecutor Andrey Vishinsky, "we can do it just as well without a trial." Alan Gross was certainly tried—but by some of Vishinsky's most devoted disciples.

Former political prisoner Armando Valladares, who somehow escaped the firing squad but spent 22 torture-filled years in Cuba's *gulag,* described his trial very succinctly: "not one witness to accuse me, not one to identify me, not one single piece of evidence against me." Mr. Valladares was arrested in 1961 for the crime of refusing to display a pro-Castro sign on his desk. Shortly after his arrival on U.S. shores, Mr. Valladares was appointed by Ronald Reagan as U.S. ambassador to the Human Rights Commission of the United Nations, a setting where both Fidel Castro and Che Guevara traditionally basked in wild ovations. Modern history records few U.S. diplomatic tweaks as slick as those of Mr. Valladares, or U.S. ambassadors as effective as he.

On July 17, 2012, Armando Valladares published a letter to Alan Gross in *The Daily Caller.* Among its highlights:

Alan P. Gross
Havana, Cuba

Dear friend:

That is how I am compelled to address you, because even though we have never met, we share a common bond: I too lived behind the iron bars now surrounding you in Cuba—in my case for 22 years.

Like you, I was convicted by the Cuban authorities without a single shred of evidence against me.

I have no doubt that your greatest pain right now must be the realization that the U.S. government has turned its back on you. There was a time when the words "I am an American citizen" meant something. They meant all the more when the individual declaring that was the target of abuse outside of the United States. It gives me great sadness to say that inside the Communist boot that now tramples upon your dignity is the foot of the American president, Barack Obama.

The more Castro's thugs oppress you and make your family suffer, the more your jailers torture you, the harder things get for you—the more this administration seeks to reward them with new concessions. Under any previous U.S. administration, Democrat or Republican, you would not still be in jail. The American president, who has made a habit of publicly bowing to foreign powers, bows to your torturers and would-be executioners. Meanwhile, the adult daughter of Cuba's dictator recently visited the U.S. to applaud and show her support for President Obama. She receives a visa to come to the United States and a Secret Service escort. And you? You suffer the torture of imprisonment.

The Obama administration must step up its efforts to press for your release through its diplomatic channels. Should those diplomatic efforts fail, then they must be followed by real action, including the suspension of flights and remittances to Cuba until such time as you are allowed to return to the United States. If the Obama administration even threatened to do this it is my considered judgment that you would be on the next flight back to your home in Washington, D.C.

By the way, introducing cutting-edge communications equipment into Cuba didn't always land Americans a 15-year gig in a torture-chamber. In 1957 ATT presented Cuban "dictator" (according to every media mention) Fulgencio Batista with a golden telephone for his regime's enthusiastic welcome of all of the company's latest technology. This Cuban dictator reveled in the fact that Cubans had better, more abundant and cheaper means of communication than most Europeans. You might recall the scene from *Goldfather II* where Hyman Roth and Michael Corleone pass the golden telephone around Batista's conference table. This one scene contains an element of historical accuracy.

OPPOSING THE "EMBARGO" FOR FUN AND PROFIT

As explained earlier, to label our current relationship with Cuba an embargo is laughable. To label it a "blockade" shows appalling ignorance, functional illiteracy or, more likely, Castro-regime advocacy, on its payroll or off. And given the absence of any person or entity registered with U.S. Department of Justice as an agent of the Cuban government, we have to assume the latter.

Payments from Castro's payroll, however, can appear in laundered form. Take the case of the oft-quoted champion of unfettered U.S. trade and travel to Cuba, Phil Peters of the Lexington Institute. A Nexus-Lexus search shows that Mr. Peters could be properly billed as the mainstream media's go-to source on the Cuba embargo issue.

Here's a sampling of how his frequent media hosts introduce Cuba embargo opponent Phil Peters:

"Philip Peters follows economic matters in Cuba for the security- and-free-market-oriented Lexington Institute in Arlington, Va." (*The New York Times*)

"Philip Peters is a scholar at the Lexington Institute." (*The Washington Post*)

Philip Peters is a Cuba expert with the Lexington Institute, a think tank in Arlington, Va. (*The Wall Street Journal*)

"Philip Peters is Cuba specialist for the Lexington Institute, a Washington-area think tank that promotes free markets." (*USA Today*)

"Philip Peters is a Cuba analyst at the Virginia-based Lexington Institute." (The Associated Press)

"Philip Peters is a vice-president of the Lexington Institute and an expert on Cuban affairs." (CNN)

Well, here's some background on the Lexington Institute's funding.

In a joint venture with the Castro regime, Canadian mining company Sherritt International operates the Moa nickel mining-plant in Cuba's Oriente province. This facility was among the thousands stolen from their U.S. managers and stockholders at Cuban-Soviet gunpoint in 1960 (when it was worth $90 million). Now here's an explosive item from a legal memo uncovered by Babalu blog as part of a court case discovery:

"Canada's Sherritt works quietly in Washington . . . recently it has given money to a former State Department employee, Phil Peters, to advance its interests. The money to Peters goes through contributions to the Lexington Institute, where Peters is a vice president. Because the Lexington Institute is a 501(c)(3) not-for-profit, there is no public record of Sherritt's funding. This has allowed Peters to advise and direct the Cuba Working Group (a Congressional anti-embargo cabal) in ways beneficial to Sherritt while presenting himself to the Group as an objective think-tank scholar with a specialization in Cuba." [21]

In brief: one of the Castro regime's top business partners funnels under-the-table payments to America's top anti-embargo publicist, who is invariably billed as an "impartial, scholarly expert" in every media mention.

Nick Schwellenbach, a former investigator for the Project on Government Oversight, also uncovered incriminating items regarding the Lexington Institute's funding. Some of these were included in an investigative report by the *Mobile Press-Register* on Phil Peters's colleague Loren Thompson, the institute's "defense expert." Thompson is consulted by the media on defense-spending matters almost as often as Peters is on Cuban matters.

"What is often not revealed in news reports, "Schwellenbach discloses, "is that almost all funding for Thompson's employer, the non-profit Lexington Institute, comes from the same defense contractors who frequently have a stake in the programs that he writes about." When confronted with the evidence, "Thompson readily confirmed that the institute receives 'quite a significant' level of support from defense contractors, including similar amounts from Boeing and Los Angeles-based Northrop. . . . That fact is not mentioned on the institute's Web site, however, and Thompson would not provide specific dollar amounts. Boeing and Northrop spokesmen later also declined to say how much their firms give...." [22]

In keeping with this time-honored Lexington Institute fund-raising tradition, might Peters's honorariums also issue from parties with a stake in the issues he writes and talks about? We hardly expect the Castro regime to fess up in the manner of Boeing and Norththrop. But the court-discovery document provides a pretty good clue.

CHAPTER 16

"Agents of Influence"—Castro's Ladies and Men in the U.S. Media

On September 20, 2001, the FBI arrested the enemy spy that had managed the deepest penetration of the U.S. Department of Defense in history. The spy's name is Ana Montes and during her 15 years in the Defense Intelligence Agency she operated as an agent for Fidel Castro. At the time of her arrest she had moled her way to the head of the DIA's Latin America division. From here, she greatly influenced (if not actually directed) the Clinton administration's Cuba policy. Today she serves a 25-year sentence in federal prison. She was convicted of "conspiracy to commit espionage," the same charge against Ethel and Julius Rosenberg carrying the same potential death sentence for what is widely considered the most damaging espionage case since the so-called end of the Cold War. Montes dodged the Rosenbergs' fate primarily through a plea bargain.[1]

""Ana Montes compromised our entire program against Cuba, electronic as well as human," admitted Joel F. Brenner, a national counterintelligence executive. She "passed some of our most sensitive information about Cuba back to Havana," disclosed then undersecretary for international security, John Bolton.[2]

Lieutenant Colonel Christopher Simmons of the DIA had a key role in uncovering Fidel Castro's "queen jewel," as she came to be known, and sending her to prison. Two years later Castro had cause to curse Simmons again. "Virtually every member of Cuba's UN mission is an intelligence agent," revealed Alcibiades Hidalgo, who defected to the U.S. in 2002 after serving as Raul Castro's chief of staff and Cuba's ambassador to the UN.[3] In 2003 Lieut. Col. Simmons helped root out 14 of those Cuban spies, who were promptly expelled from the U.S.

In 23 years as a U.S. military counterintelligence officer, Lieut. Col. Simmons has ended the operations of 80 enemy agents, many of whom are today behind bars. "I believe that the Cuban intelligence service has penetrated the United States government to the same extent that the old East German Stasi once penetrated the West German government," he said in an interview in 2008.

Retired from the DIA, Lieut. Col. Simmons is now an active reserve officer and a national security consultant who specializes in outing Castro's "agents of influence" in the U.S. "For Cuba, being able to influence policy and elite opinion-makers is equally important—possibly even more important than recruiting spies with access to intelligence information," asserts Norman Bailey, who worked for the office of the director of National Intelligence. That makes Chris Simmons a busy man.

Among the agents of influence identified by Lieut. Col. Simmons are:

*Julia Sweig, senior fellow at the Council on Foreign Relations and director of its Latin America studies division;

*Retired professor Gillian Gunn-Clissold, who headed Georgetown University's Cuba Study Group and served as assistant director of Caribbean programs at Trinity College;

*Professor Alberto Coll, ex-deputy assistant secretary of Defense (1990-93), former professor at the Naval War College, series host of the History Channel and now professor at DePaul University.

*Professor Mariteli Perez-Stable, currently teaching at Florida International University, on the editorial staff of *The Miami Herald* and Vice president of the Washington, DC-based think-tank,

Inter-American Dialogue, a frequent source on Cuba issues for the mainstream media.[4]

The media blackout on Chris Simmon's bombshell has been total and understandable. For decades some of those he describes as Castro's agents of influence have been the mainstream media's favorite go-to Cuba experts for interviews, insights, prognostications and sound-bites on Cuba.

Since Fidel Castro's health "hiccup" in the summer of 2006, a cursory search shows that Cuba "experts" from the Inter-American Dialogue have been prime sources for stories by the following news outlets: Reuters, The Associated Press, CNN, *The New York Times, The Washington Post,* ABC, PBS, MSNBC, NPR, *Time, Newsweek, The Chicago Tribune, The Christian Science Monitor, The Nation,* the *International Herald Tribune, Los Angeles Times,* the Brookings Institute, *Foreign Affairs* magazine, *Forbes* and the *Latin Business Chronicle.* Throw in the *London Daily Telegraph,* Canadian Broadcasting Corporation, Canada's *Globe and Mail* and *Der Spiegel* for good measure.

When PBS ran an "American Series" special on Fidel Castro in 2005, most of the show involved an interview with Marifeli Perez-Stable, who is also a member of the prestigious Council on Foreign Relations as well as Mexico's Council on Foreign Relations.

According to Chris Simmons, Dr. Perez-Stable also worked as an agent for Cuba's DGI until the early 90's, when a defecting Cuban intelligence officer blew her cover and ended her usefulness to the Castro regime. This defector had been Perez-Stable's Cuban case-officer and Simmons saw the document naming her.[5]

"I'm sick and tired of these McCarthyite tactics," Perez-Stable was quoted in a *Miami Herald* article regarding Simmons's accusation. "I supported the Cuban revolution in the 1970's. Over the course of the 1980's, I had a change of heart."[6]

Problem is, Chris Simmons cites a meeting by Ms. Perez-Stable with her Cuban case-officer held as late as mid-1991 in Ottawa, Canada.

"This is nothing more than a witch hunt," said *Miami Herald* editor Joe Oglesby about Simmons's charges. "This is character-assassination and these issues have been raised and dealt with in the past."[7]

Yes, the issue has been raised in the past. Problem is, the only "dealing with it" by *The Miami Herald* was to bury it, look around furtively and hope that few noticed. In a written response to *The Miami Herald*, Professor Alberto Coll said: "'These are baseless and scurrilous allegations without a shred of evidence, presented by someone eager to make a quick buck in Miami by selling his book."[8]

Problem is, in May, 2005 Professor Coll was found guilty of lying to federal authorities about the purpose of a visit to Cuba. The Naval War College then suspended his access to classified material.

So why aren't these "agents of influence" either in jail or being prosecuted? I asked retired Lieut. Col. Simmons.

"As a counterintelligence officer my job was to identify and neutralize foreign agents," he explained, "to prevent them from doing more damage to my country. One way to accomplish this is to get a conviction for not registering as agents of a foreign government. This usually takes hundreds of thousands if not millions of dollars. But it's often easier, also easier on the taxpayer, to simply neutralize them by 'outing' the ones who knowingly had contacts with Cuban intelligence agencies and putting both them and their media cohorts on full alert that U.S counterintelligence is on to their game. I've obviously received clearance to mention the above names."[9]

That element of knowing is crucial. The Castro regime is famous for the hospitality provided by the official hosts and attendants it assigns the thousands upon thousands of U.S. visitors—legislators, scholars, journalists, ecclesiastics, businessmen, cultural ambassadors—who somehow breach the brutal "U.S. blockade" every year to visit Cuba. Point is, virtually every official visitor to Cuba from the U.S. has some form of contact with Cuban intelligence. But most are unaware of the true professional identity of their charming guides, dinner companions, taxi drivers, etc.

Chris Simmons also based his accusations against the Inter-American Dialogue's vice president partly on an FBI debriefing of a Cuban intelligence defector named Jesus Perez-Mendez, who had worked closely with Dr. Perez-Stable's Cuban case-officer. This defector revealed that in the early 80's Cuba's DGI appointed Dr. Perez-Stable as head of a division within their "Cuban Institute of Friendship with Peoples" (ICAP, in Spanish), which fronted as an "educational" and "cultural-exchange" group. "The DGI prepared Perez-Stable's annual schedule in the U.S.," disclosed Perez-Mendez. "She receives $100 for every tourist that travels to Cuba with this group."[10]

This same ICAP, by the way, sponsored the Reverend Jeremiah Wright's visit to Cuba in 1984. So it's likely that Jeremiah Wright unwittingly earned Ms. Marifeli Perez-Stable a C-note—and tax-free, it appears.

JEREMIAH WRIGHT'S CUBAN FRIENDS

"I have been affiliated with the Cuban Council of Churches since the 1980s," boasted Rev. Jeremiah Wright in a sermon on July 16, 2006. "I have several close Cuban friends who work with the Cuban Council of Churches and you have heard me preach about our affiliation and the Black Theology Project's trips to Cuba. The Cuban Council of Churches has been a non-partisan global mission partner for decades. I have worked with them for two decades."[11]

Non-partisan, Reverend Wright? Not according to Cuban intelligence defector Juan Vives, who from hands-on experience reports that the Cuban Council of Churches is in fact an arm of Cuba's ICAP, itself an arm of Cuba's KGB-founded and mentored DGI. The ICAP's long-time chieftain was Rene Rodriguez Cruz, who by the Reverend Jeremiah Wright's own admission might have been one of his "friends."

Rodriguez's meteoric rise through Cuba's Stalinist bureaucracy was facilitated by his diligence as an early executioner, often beating out even Che Guevara and Raul Castro in his zeal to shatter the firing-squad victim's skull with a *coup de grace* from his .45. On November 5, 1982 a Dade County, Florida, grand jury indicted Rene Rodriguez Cruz for smuggling drugs into the U.S.

This murderer headed a Cuban agency that Jeremiah Wright "worked with for decades" by his own admission, and whose staff he regards as "friends." These friends arranged the visit for the Rev. Jesse Jackson and his 300-person entourage to Havana in 1984, which included Rev. Wright.

"Viva Fidel!" bellowed Reverend Jackson while concluding his speech at the University of Havana during that visit. "Viva Che Guevara! Long live our cry of freedom!"[12]

"He [Jesse Jackson] is a great personality," reciprocated a beaming Fidel Castro, "a brilliant man with a great talent, capable of communicating with people, very persuasive, reliable, and honest. Jackson's main characteristic is honesty. He is sincere and there is not a single bit of demagoguery in his conversations."

You gotta love that last point.

STEPHEN COLBERT'S FAVORITE CUBA "EXPERT"

"Julia Sweig is director for Latin America studies at the Council on Foreign Relations." (NPR)

"Julia Sweig heads the Latin American division for the Council on Foreign Relations." (Stephen Colbert)

"Julia E. Sweig is senior fellow and director of Latin America studies at the Council on Foreign Relations." (New York Times)

When Stephen Colbert introduced Julia Sweig on his show—July 15, 2008, and May 11, 2009—as the head of the Council on Foreign Relations Latin American division he was correct but incomplete. After all, this is the same brief bio used for Julia Sweig by the *Daily Beast*, *Foreign Affairs*, *The New York Times*, the *Los Angeles Times*, *The Washington Post*, NPR, PBS and the many other media-outlets that feature her expertise. None of these mentions that she also boasts warm friendship and close collaboration with Castroite terrorists whose plans for New York would have put the death-toll from 9/11 in second place. Some background:

On November 17, 1962, J. Edgar Hoover's FBI cracked a plot by Cuban agents that targeted Macy's, Gimbel's, Bloomingdale's and Manhattan's Grand Central Terminal with a dozen incendiary devices and 500 kilos of TNT. The explosions were timed for the following week, the day after Thanksgiving. Macy's gets 50,000 shoppers that one day.

Thousands of New Yorkers, including women and children—given the date and targets, probably mostly women and children—were to be incinerated and entombed.

At the time, the FBI relied heavily on HUMINT (human intelligence). They'd expertly penetrated the plot, identified the ringleaders and had them tapped. One by one the ringleaders were ambushed and arrested. Among these were Cuban DGI agents Jose Gomez Abad and Elsa Montero, who worked as "diplomats" in Cuba's UN mission. Alas, they enjoyed "diplomatic immunity" and were soon back in Cuba as heroes instead of in the electric chair at Sing Sing.

The FBI speculated that as many as 30 others might have been in on the plot, but the above-named were the head honchos. The intent and will of those Castroite terrorists to commit mass-murder was certainly present; only our crackerjack FBI of the time foiled it.

We turn now to the acknowledgments in Julia Sweig's award-winning book published in 2003, entitled *Inside the Cuban Revolution:*

"In Cuba many people spent long hours with me, helped open doors I could not have pushed through myself, and offered friendship and warmth to myself during research trips to the island . . . Elsa Montero and Jose Gomez Abad championed this project."

Sweig also thanks Ramon Sanchez Parodi, Jose Antonio Arbesu, Fernando Miguel Garcia, Hugo Ernesto Yedra and Josefina Vidal for their "warmth, their friendship and their kindness in opening Cuban doors."

Chris Simmons identifies every one of the above as Cuban DGI agents. Josefina Vidal was booted from the U.S. in 2003 for espionage, after Simmons himself fingered her.

"The main interest of the book," gushed London's prestigious *Financial Times* about Julia Sweig's *Inside the Cuban Revolution,* "is that it is primarily based on original interviews and previously inaccessible records."

No doubt. But might KGB-trained officials in the service of a Stalinist regime possibly have had an agenda during those interviews and in cherry-picking which records to disclose—not to mention welcoming Sweig into Cuba to begin with?

I haven't checked Guinness, but effusively thanking ten different intelligence agents of a terror-sponsoring enemy nation in your book's acknowledgements—three of whom were expelled from the U.S. for terrorism or espionage—must be some kind of record, at least for someone outside a maximum-security federal prison.

Not that in media eyes this affects Sweig's position as an impartial expert on issues pertaining to the terror-sponsoring enemy nation. "A nonpartisan resource for information and analysis," boasts the intro to the Council on Foreign Relations, which features Julia Sweig as its Latin America expert.

"In 1998, a comprehensive review by the U.S. intelligence community concluded that Cuba does not pose a threat to U.S. national security," states the Council on Foreign Relations website. Perhaps overlooked by the Council is that this comprehensive review was authored by the Clinton Defense Department's Ana Montes, who dodged the fate of the Rosenbergs with a plea-bargain and is currently serving a 25-year stretch in federal prison for the crime of espionage. The Montes case ranks as the most damaging (for us) spy case since the "end" of the Cold War.

In September 2010 *The Atlantic's* Jeffrey Goldberg's copped the first interview with Fidel Castro since the Stalinist dictator's near-death crisis in 2006. Goldberg thanked Julia Sweig for arranging the visit, describing her as "a friend at the Council on Foreign Relations" and "a preeminent expert on Cuba and Latin America."

"We shook hands," writes Goldberg about meeting Castro. "Then *he greeted Julia warmly.* They [Castro and Sweig] have known each other for more than 20 years." (emphasis mine)

CHAPTER 17

Barbara Walters, Charmed by the Hemisphere's Top Torturer of Women

"Fidel Castro is old-fashioned, courtly, even paternal, a thoroughly fascinating figure!" (NBC's Andrea Mitchell)

"Fidel Castro has brought very high literacy and great health-care to his country. His personal magnetism is powerful." (ABC's Barbara Walters)

"Why did Elian's mother leave Cuba? What was she escaping? By all accounts this young woman was living the good life." (NBC's Jim Avila, April 2000)

"[Raul Castro's wife Vilma Espin] was a champion of women's rights and greatly improved the status of women in Cuba, a society known for its history of machismo." (*The Washington Post*, June 18th 2007)

"**O**nly minutes after my arrival at the Hotel Riviera in Havana, I was told to be in his office within 15 minutes," wrote Barbara Walters about her first interview with Fidel Castro in May 1977. "There I found a very courtly, somewhat portly Fidel Castro.

He apologized for making me wait for two years and said that now he wanted to cooperate. Castro suggested that he personally escort us on a visit to other parts of the country, and he gave me the choice of places. I selected the Bay of Pigs and the Sierra Maestra . . .

"On Wednesday, Castro himself came to our hotel to pick us up. . . . Then, driving a Russian-made jeep, he took us to the Bay of Pigs, where we boarded an armed patrol boat. We thus became, according to Castro, the first Americans to cross the Bay of Pigs since the U.S.-supported invasion there in 1961."[1]

Barbara Walters's crossing of the Bay of Pigs was probably more than a historical sightseeing junket. On the other side and near the mouth of the bay sits Castro's personal island, Cayo Piedra, that houses his luxurious getaway chateau. According to defectors, Fidel Castro, when younger, often repaired to this remote, luxurious villa for spear-fishing, among other recreational pursuits.

Juan Reynaldo Sanchez, a lieutenant colonel in Cuba's armed forces who spent 17 years as Fidel Castro's bodyguard/valet, had just been promoted to the position when Barbara Walters visited Cuba for her first interview with the Stalinist dictator in May 1977. Sanchez defected to the U.S. in 2008 and explained to this writer how he was part of the Castroite entourage that accompanied Ms. Walters and Fidel to the latter's island chateau. Ms Walters does mention that:

"We stopped at a little island for a picnic lunch of grilled fish and pineapple. During which Castro swapped fish stories with the ABC crew. It was here that we taped our first but brief and candid interview with him."[2]

And speaking of candidness, when in her book *Audition* Barbara Walters confessed to an adulterous affair with Massachusetts Senator Edward Brooke, Oprah Winfrey asked if she had been in love at the time.

"I was certainly . . . I don't know . . . I was certainly infatuated," answered Walters.

"Infatuated?" asked Oprah.

"I was certainly involved," Walters says. "He was brilliant. He was exciting!"

"His personal magnetism is powerful. His presence is still commanding!" panted Barbara Walters about her 2002 interview with the hemisphere's top torturer of women.

Argentinian journalist Juan Gasparini in his Spanish-language book *Mujeres de dictadores* ("Women of Dictators") writes: "It is widely supposed that Fidel Castro had several amorous adventures with the North American reporter Barbara Walters who twice visited Cuba to interview him. It is said that she later visited Cuba more discretely for private visits."

Did her journalistic sisters envy Ms. Walters? "Fidel Castro is old-fashioned, courtly, even paternal, a thoroughly fascinating figure!" squealed NBC's Andrea Mitchell, after her interview with the dictator who established prisons for the serial torture of women.

And as earlier mentioned, during the Manhattan elite's love-fest for Fidel Castro in 1996, Diane Sawyer was so overcome in the serial murderer's presence that she lost control, rushed up, broke into that toothy smile of hers, wrapped her arms around Castro and smooched him warmly on his bearded cheek.

This phenomenon is not exactly unknown to psychologists, especially those who specialize in studying rapists, torturers and killers of women. From Charles Manson to Richard Ramirez, from the Son of Sam to O.J. Simpson, all these psychopaths— while in prison and especially on death row—have been swamped with love-letters and marriage proposals from women.

But most people don't associate Barbara Walters, Andrea Mitchell and Diane Sawyer with deranged meth-addicts.

When in a 2002 interview Fidel Castro told Barbara Walters that Cuba is "to be not only the most just society in the world but the most cultivated," Barbara Walters (whose ABC profile tells us that she "tackles the tough issues") responded with such punchy rebuttals as, "Cuba has very high literacy and you have brought great health to your country."[3]

CASTRO'S CHAMBERS FOR WOMEN

On the way to Fidel Castro's love-shack at the mouth of the Bay of Pigs, feminist icon Barbara Walters passed several prisons and torture-chambers crammed to suffocation with women political prisoners, a totalitarian horror utterly unknown in our hemisphere until her "magnetic" Cuban escort took power.

When transferring them from cell to cell, communist prison guards had to drag many of these women around like dead animals. The women prisoners were simply incapable of walking. The constant beatings had incapacitated many of them. The excrement and menstrual fluid caked to their legs and bare feet made it more difficult still. Some of the cells, called "tapiadas" or stoppages, were barely big enough to stand and walk in and were completely sealed except for a few tiny air-holes. The women were confined completely underground in total darkness and suffocating heat for weeks at a time. These were tombs by any other name, except that their occupants were still alive, if barely and if only by ultra-human perseverance.

"Chirri was just a kid," recalled prisoner Ana Lazaro Rodriguez about one of her cellmates, "barely 18. Tiny, blonde and beautiful, she should have been going to high-school dances. Instead, because her father had been involved in a plot against Castro, she was squatting in a dark filthy cell, wallowing in menstrual blood and shit."[4]

Jailing, torturing and murdering people (particularly females) for the crime of being related to "enemies of the revolution," by the way, comes straight from the Bolshevik playbook. The practice was started by the Soviet Cheka and greatly expanded upon by Stalin during the Great Terror. The Soviet Union's Cuban satraps adopted the practice with genuine gusto.

Not that at 18 Chirri was among the youngest victims of Castroism. "Mommy—MOMMY?—AY!—NO!" Ana Rodriguez recalls the shrieks of pain and horror coming from a nearby torture-chamber. "Up and down the corridor the women prisoners started pounding things—anything!—on cell bars and shouting desperate threats!" she recalls. "But the only reply was the little girl's piercing sobs."

"She's a little girl!" Ana yelled at a nearby prison guard. "How can you let this happen?" Then, Ana Rodriguez recalled, "Slowly and deliberately the guard turned her back and walked away."[5]

The victim had been a 13-year-old girl raised in a Havana Catholic orphanage named *Casa de Beneficiencia y Maternidad* ("House of Charity and Maternity"), founded in 1705. Castroite commisars, perfectly mimicking their Bolshevik mentors, had taken over the orphanage and begun hectoring the girls on how the nuns who had been raised them were actually witches preparing to sell them into prostitution. Many of the barely-pubescent girls broke a blackboard and some desks in protest against the Bolsheviks insulting the only home and motherhood they'd ever known.

So the Soviet-mentored Castroite police yanked the little girls from the orphanage, hauled them down to the women's prison and threw them into cells with common prisoners. In his *Gulag Archipelago* Alexander Solzhenitsyn writes about the tacit alliance always evident between Communist jailers and common prisoners, most of whom had been hapless victims of capitalism, after all.

In the case witnessed by Ana Rodriguez, the little girl was thrown in with "Sappho," a notorious lesbian with a multi-scarred face who was in jail for murder. "It was another half-hour before the little girl's screams finally ended," writes Ana.

When Ana Rodriguez and thousands of women political prisoners emerged from their cells, into the dark corridors of their fetid, steaming, roach- and rat-infested prisons, their eyes blazed in pain even from that feeble light. They staggered and fell, shielding their eyes with their filthy hands, though many had their eyelids almost swollen shut from hundreds of mosquito bites. "One of our games was slapping our hands in front of our faces," recalled Rodriguez, "then counting how many mosquitoes we killed. My record was almost a hundred."

In time-honored Bolshevik practice, to these physical tortures were added mental ones. One of the women's prisons was located only a few miles from La Cabana, Havana's firing squad-central. With the right wind direction, the frequent firing-squad volleys would reach the women prisoners, many of whom had male relatives in La Cabana. The guards took advantage of this to appear in the hallways and howl maliciously at the despairing, rat-bitten women. "Heard that? Heard it!" they cackled. "We just shot your husband!" Or son or dad or granddad or uncle.

According to Dora Delgado, who suffered more than a decade in Castro's torture-chambers, having to hear the firing-squad volleys that murdered their loved ones is what finally drove many of Castro's brutalized women prisoners over the edge to suicidal despair.

"They started by beating us with twisted coils of electric cable," recalls another former political prisoner, Ezperanza Pena, from exile today. She's recalling prison ordeals which occurred a few short miles from where Andrea Mitchell and Maria Shriver smilingly interviewed her jailer. "I remember young Teresita on the ground with all her lower ribs broken. Gladys had both her arms broken. Doris had her face cut up so badly from the beatings that when she tried to drink, water would pour out of her lacerated cheeks."[6]

"On Mother's Day they allowed family visits," recalls Manuela Calvo from exile today. "But as our mothers and sons and daughters were watching, we were beaten with rubber hoses and high-pressure hoses were turned on us, knocking all of us on the floor and rolling us around as the guards laughed and our loved ones screamed helplessly."

"When female guards couldn't handle us, male guards were called in for more brutal beatings. I saw teenage girls beaten savagely, their bones broken, their mouths bleeding," recalled Polita Grau.[7]

You'll please excuse these Cuban ladies if they regard the "struggles" of Betty Friedan and Gloria Steinem as a trifle overblown. They're still awaiting that call from the producers of The History Channel, Oxygen or "The View." But they probably understand how "The Real Grandmaws of Miami" just doesn't click with Bravo TV.

"Anything that I and my friends might have experienced is nothing—nothing—compared with what some of the men in this room went through." The statement came from presidential candidate John McCain during a campaign stop in Miami in October 2008. The Republican candidate was the guest of Bay of Pigs veterans and former Cuban political prisoners. "I'm introducing a man who suffered the prisons, as I did," said Roberto Martin-Perez, who introduced McCain on the podium. "This honor that's been conferred upon me is not only mine but the thousands of victims who have suffered because of this terrible doctrine, communism."[8]

Mr. Martin-Perez suffered 28 years in Castro's prisons and torture-chambers. Indeed, he probably qualifies as the longest-suffering political prisoner alive today in the Western Hemisphere, perhaps the world—not that you'd know this from any media coverage. Even at age 23, Martin-Perez was known among his communist captors and prison guards as *el cojonudo* ("the ballsy one"). "One day I'd gotten particularly smart-mouthed, I guess," he remembers. "So they dragged me down to the torture cell and hung me by my wrists behind my back, with my feet exactly an inch from the floor. I could touch it with my tippy-toes every now and then. They had the elevation exactly right. They hung me there for 17 days—exactly 17. I still remember it well."[9]

Martin-Perez emerged from his prison ordeal, which included more than a decade in solitary confinement, with scars from multiple beatings along with six bullet-wounds, one of which destroyed a testicle. After his first eight years of Castroite prison and torture, Martin-Perez was being moved from one KGB-designed prison to another. During the transfer he was briefly thrown into one of the cells in the women's prisons, where he noticed a crude cross scratched on a cell wall with some notes underneath.

He moved in for a closer look in the dim light and read: "Can God really exist?" The note was surrounded by hundreds of women's names. "The total darkness, the stench of excrement, the rats, mosquitoes and roaches all around me caused me to drop on my knees and weep uncontrollably," he recalls. "And for the first time and last time I myself also doubted His existence! After eight years in Castro's prisons, I couldn't imagine that there was anything about Castroite repression and inhumanity that was foreign to me," he recalls. "But I was wrong."[10]

The cell that confined young Cuban women in conditions that convulsed in sobs one of the toughest men alive today was a short distance from where Barbara Walters sat quivering alongside Fidel Castro cooing: "Fidel Castro has brought very high literacy and great health-care to his country. His personal magnetism is powerful! . . . But children kiss you. People shout. 'Fidel! Fidel!' You are a legend!"[11]

"Cuban women political prisoners deserve a monument to be built in their name once Cuba is free," said Mario Chanes de Armas. "They too, before and now, were beaten and tortured in prison." The late Mario Chanes de Armas suffered 30 years in Castro's prisons and torture-chambers. Far from a "Batistiano war criminal" as the media mostly describe early victims of Castroism, Chanes had been a Castro ally.[12]

From the Moncada attack on July 26, 1953, to the landing of the *Granma* in December 1956, to Batista's flight on New Year's Day 1959, Chanes had fought *alongside* Castro and *against* Batista, having being jailed alongside Castro from 1953 to 1955. In 1961 Chanes turned in rebellion against the obvious Stalinization of Cuba by his former partner and was sentenced to 30 years in prison. Until his death in 2007 in a Miami nursing home, Chanes stood as the longest-suffering political prisoner in the world. Alas, The History Channel was not interested in his story, any more than were any of the other media outlets that created "Mandela Mania" upon that South African prisoner's release eight thousand miles away.

Over the decades Fidel Castro's regime has jailed 35,150 Cuban women for political crimes, a totalitarian horror utterly unknown not just in Cuba but in the Western Hemisphere, until the regime so "magnetic" to Barbara Walters, Andrea Mitchell and Diane Sawyer took power. Some of these Cuban ladies suffered twice as long in Castro's *gulag* as Alexander Solzhenitsyn suffered in Stalin's.

Upon the death of Raul Castro's wife Vilma Espin in 2006, *The Washington Post* gushed that "she was a champion of women's rights and greatly improved the status of women in Cuba, a society known for its history of machismo." Actually, until 1959 Cuba's "glass ceiling" mainly kept women out of prison for political offenses.

This Castroite "improvement of status" and "good life for Cuban women" as trumpeted by *The Washington Post* also somehow tripled Cuban women's pre-revolution suicide rate, making Cuban women the most suicidal on earth—this according to a 1998 study by scholar Maida Donate-Armada that uses some of the Cuban regime's own figures.

Thousands upon thousands of Cuban women have drowned, died of thirst or been eaten alive by sharks attempting to flee from *The Washington Post's* dutifully-transcribed "improvement of status." This from a nation formerly richer than half the nations of Europe and deluged by immigrants from the same.

"Why did Elian's mother leave Cuba? What was she escaping? By all accounts this young woman was living the good life." Or so said NBC's Jim Avila in April 2000.

CHAPTER 18

Dan Rather on Castro:
"This Is Cuba's Elvis!"

"The truth will always be known because there are always brave reporters, like you and Herbert Matthews, who will always risk your lives for seeking the truth!" (Fidel Castro to CBS's Bob Taber, 1957)

"Castro could have easily been Cuba's Elvis. He's very popular in Cuba. And the adulation for him seems genuine." (Dan Rather, 1978)

"From these mountains, Castro's guerrilla army took a dream and *gave it life."* (Dan Rather in Cuba, 1996)

Two months after Herbert Matthews's visit to Cuba, CBS dispatched anchorman Robert Taber and a camera-crew to Castro's camp in Cuba's Sierra Maestra. After his death-defying odyssey to Castro's camp (see the earlier adventure of Herbert Matthews), Taber emerged from Cuba's hills with a long reel and tape of sight and sound that his editor and producer, the late Don Hewitt, fashioned into a 30-minute Castro snow-job. Entitled "Rebels of the Sierra Maestra: The Story of Cuba's Jungle Fighters," it aired on May 19, 1957. Fully half of the report consisted of Fidel

Castro facing the camera and announcing his plans for Cuba. No rebuttal was heard on this blockbuster investigative report.

Two years later, while Castro's firing-squads murdered hundreds of Cubans per week, Don Hewitt was again on duty. This time he was producer of Edward Murrow's CBS show "See It Now," which on February 6, 1959 featured an interview with Castro. By this time Castro had abolished *habeas corpus*, had filled Cuba's jails with five times the number of political prisoners as under Batista, and was killing hundreds without due process. Surely he would be pressed on those human-rights issues by the celebrated scourge of Sen. Joe McCarthy.

"That's a very cute puppy, Fidelito," Murrow cooed to Castro's son, who skipped merrily on camera at their "home" in the Havana Hilton and plopped the dog on the lap of his loving and pajama-clad papa. "When will you visit us again?" an uncharacteristically smiling Murrow asked a *very* uncharacteristically smiling Fidel. "And will that be with the beard or without the beard?" In this broadcast, CBS did not raise a single issue of substance.[1]

Every night during the week that Murrow interviewed him, Castro and company repaired to their respective stolen mansions and met with Soviet GRU agents to advance the Stalinization of Cuba. That February of 1959, Murrow was fresh from a harangue to the Radio and Television News Directors Association of America, in which he blasted the television industry for "being used to delude" the public.

By April 16, 2000 most people with eyes, ears and functioning brains had noticed that, for going on 40 years, practically everything CBS had broadcast regarding Castro was indeed delusional. (During an interview with Castro in 1978, for instance, Dan Rather had referred to his host as "Cuba's own Elvis!") But it was on that April date that Don Hewitt's brainchild, "60 Minutes," truly went the extra mile for Castro, featuring a Dan Rather interview with Juan Miguel Gonzalez, Elian's father. America saw a bewildered and heartsick father simply pleading to be allowed to have his motherless son accompany him back to Cuba, his cherished home-land. How could anyone oppose this? How could simple decency and common sense allow for anything else?

"Did you cry?" the pained and frowning Dan Rather asked the bereaved father during the "60 Minutes" drama. "A father never runs out of tears," Juan (actually, the voice of Juan's drama-school-trained translator) sniffled back to Dan. And the "60 Minutes" prime-time audience could hardly contain its own sniffles.

Here's what America didn't see.

"Most of the questions Dan Rather was asking Elian's father during that '60 Minutes' interview were being handed to him by Gregory Craig," recalls Pedro Porro, who served as Rather's in-studio translator during the taping of the famous interview. Dan Rather would ask the question in English into Porro's earpiece and Porro would translate it into Spanish for Elian's heavily-guarded father. "Juan Miguel Gonzalez was surrounded by Castro security-agents the entire time he was in the studio with Rather and Craig."[2]

Officially Craig served as attorney for Elian's father, Juan Miguel Gonzalez. The humble Cuban worked as a hotel doorman in a nation where the average monthly salary is $16. The high-rolling Gregory Craig, a Clinton crony, worked for an elite Washington law-firm, Williams & Connolly, one of America's priciest.

Upon accepting the case, Gregory Craig had flown to Cuba for a meeting with Fidel Castro. Craig's remuneration, we learned shortly after his return, came from a "voluntary fund" set up by the United Methodist Board of Church and Society and admin-istered by the National Council of Churches. The same reporters and pundits, who routinely snicker through any statement by a Republican, reported this item with a straight face.

In an interview with Tim Russert on June 6, 2000, Gregory Craig explained his motivation for accepting the case: "What I want to do is to set Juan Miguel free. I want the father to make a decision uncoerced from Havana, uncoerced from Miami, uncoerced by the press, independently and freely to make a decision where and how he wants to raise his family. That's all I'm concerned about."

Unfortunately for Mr. Craig, we have an eyewitness to this non-coercion: Pedro Porro, who saw the taping of Dan Rather's interview with Juan Miguel Gonzalez. "Gregory Craig led the Juan Miguel-Cuban-security entourage into the studio, then presided over the interview like a movie director," says Mr Porro. "It was obvious that Gregory Craig and Rather where on very friendly terms. They were joshing and bantering back and forth, as Juan Miguel sat there petrified. Craig was stage-managing the whole thing. The taping would stop and he'd walk over to Dan, hand him a little slip of paper and say something into his ear. Then Rather would read straight from the paper.

"Juan Miguel was never completely alone," continues Porro. "He never smiled. His eyes kept shifting back and forth. It was obvious to me that he was under coercion. He was always sur-rounded by security agents from the Cuban Interests Section, as they called it. When these agents left him alone for a few seconds, Gregory Craig himself would be hovering over Juan Miguel.

"At one point Craig stopped the taping almost yelling 'Cut!' I was confused for a moment," recalls Mr. Porro, "until Craig complained that Juan Miguel's answers were not coming across from his translator with 'sufficient emotion.' So Dan Rather shut everything down for a while and some of the crew drove to a drama school in New York. They hired a dramatic actor to act as a transla-tor, and brought him back."

Okay, roll 'em!

"I probably should have walked out," said Porro. "But I'd been hired by CBS in good faith and I didn't know exactly how the in-terview would be edited—how it would come across on the screen. I might've known, but you never know how these things play out until you actually see them."[3]

A week later Janet Reno's INS storm-troopers maced, kicked, stomped, gun-butted and tear-gassed their way into Lazaro Gonzalez's Miami house, wrenched a bawling six-year-old child from his family at gunpoint, and bundled him off to a Stalinist nation, almost certainly against his father's true wishes. They left 102 people injured, some seriously. Many of the injured were ladies who had brandished dangerous weapons. These weapons were rosaries.

No "60 Minutes" investigative report on that, however.

So, in effect, the man who served (however briefly) as Obama's chief White House counsel had earlier agreed to function as a fully deputized agent for a Stalinist regime and had arranged for Castro's kidnapping to be smoke-screened by his chums at CBS.

The New York Times' incomparable Thomas Friedman could not contain himself: "Yup, I gotta confess, that now-famous picture of a U.S. marshal in Miami pointing an automatic weapon . . . warmed my heart." Imagine getting the staff of a major TV network to act as unpaid aides, consultants, props and publicists for your case—and in prime time to boot. To top it off, Gregory Craig worked for the law firm Williams & Connolly that also, at the time, represented CBS.

When Gregory Craig had flown to Cuba to confer with "The Maximum Leader" (translates almost exactly to Fuhrer in German), Craig told Castro that to manage Elian's extrication he would need Juan Miguel in the U.S. According to most accounts, Castro balked at this. No plantation-owner likes his slaves traveling outside his plantation. Plus, Castro was no doubt privy to Juan Miguel's early communications with his Miami cousins, whom Juan Miguel thanked profusely and told he'd be making his own escape to join Elian.

In December 2011, "60 Minutes" featured another in its long line of joint CBS-Castro productions. This time Anderson Cooper and his production crew partnered with the Stalinist regime's Center for Marine Studies for a propaganda piece on the marvels of Cuban coral-reef conservation. The co-host of the CBS show and conduit for this fruitful communist infomercial was Dr. David Guggenheim, senior fellow at the Ocean Foundation in

Washington, D.C., who chairs its "Cuba Marine Research and Conservation Program." Dr Guggenheim toasts himself as a "Cubaphile" and toasts Castro's fiefdom (which he has visited more than 40 times in recent years) as a "magical place."

Needless to reiterate, such a gold-plated visa is not handed out haphazardly by the Castro regime. Nor is such a welcome-mat and red carpet rolled out randomly.

During the filming of Anderson Cooper's special, the country Dr. Guggenheim calls a "magical place" was immersed in three days of official mourning for Korea's Stalinist dictator Kim Jong-Il, as decreed by Cuba's Stalinist dictator Raul Castro. When Fidel Castro visited North Korea in 1986 his paeans to his hosts had sounded much like Guggenheim's. "I was astounded by the magnificent achievements of the heroic Korean people," wrote Castro. "There wasn't a single topic I could not discuss with my illustrious host [Kim Il-Sung]."

Che Guevara's worldwide diplomatic tour in 1960 included North Korea, which stole his heart. "North Korea is a model to which revolutionary Cuba should aspire," he proclaimed upon returning to Havana. Then he promptly put his aspiration into action by setting up a huge prison-camp at Guanahacabibes in westernmost Cuba. This barbed-wire enclosure, with machine-gun towers at the corners and forced labor in the broiling sun beneath Soviet bayonets, was set up specifically to house "lazy youths" and "delinquents," with whom it was quickly crammed to the point of suffocation.

After surfacing from their scuba-dive at the "Gardens of the Queen" reef off southern Cuba, Cooper and Guggenheim rhapsodized for the CBS cameras.

Guggenheim: "The corals are healthy. The fish are healthy and abundant. There are predators here, large sharks. It's the way these ecosystems really should look."

Anderson Cooper: "You're saying this is like a time capsule, almost?"

Guggenheim: "It's a living time-machine. And it's a really incredible opportunity to learn from."

Cooper: "So something here holds the key to figuring out how to save other reefs and bring them back."

Guggenheim: "It's because this ecosystem is being protected. It's got a leg up on other ecosystems around the world that are being heavily fished."[4] Yes, amazing how that works when you convert free citizens of a nation with a higher per-capita income and car owner-ship than half of Europe, who enjoyed the third-highest protein consumption in Latin America, into penurious half-starved serfs. In pre-Castro Cuba the abundant lobster, grouper and snapper that so enchanted Cooper and Guggenheim on their scuba-dive served as dietary mainstays of the humblest Cubans, who owned boats and fishing-gear and were perfectly free to use them at every whim and consume their catch. For Cuban landlubbers, pre-Castro groceries stocked seafood in abundance. Now these delicacies are reserved mostly for tourists, regime apparatchiks and valued foreign propagandists. Catching and eating a lobster can land a Castro subject in jail. And owning even a dinghy is the stuff of dreams, of escape.

"In 1996 the government of Fidel Castro, a diver himself, made this area one of the largest marine preserves in the Caribbean. Almost all commercial fishing was banned," explained a smug Cooper to his "60 Minutes" audience.

Yes, amazing how that works in Stalinist Cuba: "Ah! Think I'll decree my favorite diving and fishing site a preserve that prohibits my subjects from doing there what I do," brainstorms the Maximum Leader (translates into German almost precisely as Fuhrer). One fine afternoon, he presents it to his parliament. "Now, do I hear any objections? No? OK, going once, going twice—the motion passes!"

There's just something about running a KGB-tutored Stalinist regime that encourages this type of instant and gung-ho team-playing by legislators. Many among the tens of thousands of Castro's prison, torture and firing-squad victims were his former comrades, onetime regime officials. Unlike food, clothing, shelter, feminine napkins and toilet paper, one thing there's never any shortage of in Stalinist Cuba is the rubber-stamp.

Apartheid South Africa, by the way, did a bang-up job of wildlife conservation. The segregationist governments set up many national parks and nature-preserves where vigilant police kept poaching to a minimum. When apartheid ended and South Africa's black population was enfranchised, poaching grew rampant, with the populations of many endangered species (rhinos in particular) plummeting.

But extolling apartheid South Africa's conservation consciousness was not much done by the global mainstream media. Apparently, in the view of enlightened opinion worldwide, the vileness of that government's segregationist policies negated the virtue of its conservation policies. If only Stalinist policies were regarded similarly by enlightened opinion worldwide. If only a totalitarian Cuban regime that jailed and murdered political prisoners, at ten times the rate of an authoritarian South African regime, provoked a tiny fraction of the revulsion that the latter regime produced among the enlightened of the globe.

On his website, Dr. Guggenheim hails Cuba's protection of sea turtles: "The project also includes a comprehensive sea-turtle research and conservation component focused at Cuba's western-most point, Guanahacabibes. Through *strong community involvement and education*, it has dramatically reduced turtle-poaching." (my emphasis)

And how! Just ask the former inmates of Che Guevara's forced-labor camp nearby. That sort of incentive-program will easily engender community involvement.

Endnotes

Preface: The Connections You Don't See

1. Georgie Ann Geyer, *Guerrilla Prince*, Little Brown, 1991, p. 171
2. Antonio Rafael De la Cova, *The Moncada Attack: Birth of the Cuban Revolution*, University of South Carolina Press, p. 239
3. Castro Speech Data Base, Latin American Network Information Center, University of Texas at Austin
4. Ibid.
5. Humberto Fontova, *Exposing the Real Che Guevara*, Sentinel, 2007, p. 70
6. Carlos Alberto Montaner, "Castro and the JFK Assassination," *The Miami Herald*, May 28, 2012
7. Kenneth Timmerman, "More Cuban Spies Lurking In U.S.," *Newsmax*, May 19, 2007
8. Yuri Bezmenov, interview with Edward Griffin, *American Media*, 1984
9. Nicholas Horrock, "FBI Asserts Cuba Aided Weathermen," *The New York Times*, October 9, 1977
10. Chris Simmons, "The Communist Roots of a 'Cuba Expert,'" Cuba Confidential weblog, May 24, 2012
11. Dinita Smith, "No Regrets for a Love Of Explosives: In a Memoir of Sorts, a War Protester Talks of Life With the Weathermen," *The New York Times*, September 11, 2001
12. Larry Grathwohl, interview with the author
13. Ibid.
14. Ibid.

1. The Golden Anniversary: A Half-Century of Loyal Service

1. Trevor Armbrister, "Fawning Over Fidel," *Reader's Digest*, May 1996
2. Andrew Malcom, "Fidel Castro to Congressional Black Caucus members: 'How can we help President Obama?'" *Los Angeles Times*, April 7, 2009

3. Humberto Fontova, "Jimmy Carter Does Havana," *The Washington Times*, April 6, 2011

4. Rana Foroohar, "How We Ranked the World," *Newsweek*, August 10, 2010

5. Frances Robles, "Castro's Victims," *The Miami Herald*, December 31, 2007

2. Communist Omelet: The Unreported Cost in Life and Treasure

1. "Historians Have Absolved Fidel Castro," Newsmax.com, August 15, 2006

2. Eusebio Penalver, interview with the author

3. Irvine, "Mandela Mania," Accuracy in Media, July 1990

4. Juan Tamayo, "Suicide Epidemic Exists Under Castro," *The Miami Herald*, June 18, 1998

5. Ninoska Perez Castellon, "Serenading a Wicked Friend," *The Miami Herald*, February 21, 2002

6. Andres Suarez, *Cuba, Castroism and Communism, 1959-1966*, MIT Press, 1967

7. Yosvani Anzardo Hernandez, "Una haitiana en Cuba," http://www.cubanet.org/CNews/y09/agosto09/06_C_3.html

8. Alberto Bustamante, "Notas y Estadisticas Sobre Los Grupos Etnicos en Cuba," *Revista Herencia*, Volume 10, 2004

9. Mario Lazo, *Dagger in the Heart; American Policy Failures in Cuba*, Funk & Wagnalls, 1968

10. Andres Suarez, *Cuba, Castroism and Communism, 1959-1966*, MIT Press, 1967

11. Jeffrey Goldberg, "America's Absurd and Self-Defeating Cuba Policy," *The Atlantic*, September 16, 2010

12. Pablo Neruda, "Saludo a Batista," *El Siglo*, November 27, 1944

13. Lorraine Lees, *Keeping Tito Afloat: The United States, Yugoslavia, and the Cold War*, Pennsylvania State University Press, 1997

14. Julio Alvarado, *La Aventura Cubana*, Artes Graficas y Ediciones, 1977

15. Ibid.

3. The "World's Luckiest People," or So Says *Newsweek*

1. Javier Barroso, "Un Joven Muere en el Tren de Aterrizaje de un Vuelo de Cuba," *El Pais* (Madrid), July 14, 2011

2. Wilfredo Cancio Isla, "Solo Dos Cubanos Han Logrado Sobrevivir a Fugas Clandestinas en Aviones Desde la Isla," cafefuerte.com, July 13, 2011

3. Christopher Marquis and David Hancock, "U.S. Rips Extreme Cruelty, Protests 3 Killings Near Base," *The Miami Herald*, July 7, 1993

4. Juan Tamayo, "Suicide Epidemic Exists Under Castro," *The Miami Herald*, June 18, 1998

5. Mario Lazo, *Dagger in the Heart; American Policy Failures in Cuba*, Funk & Wagnalls, 1968, p. 397

6. Arturo Cobo, interview with the author

7. *Granma*, July 6, 1989; see also Enrique Encinosa, *Unvanquished: Cuba's Resistance to Fidel Castro*, Pureplay Press, 2004.

8. Maria Werlau & Armando Lago, Cuba Archive Truth and Memory Project

9. Ronald Bergan, *Francis Ford Coppola, Close Up: The Making of His Movies*, Thunder Mouth Press, 1993, p. 530

4. Here Come the Sharks. Where's the Discovery Channel?

1. Matt Lawrence, interview with the author

2. Diana Nyad, "Sharks Need Our Help," CNN, July 28, 2011

3. Diana Nyad, "Cuba on Independence Day," *The Huffington Post*, July 5, 2012

4. Timothy Smith, "Cuban Aims for Big Escapes in Ring," *The New York Times*, May 28, 1998

5. G. Fernandez and M.A. Menendez, "Castro Graba Intimidades de Visitantes," March 12, 2001, http://www.autentico.org/oa09669.php

5. The Discovery Channel Spins the Missile Crisis

1. Sergei Khrushchev, "How My Father and President Kennedy Saved The World: The Cuban Missile Crisis as Seen From the Kremlin," *American Heritage*, October 2002

2. Che Guevara to Sam Russell, *London Daily Worker*, November 1962

3. Khrushchev, Op. cit.

4. Elliott Abrams to Antonio De la Cova, May 27, 1993

6. Castro's Running-Dogs: Herbert Matthews and *The New York Times*

1. Anthony DePalma, *The Man Who Invented Fidel*, Perseus Book Group. 2006, pp 74-75
2. Committee on the Judiciary, United States Senate, Eighty Sixth Congress, Second Session, Part 9, August 27, 30, 1960
3. Manuel Marquez-Sterling, interview with the author
4. *Bohemia* magazine, Havana, February 27, 1957
5. Ibid.
6. Oscar Yanes, *Pura Pantalla*, Planeta, 2000
7. Anthony DePalma, Op. cit. p. 158
8. Julio Lobo, Commencement Speech to graduating class, Louisiana State University, 1963
9. Javier Arzuaga, Op. cit.

7. To Kill a Labor Leader: Manhunt in Buenos Aires

1. Carlos Bringuier, interview with the author
2. Enrique Ros, *Che: Mito y Realidad*, Ediciones Universal, 2002, p. 189
3. Rufo Lopez Fresquet, *My Fourteen Months With Castro*, World Publishing Company, 1966
4. Harry Truman, *The Washington Post*, July 31, 1959
5. Dwight Eisenhower, presidential press conference, July 15, 1959
6. Anthony DePalma, *The Man Who Invented Fidel*, Perseus Book Group, 2006, p. 178
7. U.S. Department of State, *Bulletin*, Volume XLVII, No. 1213, September 24, 1962
8. Roger Hilsman, *The Cuban Missile Crisis: The Struggle Over Policy*. Praeger, 1996, p. 39
9. Michael Beschloss, *The Crisis Years: Kennedy and Khrushchev, 1960-63*, Harper Collins, 1991, p. 27
10. Anthony DePalma, Op. cit. p. 175

8. Papa Hemingway Admires Death in the Cuban Afternoon

1. Anthony DePalma, *The Man Who Invented Fidel*, Perseus Book Group, 2006, p. 198
2. Humberto Fontova, *Exposing the Real Che Guevara*, Sentinel, 2007, p. 31
3. James Scott Linville, *Shooting Script*, Standpoint Magazine, January 2009

9. Castro's "Revolution of Youth"—Imprisoning the Young

1. Anthony DePalma, *The Man Who Invented Fidel*, Perseus Book Group, 2006, p. 201

2. Arthur M. Schlesinger, Jr., *A Thousand Days*, Houghton Mifflin Harcourt, 2002, p. 220

3. Daniel James, *Che Guevara: A Biography*, Stein & Day, 1969, p. 276

4. Jon Lee Anderson, *Che: A Revolutionary Life*, Grove Press, 1997, p. 617

5. Bay of Pigs Veterans Association, interviews with the author

6. Association of ex-Cuban Political Prisoners, interviews with the author

7. "Equal opportunity killing: Victims under age 18 of the Castro regime in Cuba," CubaNet, http://www.cubanet.org/ref dis/05210401.htm

8. Leo Sauvage, *Che Guevara, The Failure of a Revolutionary*, Prentice Hall, 1973, p. 126

9. Letter from Paquito D'Rivera to Kris Kristofferson and Stephen Stills, Latin American Studies, May 21, 2005

10. Dave Zimmer, *Crosby Stills and Nash: The Biography*, Da Capo Press, 2008, p. 209

11. Ibid.

12. Canek Sanchez Guevara, *Revista Proceso*, October 2004

10. Jon Stewart to Don Fidel: Thank You, Godfather

1. http://www.latinamericanstudies.org/espionage/Perez-Mendez-debriefing.pdf

2. A. Padilla, "The Tourism Industry in the Caribbean After Castro," Association for The Study of the Cuban Economy (ASCE), June 19, 2003. http://www.ascecuba.org/publications proceedings/volume13/pdfs/padilla.pdf

3. Julio Alvarado, *La Aventura Cubana*, Artes Graficas y Ediciones, 1977. pp. 794-95. Julio Alvarado was a Bolivian-born economist who served as an executive for Cuba's National Bank from 1948 to 1959. Like most of his colleagues he was adamantly anti-Batista; but the barrage of Castroite propaganda regarding economic conditions in pre-Castro Cuba inspired him to compile this 885-page statistical book in order to set the record straight.

4. Ibid.

5. U.S. Department of Commerce, Bureau of Foreign Commerce, *Investment in Cuba: Basic information for United States Businessmen*, 1956

6. Alvarado, Op. cit.

7. U.S. Department of Commerce, Bureau of Foreign Commerce, Op. cit.

8. Statement by the President on United States Commitment to Open Investment Policy, The White House Office of the Press Secretary, June 20, 2011

9. Carlos Alberto Montaner, *Fidel Castro y La Revolucion Cubana*, Piscataway, NJ, Transaction Publishers, 1984

10. Kirby Smith and Hugo Llorens, "Renaissance and Decay: A Comparison of Socioeconomic Indicators in Pre-Castro Cuba and Current-Day Cuba," The Association for the Study of the Cuban Economy (ASCE), August 1998

11. Mario Lazo, *Dagger in the Heart: American Policy Failures in Cuba*, Funk & Wagnalls, 1968

12. Ibid.

13. Ibid.

14. Julio Alvarado, Op. cit.

15. Ibid.

16. Ibid.

17. Ileana Fuentes, "De Casa Marina a Casa Mariela," *Diario de Cuba*, August 11, 2011

18. http://www.juventudrebelde.co.cu/culture/2010-03-16 cuban-writer-enrique-cirilo-accuses-us-writer-of-plagiarism

19. Lazo, Op. cit.

20. Eusebio Penalver, interview with the author

21. One of the delegates exclaimed: "Castro is a very engaging, down-to-earth and kind man, someone I would favor as a neighbor!"

11. Not Your Father's Hit-Men: Gangsters in Cuba Today

1. Humberto Fontova, *Fidel; Hollywood's Favorite Tyrant*, Regnery, 2005

2. Ibid.

3. Frederick Tempe, *Divorcing the Dictator: America's Bungled Affair with Noriega*, Putnam, 1990, p. 192

4. Ibid.

5. Tim Weiner, "Bay of Pigs Enemies Finally Sit Down Together," *The New York Times*, March 23, 2001

6. Georgie Ann Geyer, *Guerrilla Prince*, Little Brown & Co. 1991, p. 240

7. T. Smith, *The Fourth Floor: An Account of the Castro Communist Revolution*, Random House, 1962, pp. 30-52

8. Tempe, Op. cit.

9. Alba Escobar and Nelson Rubio, "Programa Actualidad," October 24, 2011

10. Karla Zabludovsky, "Police Find 49 Bodies by a Highway in Mexico," *The New York Times*, May 13, 2012

11. "No end to violence in Mexico, experts say," FoxNews Latino, May 15, 2012

12. Jess Hill and George Grayson, "Fears Mexican drug gan spreading to other countries," ABC Radio, February 11, 2011

13. FoxNews Latino, Op. cit.

14. "Mexico investigates massacre of 72 illegal immigrants," Associated Press, August 26, 2010

15. Jerry Seper, "Brutal Mexican drug gang crosses into U.S.," *The Washington Times*, April 19, 2011

16. Juan Tamayo, "Alarma por creciente influencia de Cuba en Cancun," *El Nuevo Herald*, June 27, 2010

17. Ibid.

18. "Relacionan a Niurka con tráfico de ilegales," Servicios Informativos y Publicitarios del Sureste (SIPSE), June 7, 2010

19. Ibid.

20. Jerry Seper, "Brutal Mexican drug gang crosses into U.S.," *The Washington Times*, April 19, 2011

21. Menachem Gantz, "Hezbollah Opens Base in Cuba," Ynet News, September 9, 2011

22. Michael Ware, "*Los Zetas* called Mexico's most dangerous drug cartel," CNN, August 6, 2009

23. "Napolitano: Border security better than ever," CBS News, March 25, 2011

24. Mary Ellen Resendez, ABC 15 News, June 14, 2010

25. KVOA News, "Bureau of Land Management warns motorists who travel along I-8," June 16, 2010

26. Resendez, Op. cit.

27. Jerry Seper, "Brutal Mexican drug gang crosses into U.S.,"
The Washington Times, April 19, 2011

28. Ed Vulliamy, *Amexica; War Along the Borderline,* Bodley Head, 2010

29. Marc Lacey, "Escalating drug violence traumatizes Mexico's
children," *The New York Times,* October 21, 2008

30. Vera Chan, "Big Story: Mexico's six-year drug war behind the
Mother's Day massacre," *Yahoo News,* May 15, 2012

31. Ibid.

32. Jess Hill & George Grayson, "Fears Mexican drug gang spreading
to other countries," ABC Radio, February 11, 2011

12. How Barack Obama Tried to Lose Honduras to the Dictators

1. Humberto Fontova, *Fidel: Hollywood's Favorite Tyrant,*
Regnery, 2005, p. 50

2. "Los tentaculos de las Farc en Venezuela," *El Espectador,* May, 8, 2010

3. Catherine E. Shoichet, "One word with many meanings translates
into sports controversy," CNN, November 17, 2011

4. President Roberto Micheletti, interview with the author

5. "The Refuseniks of Cuba," May 20, 2012

6. Cliff Kincaid, interview with the author

7. "Cuba Dissident Released from Jail after Alleged Beating,
Rubio Says," FoxNews Latino, June 14, 2012

13. Keep Your Pants On, Stephen Colbert. Che Wasn't That Hot

1. "Benicio Del Toro, 'Latino Brad Pitt', wins Cannes award as 'Che',"
Agence France-Presse (AFP), May 25, 2008

2. Simon Hattenstone, "Dammit, this guy is cool", *The Guardian,*
November 28, 2008

3. "Havana Hails 'Che' and Benicio Del Toro's Performance,"
Latin American Herald Tribune, December 8, 2008

4. http://www.latinamericanstudies.org/espionage/Perez-Mendez
debriefing.pdf

5. *CNN Entertainment,* January 1, 2009

6. Paul Bethel, *The Losers: The Definitive Report, by an Eyewitness, of
the Communist Conquest of Cuba and the Soviet Penetration in Latin
America,* Arlington House, 1969, p. 51

7. Nestor Carbonell, *And the Russians Stayed: The Sovietization of Cuba*, Morrow, 1989

8. Castro Speech Database, Latin American Network Information Center, University of Texas at Austin

9. Humberto Fontova, *Exposing the Real Che Guevara*, Sentinel, 2007

10. Ibid.

11. Felix Rodriguez, interview with the author

12. Roberto Martin-Perez, interview with the author

13. http://archive.frontpagemag.com/readArticle aspx?ARTID=33786

14. Fursenko and Timothy Naftali, *One Hell of a Gamble: Khrushchev, Castro, and Kennedy, 1958-1964: The Secret History of the Cuban Missile Crisis*, Norton, 1998, p. 87

15. Miguel Sanchez in interview with Oscar Haza, "A Mano Limpia," America TeVe, October 27, 2009

16. Ibid.

17. Javier Arzuaga, *Confesiones de un sacerdote*, El Veraz, 2006

18. Dariusz Tolczyk, *See No Evil*, Yale University Press, 1999

19. Humberto Fontova, *Fidel; Hollywood's Favorite Tyrant*, Regnery, 2005

20. Daniel Frankel & Sharon Waxman, "Veteran Hollywood/D.C. Publicist Stephen River Dies," *The Wrap*, June 8, 2010; http://www thewrap.com/deal-central/ind-column/veteran-hollywooddc-publicist stephen-rivers-dies-18154?page=0,1

21. Margarita Alarcon, "A Life Worth Living," *The Huffington Post*, June 8, 2010; http://www.huffingtonpost.com/margaritta alarcon/a-life-worth-living_b_604873.html

22. See note 4, above.

14. Sickos! The Cuban Health-Care Hoax, Directed by Michael Moore

1. Juan Tamayo, "Coverage comes with price of self-censorship," *The Miami Herald*, February 28, 2010

2. Humberto Fontova, *Fidel; Hollywood's Favorite Tyrant*, Regnery, 2005

3. Rene Rodriguez, "Cuban healthcare is painted rosy in 'Sicko,' critics say," *The Miami Herald*, June 23, 2007

4. *The Wall Street Journal*, July 23, 1999

5. Gonzalo Guimaraens, "Vacuna Cubana Contra la Menningitis Ineficacia Comprobada," *Revista Guaracabuya*, July 2000

6. Katherine Hirschfeld, *Health, Politics, and Revolution in Cuba Since 1898,* Transaction Publishers, 2006

7. Ibid.

8. "Megaphone for a Dictator: CNN's Coverage of Fidel Castro's Cuba," Media Research Center, May 9, 2002

9. Ibid.

10. Melisa Scott, "Healthy in Cuba, Sick in America?" ABC News, September 7, 2007

11. "Medical Journal Exposes Cuba's Failed Doctor Diplomacy," Association of American Physicians and Surgeons, October 2000

12. Ibid.

13. Lynn Davidson, "Did CNN Instruct Reporters to Sanitize Coverage of Fidel Castro?" *Newsbusters,* February 20, 2008

15. The Cuban "Embargo"—Are You Kidding?

1. Humberto Fontova, *Fidel; Hollywood's Favorite Tyrant*, Regnery, 2005

2. Julio Alvarado, *La Aventura Cubana*, Madrid, Artes Graficas y Ediciones, 1977

3. Ibid.

4. Ibid.

5. Nick Miroff , "U.S. Travel To Cuba Grows As Restrictions Are Eased," NPR , February 6, 2012

6. "U.S. food sales to Cuba continued decline in 2011," Reuters, February 22, 2012

7. Pascal Fletcher, "Cuba will not accept 'IMF-imposed' debt solution," Reuters, July 7 1999

8. "Statement issued by Geordin Hill Lewis, DA, Shadow Deputy Minister of Trade and Industry, South Africa," Politics Web, February 6, 2012

9. Juan Tamayo, "WikiLeaks: Even China complained Cuba wasn't paying its bills," *The Miami Herald,* December 10, 2010

10. "Cuban authorities arrest British man in corruption probe," *The Miami Herald,* April 25, 2012; see also http://www.economist. com/node/21555590

11. Americans for Humanitarian Trade with Cuba, May 24, 2000

12. "Defector Warns of Social Explosion in Cuba," *The Washington Post,* August 13, 2002

13. Nestor Carbonell, *And the Russians Stayed; The Sovietization of Cuba*, William Morrow & Co., 1989

14. Department of State, *Foreign Relations of the United States, 1961-63,* Volume X, Cuba

15. Daryl Lembke, "Cuban Spy Link to Ford, Reagan Death Plot Probed," *Los Angeles Times,* March 19, 1976

16. "Clinton Receptive to Castro Overture to Discuss 'Everything,'" Fox News, April 17, 2009

17. Jose Azel, "Cuba's Internet Repression Equals Groupthink," *The Miami Herald,* February 27, 2011

18. "Cuba's communist secret agent betrays the Grand Lodge of Cuba," *Masonic Times,* April, 2, 2011

19. *Soviet Archives* of Vladimir Bukovsky

20. Paul Haven, "Cuba finds American guilty of crimes against the state," Associated Press, March 12, 2011

21. Humberto Fontova, "Why we remain resolute against traveling to Cuba," *The Miami Herald,* March, 10, 2012

22. Sean Reilly, "Analyst's switch stirs tanker talk," *Mobile Press-Register,* June 9, 2008

16. "Agents of Influence"—Castro's Ladies and Men in the U.S. Media

1. George Gedda, "Official: Cuba May Help Rogue States With Biological Expertise," Associated Press, May, 6, 2002

2. Joel Brenner, "Strategic Counterintelligence," American Bar Association Standing Committee on Law and National Security, March 29, 2007

3. "Huye a Miami Alcibiades Hidalgo, ex embajador de Cuba en la ONU," *ABC* (Madrid), June 28, 2002

4. Armando Valladares, "Their men in higher ed," *The Washington Times,* June, 18, 2009

5. Ibid.

6. Alfonso Chardy, "Spy Catcher claims four are agents for Cuba," *The Miami Herald,* August, 8, 2008

7. Ibid.

8. Ibid.

9. Col. Simmons, interview with the author

10. Jesus Perez Mendez debriefing, latinamericanstudies.org
11. Humberto Fontova, "Obama's Lovefest with Cold War Foe,"
    The Washington Times, May 12, 2012
12. Jeff Jacoby, "Castro's Cheerleaders," *The Boston Globe,*
    May 8, 2003

17. Barbara Walters, Charmed by the Hemisphere's Top Torturer of Women

1. Barbara Walters, "An Interview with Fidel Castro," *Foreign Policy,*
   September 1977
2. Ibid.
3. Barbara Walters, interview with Fidel Castro, "ABC 20/20,"
   October 11, 2002
4. Ana Rodriguez and Glenn Garvin, *Diary of a Survivor: Nineteen Years
   in a Cuban Women's Prison,* St Martin's Press, 1995
5. Ibid.
6. Mignon Medrano, *Todo lo dieron por Cuba,* Fundacion Nacional
   Cubano Americana, 1995
7. Ibid.
8. Beth Reinhard, "McCain: Keep Cuba embargo in place,"
   The Miami Herald, May 20, 2008
9. Roberto Martin-Perez, interview with the author
10. Medrano, Op. cit.
11. Walters, *Foreign Policy,* Op. cit.
12. Medrano, Op. cit.

18. Dan Rather on Castro: "This Is Cuba's Elvis!"

1. Edward Murrow, "See it Now," CBS, February 6, 1959
2. Pedro Porro, interview with the author
3. Ibid.
4. "The Gardens of the Queen," CBS, December 18, 2011

INDEX

A

A&E (Arts & Entertainment Network), 146

Abascal, Gerardo, 68

ABC (Madrid), 233

ABC (American Broadcasting System), 11, 32, 73, 104, 107, 132, 146, 159, 160-65, 171, 197, 205-207, 229, 230, 232, 234

Abrams, Elliott, 50, 225

Abyssinian Baptist Church, 106

Acevedo, Jose, 21

Acosta, Antonio Ruiz, 85

Acosta, Felicito, 85

Acosta, Ruben, 85

Acosta, Teofilo, 130

Accuracy in Media, 10, 130, 224

"Adonis G.B.," Cuban refugee, 21, 24

Aerogaviota, 29-30

Africa, Cuban military intervention in, 185

African National Congress (ANC), 11

Against All Hope (see also Valladares, Armando), 8

"Age of Aquarius," xiii

Agence France-Presse, 168, 230

Agency for International Development (U.S.), 187

Aguilera, Hermes, 128

Ahmadinejad, Mahmoud, 156

Al Jazeera, 187, 188

Al Qaissia, Moutaz, 188

Alarcon, Margarita, 155-57, 231

Alarcon, Ricardo, 156-57

Alarcon Ramirez, Dariel, 144-46

Albright, Sec. Madeleine K., 112, 166

Alfonso, Julio Cesar, 165, 173

Alien (film), 24

Aliens, Special Interest (SIAs), 117

Alis, Krupskaia, 131

Allen, Woody, 147

Allende, Salvador, 145

Almeida, Joaquim de, 136

Alvarado, Julio, 224, 227-28, 232

Alvarez, Yisel, 32

Alvarez Cardentey, Miguel, 24
Amanpour, Christiane, 131-32
Ambrosino, Christine, 37
American Film Institute, 136
American Journal of Nursing,
    104
"American Series" (PBS), 197
Americans for Humanitarian
    Trade with Cuba
    (AHTC), 181, 232
Amoedo, Ambassador Julio,
    66
Analisio, Placido, 58
"Anatomy of a Sharkbite" (see
    Discovery Channel), 42
Anaya, Carlos, 32
Anderson, Howard, 184-85
Andreas, Dwayne, 3, 181-82
Angola, 179
Animal Farm, 44, 129
"Anti-Fascist Protection
    Rampart" (see also Berlin
    Wall), 23
AP (see Associated Press), 61,
    107, 153, 192, 197, 229, 233
Apartheid (Cuba), 30, 106, 163
Apartheid (South Africa; see
    also Mandela, Nelson), 10,
    106, 163, 222
Archer Daniels Midland,
    181-82
Argentina, 7, 66, 69-71, 74-75

Arizona (U.S.), 23, 117, 119, 121,
    124
Armed Forces, Cuban, 29, 206
Artime, Manuel, 86
Arzuaga, Javier, 151-53, 226, 231
Aspillaga, Florentino, x
Assad, Hafez, 154, 188
Associated Press, 61, 107, 153,
    192, 197, 229, 233
Association of American
    Physicians and Surgeons,
    168, 173, 232
Atilano, Pablo, 58
Atkinson, Michael, 15
Atlanta (Georgia), 123
Atlantic, The, 16-17, 203, 224
Avila, Jim, 38, 205, 213
Ayers, William Charles "Bill,"
    xi-xiv

B

Babalu, 193
Babeu, Paul, 121
Bacardi, Ltd., 17-18
Bagasse, 18
Baghdad, Iraq, murder rate,
    121
Bahamas, 26, 50
Bahamian Coast Guard, 26-27
Bailey, Norman, x, 196
Baker, Sen. Howard Henry,
    Jr., 27
Baker, Peter Edward "Ginger,
    88"

Ball, George, Undersecretary, 73

Bancomex, 178-79

Barletta, Amadeo, 99

Barrett, Butch, 124-25

Barrientos, Rene, 145

Barrio Azul (Juarez, MX), 24

"Barzini, Don" (see Godfather, book and film), 110, 148

Batista, Fulgencio, viii, x, 1, 14, 16-19, 45, 53-63, 66, 68, 75, 85-88, 99, 105, 109-11, 120, 137, 140-41, 148-49, 170, 183, 191, 212, 216, 224, 227

Battleship Potemkin, The (film), 139

Bay Area, 185

Bay of Pigs, 26, 41, 84, 86-88, 148, 151, 206, 208, 211

BBC (The British Broadcasting Corporation), 136, 162

Beche, Father Berba, 68

Beckel, Robert G. "Bob," 59, 89, 135, 136

Behar, Joy, 12

Benchley, Peter, 51

"Bennell, Dr. Miles" (Invasion of the Body Snatchers), 170

Berbena, Gloria, 189

Berkeley (see University of California, Berkeley), 104

Berlin Wall, 23-25, 27, 29, 33, 36, 39, 41

Bernal, Alejandro, 109

Bernal, Marcelo, 168

"Best and the Brightest," 73, 88

"Best Countries in the World" (see *Newsweek*), vii, 4, 21, 25, 35

Bethel, Paul, 140

Bezmenov, Yuri Alexandrovich, x

Biscet, Oscar Elias, 106-7

Biscet, Winnie, 107

Bishop, Maurice, xii

Black Book of Communism, The, 8, 80

Black Theology Project, 199

Blair, Anthony Charles Lynton ("Tony"), 22

Blanco, Juan, 85

Blanco, Juan Antonio, 99

Blockade (Cuban Missile Crisis), 48

"Blockade," xii, 177-78, 181, 192, 198

"Blood in the Water," 45

Bloomingdale's, New York, 201

B'nai Brith Lodge (Cuba), 31

Boadle, Anthony, 7, 16

Bolivia, 88, 91, 136, 144-47

Bolivian Army, Rangers, 143-45

Bolshevism, 89, 208, 209, 210

Bolton, Ambassador John, 195
Bosch, Jose "Pepin," 17, 18
Botin, Vicente, 43, 162
Boy Scouts of America, vii
Boys' Life magazine, vii-viii
Bradlee, Benjamin
    Crowninshield "Ben," 130
Brandenburg Gate, 32
"Brasi, Luca" (see Godfather,
    The, film & novel), 124
Bravo (TV), 12, 201
Bravo, Flavio, 148
Brazil, 167-68, 179
Bridge of the Americas, 121
Brigade 2506 (see also Bay of
    Pigs), 84-88
Bringuier, Carlos, 69-70, 74-75
British Airlines, 21, 22
British Empire, 50
British Navy, 50
Brizuelas, Efrain, 85
Brooke, Edward, 206
Brookings Institute, 197
Brothers to the Rescue, 26, 35,
    186
Brown, Tina, 3, 21, 25
Buffett, Jimmy, 93
Bukovsky, Vladimir, 189
Bundy, McGeorge, 73
Bureaus, news, Havana, 11, 38,
    107, 138, 146, 160-61, 164-67,
    171, 174-75, 178, 187, 189

Bureau of Diplomatic Security
    (U.S. Department of State),
    129
Bureau of Land Management
    (U.S.), 122
Burleson Air Force Base, 49
Burton, Rep. Dan, 112
Bush, President George W.,
    107, 156, 178, 186
Business Week, xii, xv
Butantan Institute, 167
"Butcher of Budapest," 88-89

C
Cabrera-Infante, Guillermo,
    14-15
Calderon, Felipe, 115
Calvo, Manuela, 210
Camelot (see Kennedy,
    John F.), 48, 83, 84, 151
Campaneria, Virgilio, 86
Campbell, Arthur, 141
Campesinos (Bolivia), 91
Campesinos (Cuba), 19, 148
Canada, xi, xiv, 31, 52, 104, 127,
    172, 179-180, 192-193, 197
Canadian Broadcasting
    Corporation, 197
Cancun, 115-16, 120
Cannes Film Festival, 135,
    165-66
Capuzzo, Michael, 40-41
Carlucci, Frank, 181
Carlyle Group, 181-82

Carrillo, Jesus, 85

Carter, President James Earl "Jimmy," 3, 8, 30, 160, 177, 185-86

Carter Center, 30

Casa de las Americas (Cuba; see also DGI), 97, 103-104, 156-57

Casa de Beneficienciay Maternidad, 209

Castano, Jose, Jr., 84-85

Castano, Jose, Sr., 84

Castillo, Eliecer, 39-40

Castro, Fidel, throughout (See table of contents for subject breakdowns.)

Castro, "Fidelito," 216

Castro, Manolo, 69-70

Castro, Mariela, 129-32

Castro, Raul, ix, 28-31, 47, 68, 70, 88, 106, 109, 129-31, 141, 144, 150, 157, 182, 186, 196, 200, 205, 213, 220,

"Castro's Propaganda Apparatus" (CIA document), x

"Castroism," 22, 51, 80, 208, 212

Cayman News Service, 37

Cayo Piedra, 206

CBS (Columbia Broadcasting System), viii, 11, 104, 107, 146, 157, 171, 215-20

Cell phones (Cuba), 187

"Cemetery-without-crosses," 26, 28

Center for Epidemiological Research (Brazil), 167

Center for Marine Studies (Cuba), 219

Chabat, Jorge, 113

Chanes de Armas, Mario, 10, 212-13

Chapelle, Dickey (Georgette Louise Meyer), 2

Chase, Cornelius Crane "Chevy," 163

Che (see Guevara, Ernesto "Che"), viii, ix, 9, 19, 33, 38, 39, 49, 52, 59, 61, 66-67, 70, 73, 75-76, 78, 83-93, 102, 106, 148-53, 163, 180, 184, 185, 190, 200, 220, 222

Che (film), 135-48

Cheka (see also Red Terror), 153, 208

Chicago Tribune, The, 162, 197

Chile, 7, 8, 145-46, 163, 177

China, 179, 187, 232

"Chirri," Cuban woman political prisoner, 208-209

Christian Science Monitor, The, 14, 197

Churchill, Sir Winston, 151

CIA (Central Intelligence Agency), x, xi, 70, 88, 110-11, 137, 141, 142, 144, 147, 183

Cienfuegos, Camilo, 88
Cirules, Enrique (see also
Casa de las Americas), 97, 99,
103, 105
Cleaver, Emanuel, 3
"Cleaver, June" (Leave It to
Beaver), 143
Clift, Eleanor, 159
Clinton, Sec. Hillary
Rodham, 132, 186
Clinton, President William
Jefferson "Bill," 24, 34, 110,
112, 166, 186, 195, 203, 217
Close to Shore (see also
Capuzzo, Michael), 40
CNN (Cable News Network),
xi-xii, xv, 11, 31, 102, 107,
131-32, 138-39, 159, 163,
171-72, 187, 192, 197
Coast Guard (Bahamas), 26-27
Coast Guard (Cuba), 32
Coast Guard (U.S.), 25, 27, 34,
39, 50
Cobo, Arturo, 25-27, 40-42
Coface, 178
Cohiba, 33
Colbert, Stephen, 135-36,
200-201
Coll, Alberto, 196, 198
Collera Vento, Jose Manuel,
188
Collins, Judy, 91-93
Colombia, 109-112, 127
Columbia University, 104

Columbiana, Alabama, 123
Columbus, Christopher, 32
Comintern (see also Grobart,
Fabio), 64, 75
Committee to Protect
Journalists, 175
Communism (Cuba), ix, xii,
1-2, 8, 17-18, 28, 64, 69-70,
74, 87-89, 95, 105, 137, 139,
142, 148, 150-51, 154-55,
164-65, 172, 182, 187-90,
208, 211, 219
Communism (in Latin
America), 110, 128, 136, 147
Congressional Black Caucus,
3, 106
Congressional Medal of
Freedom, 188
Constitution of 1940 (Cuba),
61-62, 69
Consulates, U.S., in Mexico
(evacuations), 121-22
Contreras, Rafael, 33-34
Cooder, Ry, 92
Cooper, Anderson, 219-221
Coppola, Francis Ford, 34, 92,
95, 225
Coral Capital, 179
"Corleone, Don Vito" (see
Godfather, book and film),
110, 148
"Corleone, Mikey" (see
Godfather, book and film),
113, 191

Cosmopolitan ("Cosmo" magazine), 12
Coulter, Ann Hart, 132
Council on Foreign Relations (Mexico), 197
Council on Foreign Relations (U.S.), 2-3, 181, 182, 196, 197, 200-203
Couric, Katherine Anne ("Katie"), 12, 132
Craig, Gregory, 217-19
Cream, 88
Creative Artists Agency, 154
Cruz, Jose Ramon, 85
CSNY (Crosby Stills Nash & Young), 89
CTC (Confederation of Cuban Workers), 64
"Cuba al Fin!" 90
Cuba Archive (see also Lago, Armando and Werlau, Maria), 9, 67, 80, 150
"Cuba Discovery Tours" (Canada), 52
"Cuba Is Way Too Cool!" (Bonnie Raitt), 92
"Cuba Prostitution Documentary, The," 104
Cuba Working Group (U.S. Congress), 193
Cuban-Americans, 11, 27, 32, 129-30, 137, 182
Cuban American National Foundation, 27

Cuban Council of Churches, 199
Cuban Film Institute (ICAIC), 139
Cuban Mission to the UN, 157, 196, 201
Cuban Refugee Center (Miami), 25
Cuesta Valle, Ignacio, 10
Cultural exchange, 116, 188, 199

D

Daily Beast, The, 201
Daily Caller, The, 190
Danilevich, Gen. Adrian, 50
De Buenza, Manuel, 112
D-Day, 149
De La Cova, Antonio, 50
DePalma, Anthony, 15, 53-54, 57, 59-60, 65
Death-squads (Cuba), 80
Debt, foreign (Cuba), 178-80
DEFCON-2 (readiness level), 47
"Defcon-2" (Discovery Channel), 47, 49
Defense Intelligence Agency (DIA, USA), 29, 43, 57, 186, 195-96
Del Busto, Alicia, 11
Del Toro, Benicio, 135-43, 146-47, 155, 163
Del Toro, Sara, 11

Del Valle, Boris "El Boris,"
115-16, 125
Del Valle, Dalia, 116
Del Valle, Sergio, 115
"Delgado" (DGI code name),
xiv
Delgado, Dora, 210
Delgado, Owen, 32
Deliverance (film), 143
Dengue fever, 162, 170-71
Der Spiegel, 197
Despair (poem; see
Espronceda, Jose), 150
DGI (Cuba), xi-xiv, 97, 103-4,
116, 128-30, 156, 197, 199,
201-2
Diaz Baez, Urselia, 59
Diaz-Balart, Rep. Mario, 130,
156
Diaz Morejon, Aida, 11
Diaz-Sanchez, Mercedes, 58
Director of National
Intelligence, U.S., office
of, x, 196
Discovery Channel, 24, 35, 39,
42-45, 47-51
Dobrynin, Anatoly
Fyodorovich, 73-74
"Doctor Diplomacy," 167-68
Dr. Strangelove (film), 49
Dodd, Senator Thomas J.,
55-56, 71-72
Dog Rock, 26
Dohrn, Bernardine Rae, xi-xiv

Donate-Armada, Maida, 213
Doors, The, 88
"Doris," Cuban woman
political prisoner, 210
Dos Passos, John, 77
Dotres, Dr. Carlos, 166
"Down with Communism!" 87
"Down with Fidel!" 90
D'Rivera, Paquito, 90
Droller, Gerard "Gerry," 70
Drug Enforcement Agency
(DEA, U.S.), 118, 120, 127
Drug-trafficking, 109-124,
127-28, 133, 162, 200
Dunn, Anita, 72
Dzerzhinsky, Felix, 153

E
Economist Intelligence Unit,
179
Educational Commission for
Foreign Medical Graduates
Eisenhower, President
Dwight, 70, 83-84, 183
El Espectador, 127
El Paso, TX, 118, 121-22
El Salvador, 7, 125, 186
El Universal, 162
"Elian" (see Gonzalez, Elian),
24, 38, 205, 213, 216-19
"Elvis" (Fidel Castro), 215-16
Embargo, U.S. arms (Cuba),
141

Embargo, U.S. trade (Cuba),
  vii, 155, 166, 174, 178-86,
  192-93
Emiliano Zapata Unit, 185
English, T.J., 96-105, 109, 113
Enriquez, Lesley A., 122
Erin Brockovich (film), 142
Escobar, Alba, 112
Escobar, Pablo, 111
Espin, Vilma, ix, 205, 213
Espino, Lorenzo, 85
Espronceda y Delgado,
  Jose de, 150
Estefan, Gloria, 149
Evans, Sir Harold, 3
Executions (see also Paredon),
  9, 23, 52, 65-68, 78-80, 87,
  151, 153, 180, 185, 191, 200

F
Fahrenheit 9-11, 161
Fallaci, Oriana, 13
FARC ("Revolutionary
  Armed Forces of
  Colombia"), 120, 127-28,
  133, 166, 173
Faulkner, William, 79
FBI (Federal Bureau of
  Investigation, U.S.),
  xii-xiv, 81, 97, 99, 118, 123,
  156, 195, 199, 201
FDA (U.S. Food and Drug
  Administration), 166
Feminists (& Fidel Castro), 13

Fernandez, Delfin, 43
Fernandez, Marzo, 169
Ferrer, Darsi, 164-65
Fibla, Alberto, 10
Fidelity! 92
Financial Times, 202
Finca Vigia, 78
Flat Earth Society, The, 15
Flexner, Allison, 174
Florida Straits, 24-25, 35, 38,
  40, 42, 49, 186
Fonda, Jane, 155
Fonseca, Miguel, 21
"For What it's Worth," 90
Forbes, 197
Ford, President Gerald R., Jr.,
  185
Foreign Affairs, 197, 201
Foreign Affairs
  Committee, U.S. House
  of Representatives, 29,
  129, 156
Foreign Policy Research
  Institute, 114
Foreign terrorist organizations
  (FTO's), 125
Fortress of San Carlos de
  la Cabana (see La Cabana
  Fortress), 52, 66, 78, 87, 151,
  153, 210
Fox News, 59, 72, 135, 165
France, 9, 15, 102, 145, 162, 168,
  178-80
Frasch, Dr. Carl, 166

Frazier, Steven, 171
Freemasons, 188
"Free-Speech Tour," 89
Friedan, Betty, 211
Friedman, Thomas, 219
Frondizi Ercoli, Arturo, 184
Fuller, Katy, 184
Fuller, Robert Otis, 184

G
Gaddafi, Muammar-al, 187-88
GAESA (Grupo de
    Administracion
    Empresarial S.A.), 29-30
Garcia, Andy, 14-15, 19
Garcia, Felix Julian, 22
Garcia, Fernando Miguel, 202
Garcia, Juan Felipe, 172
Garcia, Jerome John "Jerry," 88
Garcia, Justo, Jr., 85
Garcia Perez, Jorge Luis, 132
Garcia Quinta, Roberto, 22
"Gardens of the Queen" reef
    (Cuba), 220-21
Gardner, Ambassador Arthur,
    55-57, 71-72
Gasparini, Juan, 207
Gaviota tourism group, 29-30
Gaynor, Gloria, 12
Geist, William Russell
    "Willie," 135
Gelbard, Robert S., 24
Georgetown University Cuba
    Study Group, 196

Gibbs, Stephen, 162
Gimbel's, New York, 201
"Gladys," Cuban woman
    political prisoner, 210
"Glass ceiling" (in Cuba), 213
Gleaner, The (Jamaica), 167
Globe and Mail (Toronto), 197
Glover, Danny, 92
Godfather, The (novel), 105
Godfather II, The (film), 17,
    95, 97, 105, 113
Goldberg, Jeffrey, 16-17, 203
Goldberg, Whoopi (Caryn
    Elaine Johnson), 12, 163
Goldwater, Sen. Barry M., 74
Gomez Abad, Jose (DGI),
    202-202
Gomez Farias Elementary
    School, Tijuana, 123
Gonzalez, Elian, 24, 38, 205,
    213, 216-19
"Gonzalez, Elian's mother"
    (Elizabet Brotons
    Rodriguez), 38, 205, 213
Gonzalez, Juan Miguel,
    Elian's father, 216-19
Gonzalez, Lazaro, 218
Gonzalez, Loamis, 32
Gonzalez, Luis, 85
Gonzalez, Rogelio, 86
Gonzalez, Sigifredo "Sigi,"
    119, 122-23
Gonzalez, Teodoro, 10
Gonzalez-Calero, Cesar, 162

Gonzalez Tovar, Miguel
  Angel, 123
Goodfellas (film), 113
Grand Central Terminal,
  New York, 201
Granma (newspaper), vii
Granma (yacht), 212
Grateful Dead, 88
Grathwohl, Larry, xi-xiv
Grau, Maria Leopoldina
  "Polita," 210
Grauman's Chinese Theater
  (Hollywood), 136-37
Grayson, George, 114-15, 125
Great Terror (see also Stalin,
  Stalinism), vii, 8, 136, 208
Grenada, xii, 186
Griffin, Kathleen Mary
  "Kathy," 163
Grobart, Fabio, 64
Gross, Alan Phillip, 187-90
GRU (Soviet military
  intelligence), ix, 216
Grumman Corp, 25
Guanahacabibes labor camp,
  220, 222
Guantanamo Naval Base, 24,
  111, 162
Guerrilla war, 19, 120, 140-41,
  144-49, 151
"Guerrillero Heroico" ("The
  Heroic Guerrilla," photo),
  147

Guevara De La Sernay
  Lynch, Ernesto, a.k.a.
  "Che," viii, ix, 9, 19, 33,
  38, 39, 49, 52, 59, 61, 66-67,
  70, 73, 75-76, 78, 83-93, 102,
  106, 148-53, 163, 180, 184,
  185, 190, 200, 220, 222
Guggenheim, David, 219-22
Gulag (Cuba & U.S.S.R.),
  8-9, 28, 189-90, 209, 213
Gulag Archipelago
  (Solzhenitsyn), 209
Gulf cartel, 115
Gunn-Clissold, Gillian, 196

H
Habeas corpus (Cuba), 9, 216
Haig, Alexander M., Jr., 186
Haight-Ashbury, 88
Hannity, Sean, 165
"Happy island" (see also
  Matthews, Herbert), 2,
  25, 76
Harvard University, 8, 83, 104
"Haskell, Eddie" (Leave It to
  Beaver), 143
Havana Film Festival, 138
Havana Hilton, 216
"Havana Jam," 90, 92
Havana Nocturne (see also
  English, T.J.), 96-105
Hayden, Tom, 155

Health, Politics, and
    Revolution in Cuba Since
    1898 (see also Hirschfeld,
    Katherine), 171
Hemingway, Ernest, 45, 65,
    77-80
"Hemingway Fishing
    Festival" (Cuba), 24
Hemingway Marina (Cuba),
    44, 112
Hendrix, James Marshall
    "Jimi," 83
Hernandez, Alexis, 21
Hernandez, Gilberto, 86
Hernandez, Melba, viii
Hernandez Pena, Indasio, 10
Hewitt, Don, 215-16
Hidalgo, Alcibiades, 157, 182,
    196
Hill, Faith, 149
Hill-Lewis, Geordin, 179
Hirschfeld, Katherine, 169-71
History Channel (TV), 12,
    146, 196, 211, 213
Hitler, Adolf, vii, 8, 90, 136,
    139
"Hogar de Transito para los
    Refugiados Cubanos" (see
    also Cobo, Arturo), 25
Holden, Stephen, 15
Hollywood, 15, 49, 80, 136-38,
    146, 154-55, 163
Holocaust (Caribbean), 25-26
Holocaust (European), 28

Holocaust (Ukrainian), 148
Homeland Security,
    Department of (U.S.),
    117-23
Honduras, 121, 125, 127-33
Honecker, Erich, 23
Hoover, J. Edgar, 74, 81, 201
"Hotel California," 88
Hu Jintao, 18, 187
Huffington Post, The, 36, 38,
    156-57
"HUMINT," 201
Hussein, Saddam, 188
Huxley, Aldous, 33
Hynde, Chrissie, 92-93

I
"I Hate the Sea," 33
"I Will Survive," 12
Ibarruri, Dolores ("La
    Pasionaria"), 17
ICAP (Cuba), 199
ICE (U.S. Immigration and
    Customs Enforcement),
    114
I.F. Stone's Weekly (see also
    Stone, I.F.), 81
Infant mortality, xi, 13, 95,
    100-101, 172-73
INS (U.S. Immigration &
    Naturalization Service),
    218
Inside the Cuban Revolution,
    202

Inter-American Dialogue, 30, 197, 199
Interests Section, Cuba (in U.S.), 130, 218
Interests Section, U.S. (in Cuba), 43, 178, 189
International Bank for Reconstruction and Development ("World Bank"), 4
International Herald Tribune, 197
International Labor Organization (ILO), 15, 65, 102
Internet (in Cuba), 14, 187
Invasion of the Body Snatchers, 170
Iran, 117, 119, 125, 133, 177, 179
Irvine, Reed, 130, 224
"Island in the Storm," xii
Italy, 172, 179-80

J
Jackson, Rev. Jesse, 106, 200
Japan, 16, 172, 179
Jaws (film), 24, 47
Jaws (novel), 51
Jefferson Airplane, 88
Jennings, Peter, 3, 159
Jerez, Urbino, 58
Jesus Christ (see also Mandela, Nelson), 11
Jews (in Cuba), 153-54, 187-89

Jewison, Norman, 92
Joel, William Martin "Billy," 90
John Birch Society, 77
John Paul II, Pope (Karol Józef Wojtyła), 11, 181
Johnson, Paul, 141
Juarez, MX (drug trade), 121-22, 124
Judiciary Committee, U.S. Senate, 55-56, 71-72
"Judy Blue Eyes," 91
Justice, Department of (U.S.), 31, 192

K
Katyn massacre, 67, 69
Keating, Sen. Kenneth B., 74
Kelly, Ian, 128
Kennedy, President John Fitzgerald, "JFK," 49-50, 72-74, 88, 185
Kennedy, Sen. Robert Francis, 73-74
Kerouac, Jack, 79, 83
Key West, 25-27, 36, 40-41, 45
KGB, ix-xi, xv, 12, 41, 73, 77, 80-81, 87-89, 97, 103-104, 106, 116, 120, 132, 139, 147, 154, 163, 184, 189, 199, 202, 212, 221
Khrushchev, Premier Nikita S., 47-50, 74, 88, 148
Khrushchev, Sergei, 47-49, 225

Kim Il-Sung, 220
Kim Jong-Il, 220
Kincaid, Cliff (see also Accuracy in Media), 130
King, Carole, 13, 93
King, Jr., Rev. Martin Luther, 106
Kissinger, Henry A., 185
Kolkhoz, 85, 148, 184
"Kong, Maj. T.J. 'King'" (see also Dr. Strangelove), 49
Koppel, Edward James Martin "Ted," 11, 32
Korbel School of International Studies, 31
Korda, Alexander, 147
Korean War, 149
Kremlin (see also Soviet Union), 86-88
Kristofferson, Kris, 90, 93
Kubrick, Stanley, 49
Kulaks, 148

L
La Cabana Fortress (see also Executions), 52, 66, 78, 87, 151, 153
Lago, Armando, 9, 67, 150
Lansky, Meyer, 98-99, 105, 109
"Lara," Cuban consul in Argentina, 75
Las Vegas Convention and Visitors Authority, 98
Latin Business Chronicle, 197

Latin American Studies Association, 129
Latsis, Martin, 153
"Law of National Dignity," 163-64
Lawrence, Matt, 35, 41-42
Lee, Rep. Barbara, 3
Lehder, Carlos, 109
Lenin, Vladimir, 60
Leonard Marks Essay Award, American Academy of Diplomacy (see Lopez, Arturo), 30
Lexington Institute, 192-94
Life magazine, viii
Lifetime (TV), 12
Lima, Ariel, 152-53
Lindy, Andrew, 104
Linville, James S., 78-80
Lippmann, Walter, 2
Llerena, Mario, 61
Lobo, Julio, 17-18, 65
Looe Key, 39
Look magazine, viii
London Daily Telegraph, The, 67, 130, 197
London Sunday Times, The, 7-8, 206
Lopez Levy Callejas, Arturo, 30-31
Lopez Munoz, Antonio, 10
Lost City, The, 14-19
Lubyanka (see also La Cabana Fortress), 66, 69

Lue, Dr. Albert, 168
Lugo, Maritza, 11

M
M-19 (Movement of April 19,
    Colombia), 110-11
McCarthyism (McCarthyite),
    78, 197, 216
McCaul, Michael, 125
McDonald, Country Joe, xi,
    92
McDonnell, S.F.P.D. officer
    Brian V., xiii
McGuire, Joe, 140
Machado, Carlos, 85
"Machismo" in Cuba (see
    Washington Post, The),
    205, 213
McKinsey & Co., 4
"The McLaughlin Group"
    (PBS), 159
McNamara, Robert S., 3
Macuran, Pastor, 10
Macy's, New York, 201
Maher, William "Bill" Jr., 163
"Mal Sacate" (see also
    Kristofferson, Kris), 92
Man Who Invented Fidel,
    The (see also DePalma,
    Anthony), 53, 59
Mandela, Nelson, 9-11, 87, 90,
    106-107, 132, 213
"Mandela Mania," 10, 213
Manyika, James, 4

March (de Guevara), Aleida,
    163
Mariel boatlift, 186
Marin, Olga Lucia (see also
    FARC), 128
Marquez-Sterling, Carlos,
    56-57, 61-69
Marquez-Sterling, Manuel,
    56-57, 62-63, 65-67
Martin-Perez, Roberto, 10, 24,
    145, 211-12
Martinez, Helen, 32
Martinez, Sebastian, 162-63
Martinez Rodriguez, Camila,
    27
Marx, Gary, 162
Marx, Groucho, 104, 170
Marxism, 85
Mata, Miriam, 57
Matthews, Christopher John
    "Chris," 95
Matthews, Herbert Lionel, 1,
    2, 15, 25, 53-67, 69, 71-74,
    76-77, 81, 83, 85, 87-88, 215
Mayo, Mario Enrique, 173
Meany, George, 76
Medellin cartel, 109-110, 120
Medical Education
    Cooperation, xii
Meehl, Gilbert, 122
Mendoza, Dessy, 162
Menendez, Manel, 84, 86, 151
Meningitis B vaccine (Cuba),
    166-67

Mercader, Ramon, 75-76
Mexican armed forces, 115
Mexico, 75, 110, 113-21, 125, 144,
    149-50, 160, 178, 180
Miami, 10, 12, 25, 27, 38-39, 45,
    136-37, 141, 145, 149, 159-60,
    162, 182, 198, 211, 213, 217-19
Miami Herald, The, 39-40, 96,
    109, 165, 196-98
Micheletti, Roberto, 121,
    128-33
Milanes, Ernesto, 189
Military Review (U.S. Army),
    29
Militia (Castro), 103
Miller, Tom, 51-52, 96, 99, 109
Mitchell, Andrea, xii, 11, 13,
    60, 205, 207, 210, 213
Mobile Press-Register, 193
Mogadishu, Somalia, murder
    rate, 121
Molina, Ivette, 26
Monje Molina, Mario, 136, 147
Monserratte, Joaquin, 189
"Montana, Tony" (see
    Scarface, film), 110, 113, 123
Montero, Elsa (DGI), 201-202
Montes, Ana Belen, 186, 195,
    203
Montseny, Demetrio, 111
Moore, Michael, xi, 155,
    160-62, 164-66, 168, 171-72,
    174
Morgan, Olga, 11

Morrison, Jim, 88
Morrow, William (publisher),
    96
Moses (see Mandela, Nelson),
    11
Motorcycle Diaries (Che
    Guevara), 78, 150
Motorcycle Diaries, The
    (film), 91, 137, 163
MSM (mainstream media),
    105, 107, 174, 183
MSNBC (Microsoft and
    the National Broadcasting
    Company), 95, 135, 197
MTV (Music Television), 34
Mujahedeen (Afghanistan),
    149
Mujal, Eusebio, 64-65, 69-71,
    74-76
Mujeres de dictadores
    ("Women of Dictators"),
    207
Murrow, Edward R. "Ed," 60,
    216
"Music Bridges Over
    Troubled Waters," 92

N
Nabokov, Vladimir, 79
Nacional, Hotel, 98
Naipaul, V.S., 79
Napolitano, Janet, 121
Nation, The, 197

National Council of
   Churches, 217
National Geographic, 51, 99
NBC (National Broadcasting
   Company), xii, xv, 38, 104,
   107, 146, 163, 171, 205, 207,
   213
Neill, Morgan, ix, xii, 159, 172
Neruda, Pablo, 17
New Deal, 16
"New Man," 33, 92
New York City, 10, 104, 137, 157
New York Observer, The, 15
New York Post, The, 156
New York Public Library, 129
New York Times, The, viii, x,
   1-2, 4, 11, 15, 22, 25, 30-31,
   53-54, 56-67, 71-72, 76, 81,
   86, 96, 99, 102, 123, 136, 140,
   192, 197, 200-201
Newman, Lucia, 171, 187
"Newsstand" (CNN), 171
Newsweek, vii, 2, 4-5, 13, 19, 21,
   23, 25, 35, 159, 197
Nicaragua, 7-8, 50, 177, 186
Nicholas Romanov, Czar, 154
Nicholson, Jack, 35, 92
Night of the Long Knives
   (Germany), 136
"Nightline" (see also ABC), 32
Nixon, President Richard M.,
   49, 74
Nobel prize, 4
Noel, James A. "Jim," 70

Nomenklatura, 90, 109, 189
Noriega, Manuel, 109, 111
Noriega, Roger, 119
North Korea, 220
NPR (National Public Radio),
   104, 107, 146, 197, 200, 201
Nuremberg trials, 67
Nyad, Diana, 36-39

O
Obama, President Barack H.,
   xiii, xiv, 3, 18, 72, 101, 116,
   121, 128-29, 186, 189-91, 219
Observer, The (U.K.), ix
Ocean Foundation, 219
Ochoa, Fabio, 110
"Occupy" movement, 17, 76,
   83, 89
O'Farrill, Albertina, 11
Oglesby, Joe, 198
Old Man and the Sea, The, 45
Oliva, Erneido, 86
"Oprah" (Oprah Gail
   Winfrey), 206
O'Reilly, William James
   "Bill," 7
"Organization Man," 83-84
Organization of American
   States (OAS), 97, 119, 180,
   185
Oropeza, Olga, 173
Ortega, Daniel (see also
   Sandinistas), 131
Ortega, Miriam, 11

Ortez, Enrique (see also Honduras), 128-29

Orwell, George (Eric Arthur Blair), 33, 102, 129

OTMs (Other Than Mexicans), 117

Oxygen (TV), 12, 211

P

Pacific Gas & Electric Company (see also Erin Brockovich), 142

Palfrey, Penny, 37-38

Palmerola U.S. Air Base (see also Honduras), 128, 132

Papua New Guinea, 14, 187

Paraguay, 177

Paredon (see also Executions), 151

Paris Review, The, 78-80

Park Police Station bombing, San Francisco, xiii

Patton, George S., Jr., 151

PBS (Public Broadcasting System), 146, 159, 163, 169, 197, 201

Peabody Award, 96-97

Pedrick, Kathy, 122

Pelaez, Lorenzo, Jr., 85

Pena, Esperanza, 210

Pena, Mercedes, 11

Penalver, Eusebio, 10, 106-107

Perdomo, Roberto, 10

Perez, Jorge, 22

Perez Mendez, Jesus Raul, 97, 137, 156, 199

Perez, Stable, Marifeli (see also DGI), 196-97, 199

Perfect Storm, The (film), 24

Peso, 13, 18, 165

Peters, Philip "Phil," 192-94

Phillips, Lou Diamond, 136, 147

Pinal County, AZ, 121-22

Pinochet Ugarte, General Augusto, 8, 80, 163

Playboy, 162

"Plaza," 114

Plimpton, George, 78-80

Pliyev, Issa Alexandrovich, 48

Plymouth (N.H.) State University, 62

Politburo (Cuba), 29

Polk Award, 65

Pollack, Sidney, 92, 104

Porro, Pedro, 217-18

Powell, Gen. Colin Luther, 27

Prado Salmon, Captain Gary, 143

Prague Spring, 89

Pravda, xii

Prensa Libre, 75

Presidential Medal of Freedom, 107

Proceso, 93

Project on Government Oversight (POGO), 193

Propaganda, viii, x, xii, 15, 17,

51, 60, 97, 105, 138-39,
142, 153, 155, 157, 161-62,
164-65, 168-69, 219
Propaganda Ministry (Cuba),
138-39, 142, 155
Pujals, Jose L., 10
Pulitzer Prize, 2
Puller, Lewis Burwell
"Chesty," 151
Puzo, Mario, 95

Q
Quevedo, Miguel Angel, 60
Quintana Roo, 115-16

R
Radio and Television News
Directors Association of
America, 216
Radio Rebelde (Rebel Radio),
141-42
Rafters (Cuban), 24, 26, 34-36,
40, 42-43
Raitt, Bonnie, 35, 92-93
Ramirez, Leonardo, 173
Ramirez, Richard, 207
Rangel, Charles Bernard
"Charlie," 92, 106, 182
Rather, Daniel Irvin "Dan"
(a.k.a. "Gunga Dan"), 3, 11,
60, 215-18
Raw, Dr. Isaias, 167
Reader's Digest magazine,
viii, 2

Reagan, President Ronald
Wilson, 8, 27-28, 49-50, 87,
185-86, 190
Red Terror, 153
Redbook, 12
Redelfs, Arthur H., 122
Redford, Robert, 137, 150, 155,
163
Reed, Gail, xii, xv
Reed, Rex, 15
"Reign of terror" (Cuba) 1-2,
58-59, 67, 87
Reiner, Peter, 14
Reminiscences of the Cuban
Revolutionary War (see
also Guevara, Ernesto),
viii, 150
Reno, Janet, 218
Republican National
Convention (1976), 185
Reuters, 7, 107, 166, 197
Revolution (Cuban), 9, 14-15,
18-19, 33, 51, 60, 77-78
"Revolution of youth," 83-93
Revolutionary tribunals (see
also Guevara, Ernesto), 152
Reyes, Ralph, 120
Reynolds, Burt, 143
Reynolds, Robert, 110, 141, 183
Rhodesia, 177
Richardson, Rep. Laura, 3
Riefenstahl, Leni, 139

"Ripper, Brig. Gen. Jack D."
 (see also Dr. Strangelove),
 49
Rivas, Leonin, 27
Rivera, Rep. David M., 130
Rivero Aguero, Andres, 66
Rivers, Stephen, 154-55
Riviera, Hotel (Havana), 205
Riviera Casino (Las Vegas), 98
"Roberto," Cuban rafter, 33-34
Rockefeller, David, 3, 181-82
Rodon, Felipe, 86
Rodriguez, Ana (Lazaro), 11,
 208-209
Rodriguez, Carlos, 39
Rodriguez, Carlos Rafael, 186
Rodriguez, Emeterio, 85
Rodriguez, Felix, 144-46
Rodriguez-Bueno, Juan
 Carlos, 39
Rodriguez Cruz, Rene,
 199-200
Rodriguez Lopez-Callejas,
 Luis Alberto, Maj., 30
Rojas, Nelly, 11
Roosevelt, President Franklin
 Delano, "FDR," 16
Roosevelt, President Theodore
 "Teddy," 183
Roque, Caridad, 11
Rosenberg spy case, 195, 203
Rosetta Stone, 96, 98
Ros-Lehtinen, Rep. Ileana, 156
Roth, Philip, 79

Rubio, Senator Marco, 129,
 156-57, 186-87
Rubottom, Roy R., Jr., 71
Ruiz Acosta, Antonio, 85
Rusk, Dean, 180
Russert, Timothy John
 "Tim," 217
Russia, 64, 72-74, 90, 117, 154,
 206

S
Saliva, Niurka, 116
Samizdat (Cuba), 106, 171, 173
San Roman, Jose Antonio, 86
Sanchez, Gregorio, 116-17
Sanchez, Juan Reynaldo, 206
Sanchez, Miguel, 149-50
Sanchez, Yanet, 173
Sanchez Guevara, Canek, 93
Sanchez Parodi, Ramon
 (DGI), 202
Sanchez Wood, Daniel, 58
Sandinistas, 131
Santa Clara, battle of, 140
Santana, Carlos, 91
"Sappho," Cuban common
 prisoner, 209
Sardinas, Tito, 85
Sartre, Jean-Paul, 83, 86, 89
Satraps, as applied to Cuba,
 48, 74, 88, 90, 186, 208
Sawyer, Diane, 3, 11, 207, 213
Scarface (film), 113

Schlesinger, Arthur Jr., 83-84, 86, 89

Schwellenbach, Nick, 193

Science Daily, 43

"See It Now" (CBS), 216

Shah Mohmmad Reza Pahlavi, 177

"Shark Week" (see Discovery Channel), 39-40, 42, 49

"Sharkbite Summer" (see Discovery Channel), 42

Sharpton, Rev. Alfred Charles "Al" Jr., 130

Shaw, Bernard (newscaster), 3

Sherritt International, 192-93

Shoah Foundation (see Spielberg, Steven), 154

Shriver, Maria, 13, 210

Sicko (film), xi, 160-62, 165-66, 172

Sierra Maestra, 54, 58, 63, 110, 206, 215

Simmons, Lt. Col. Christopher "Chris," 29, 43, 57, 195-99, 202

Simon, Joel, 175

Simpson, O.J., 207

"60 Minutes" (CBS), 216-17, 219, 221

Smith, Ambassador Earl T., 71-72, 111, 141, 183

SmithKline Beecham, 166

Smoker's Club of Cuba, 189

Socorras, Armando, 22

Soderbergh, Steven Andrew, 104, 113, 135-44, 147, 155, 163

Solzhenitsyn, Alexander, 9, 209, 213

Somalia, 14, 117, 178

Somoza Debayle, Anastasio, 8, 177

"Son of Sam," 207

Soros, George, 181-82

"Sosa, Alejandro" (see Scarface, film), 110

South Africa, Republic of, 9-11, 87, 106, 132, 163, 177, 179-80, 213, 222

South Africa (segregation), 92, 222

"Soviet Intentions 1965-1985" (Pentagon study), 50

Soviet Union (U.S.S.R.), 28, 29, 181, 208

Spain, 13, 16, 43, 71, 172, 179

Special Interest Aliens (SIAs), 117

"Special Interest Nations," 117

Spielberg, Steven, 92, 153-55

Stalin, Joseph, vii

Stalinism, ix, 8-10, 13, 17, 21, 23, 28-29, 39, 43-45, 51, 60, 64, 66-67, 70, 74, 76, 83, 85-86, 88-90, 92, 106, 107, 117, 129-31, 136, 138-40, 142, 144, 148, 153, 154, 157, 163, 168, 181, 187-89, 200, 202-203, 206, 208,

212-13, 216, 219-22

Standard & Poors, 179

Stasi (East German State
    Security), 7, 85, 120, 154, 196

State, Department of (U.S.),
    11, 18, 24, 50, 57, 70-72,
    110-12, 116, 120-22, 125,
    128-31, 141, 166, 180, 183,
    185-86

State Sponsor of Terrorism
    (Cuba), 11, 125

Steinem, Gloria, 211

Stern, Laurence "Larry," 130

Stewart, Jon, 95-97, 103-104,
    163

Stiglitz, Joseph E., 4

Stills, Stephen, 89-93

Stipp, Christopher, 148

Stone, Isidor Feinstein "I.F."
    (see also I.F. Stone's
    Weekly), 81

Stone, Oliver, 104, 155, 163

Stossel, John, 165

Streicher, Julius, 97

Students for a Democratic
    Society (SDS), xii

Suarez, Ray, Jr., 159

Suicide rate (Cuba), vii, 12, 13,
    25, 213

Sullivan, Edward Vincent
    "Ed," 67, 69, 88

Summers, Andy, 93

Sundance Institute, 155

Supreme Court of Colombia,
    111

Supreme Court of Honduras,
    128

"Survivor," 34

Sweig, Julia, 196, 200-203

Syria, 125, 154

Szulc, Tad, 2, 15

T

Taber, Robert "Bob," 215

Tamayo Rodriguez, Adianet,
    27

Tapia, Alberto, 86

"Tapiadas," women's prison-
    cells, 208

Tarantino, Quentin, 147

"Tattaglia, Don" (see
    Godfather, book and film),
    110

"Teeth of Death" (see
    Discovery Channel), 42, 45

Tegucigalpa (Honduras), 121,
    128, 131

Tejera, Isabel, 11

Telegraph, London Daily, 67,
    130, 197

Telephones (in Cuba), 187, 191

Television Critics Association,
    97

Television Espanola, 43

Televisions (TV's, in Cuba),
    187

Tello Quinones, Enrique, 115

Teresa of Calcutta, "Mother
  Teresa" (see Mandela,
  Nelson), 11
"Teresita," Cuban woman
  political prisoner, 210
Tetlow, Edwin, 67
Thomas, Hugh, 16
Thompson, Loren B., 193-94
Tiger, Lionel, 33
Tiger sharks, 23-24, 28, 33, 39
Tijuana, MX (drug trade), 119,
  121, 123-24
Time magazine, 2, 197
"Tirofijo" (Pedro Antonio
  Marin Marin, FARC), 127
Tito, Marshal Josip Broz, 17
Tocantins (Brazil) Regional
  Council on Medicine, 168
Torres Rizo, Julian (DGI),
  xii, xv
Trading With the Enemy
  (see also Miller, Tom), 51
Traffic (film), 113
Transparency International,
  125
Travieso, Orlando, 32
Triumph of the Will, 139
TRD-Caribe, 29
Tropicana Club, 98
Trotsky, Leon, 75
Troyanovsky, Oleg
  Aleksandrovich, 47-48
Truman, President Harry S.,
  70

Turner, Robert Edward "Ted,"
  7, 60
"20/20" (ABC), 162, 164-65

U

Uganda, 14, 187
Ukraine (see Holocaust), 51,
  148, 153
Union of Soviet Socialist
  Republics (see Soviet
  Union), 28, 29, 181, 208
United Methodist Board of
  Church & Society, 217
United Nations (UN), 103,
  106, 190
United Nations Commission
  on Human Rights, 8, 87
United Nations Declaration of
  Human Rights, 106
UNESCO (United Nations
  Educational, Scientific and
  Cultural Organization),
  101, 172
UNWHO (World Health
  Organization), 159, 168, 172
U.S. Agency for International
  Development (USAID),
  187
U.S. Coast Guard, 25, 27, 34,
  39, 50
U.S.-Cuba Trade and
  Economic Council, 181
U.S. Export-Import Bank, 180

University of California,
Berkeley, 104
University of Denver, 30-31
University of Havana, 61, 69,
106, 160, 200
University of Hawaii, 37
Uruguay, 75, 177, 180, 185
Utset, George, 160-61, 165

V
Valladares, Armando, 8, 87,
189-90
Vassiliev, Alexander, 77
Vazquez, Alberto, 21
Vesco, Robert, 112
Venceremos Brigades, xi-xv
Ventura, Jesse, 148
Verde Olivo, 49
Vidal, Josefina (DGI), 202
Villa Marista, 163
Village Voice, The, 15
Villarquide, Agata, 11
Viet Cong (Vietnam), 149
"View, The," 132, 211, 222
Vishinsky, Andrey, 189
Vives, Juan, 199
Vogue (magazine), 12

W
Walker, Gov. Scott, 17
Wallace, Mike, 3
Walsh, Joseph Fidler "Joe," 88
Walters, Barbara, 3, 11-13, 60,
159, 160, 205-208, 212, 213

Walters, Vernon, 186
Washington, George, 149
Washington Post, The, 96,
99, 109, 130, 192, 197, 201,
205, 213
Waters, Rep. Maxine, 92
Wavy Gravy, 83, 92
Weathermen, Weather
Underground, xi-xiv, 185
Webster's Dictionary, 177
Weicha, Robert, 111, 141, 183
Werlau, Maria, 9
Western Hemisphere
Subcommittee, U.S.
House of Representatives,
175
White, Peter, 51
Wieland, William A., 71
Wikipedia, "Wikileaks,"
"Wiki space," 149, 179, 232
"Wilfredo D.," Cuban refugee,
22
Williams & Connolly, 217, 219
"Willy" (Simeon Cuba
Sarabia), 143
Wilson, Edward O., 35
Winfrey, Oprah Gail (see
Oprah), 206
Wolfe, Thomas Kennerly
"Tom," 79
Wollam, Park, 141
Wood, Alcides, 58
Woodstock, Woodstocker, xi,
89, 91

"World Bank" (see International Bank for Reconstruction and Development), 4
"World News Tonight" (ABC), 159
"World's luckiest people" (see also Newsweek), 4-5, 21
Wright, Rev. Jeremiah, 106, 199-200

X
"X-treme sports," 34

Y
Yale University, 104
Yale University Press, 77, 81
"Yankee heepee," 89
Yarama, 112
Yasgur's farm (see alo Woodstock), 91
Yedra, Hugo Ernesto (DGI), 202
YouTube, 37
"You've Got a Friend" (see also King, Carole), 13, 93

Z
Zapata County (TX), 114, 119
Zapata Tamayo, Orlando, 106-107
Zelaya, Jose Manuel "Mel," 128-33
Zenteno, General Joaquin, 145

Zetas, Los ("The Z's") cartel, 109, 113-18, 120, 123, 125
Zuckerman, Mortimer Benjamin "Mort," 3